AmericanHeritage ®

HISTORY OF THE BATTLE OF

GETTYSBURG

AmericanHeritage®

HISTORY OF THE BATTLE OF
GETTYSBURG

BY

CRAIG L. SYMONDS

A BYRON PREISS BOOK

HarperCollins*Publishers*

AMERICAN HERITAGE® HISTORY OF THE BATTLE OF GETTYSBURG.
Copyright © 2001 by American Heritage Inc., Byron Preiss Visual Publications, and
Craig L. Symonds. All rights reserved. Printed in Hong Kong. No part of this book may
be used or reproduced in any manner whatsoever without written permission from the
copyright owner and the publisher except in the case of brief quotations embodied in
critical articles and reviews. For information, address HarperCollins Publishers Inc.,
10 East 53rd Street, New York, NY 10022.

HarperCollins books may be purchased for educational, business, or sales promotional use.
For information, please write: Special Markets Department, HarperCollins Publishers Inc.,
10 East 53rd Street, New York, NY 10022.

American Heritage is a registered trademark of American Heritage Inc. Its use is pursuant
to a license agreement.

FIRST EDITION

A Byron Preiss Book

Editor: Dwight Jon Zimmerman
Associate Editor and Photo Editor: Valerie Cope
Designer: Gilda Hannah
Maps: J. Vita

The publishers have generously granted permission to use excerpts from the following
copyrighted works. From *The Civil War Recollections of General Ellis Spear*, by Ellis Spear.
Copyright © 1997 by the University of Maine Press. Used by permission of the publisher.
From *Edward Porter Alexander, Fighting for the Confederacy: The Personal Recollections of General
Edward Porter Alexander*, edited by Gary Gallagher. Copyright © 1989 by the University of
California Press. Used by permission of the publisher. From *John Dooley, Confederate Sol-
dier: His War Journal*, edited by Joseph T. Durkin. Copyright © 1943 by Georgetown Uni-
versity Press. Used by permission of the publisher.

Printed on acid-free paper.

Library of Congress Cataloging-in-Publication Data

Symonds, Craig L.
    American Heritage history of the Battle of Gettysburg / by Craig Symonds.
        p. cm.
    ISBN 0-06-019474-X
    1. Gettysburg (Pa.), Battle of, 1863. I. Title.

E475.53 .S96 2001
973.7'349—dc21   2001039187

01 02 03 04 05 TOP 10 9 8 7 6 5 4 3 2 1

CONTENTS

Prologue	A Town at the Crossroads	7
Chapter 1	Taken at the Flood	13
Chapter 2	The Eyes and Ears of the Army	29
Chapter 3	Invasion	49
Chapter 4	McPherson's Ridge	69
Chapter 5	The Shadow of Stonewall	89
Chapter 6	The Best-Laid Plans	109
Chapter 7	A Tale of Two Generals	121
Chapter 8	The Assault Begins: Devil's Den and Little Round Top	135
Chapter 9	Confederate Breakthrough: The Wheat Field and the Peach Orchard	155
Chapter 10	The Struggle for the High Ground: Cemetery Hill and Culp's Hill	173
Chapter 11	The Calm Before the Storm	195
Chapter 12	The Grand Assault	213
Chapter 13	The Cavalry	243
Chapter 14	The Endgame: Retreat and Pursuit	261
Epilogue	The Last Full Measure	283
	Order of Battle	294
	A Portfolio of Gettysburg Battlefield Monuments	298
	Selected Bibliography	308
	Acknowledgments	310
	Illustration Credits	311
	Index	313

A Town at the Crossroads

T he column advanced rapidly considering the rough roads and the darkness, and from almost every wagon for many miles issued heart-rending wails of agony. For four hours I hurried forward on my way to the front [of the column], and in all that time I was never out of hearing of the groans and cries of the wounded and dying. Scarcely one in a hundred had received adequate surgical aid, owing to the demands on the hard-working surgeons from still worse cases that had to be left behind. Many of the wounded in the wagons had been without food for thirty-six hours. Their torn and bloody clothing, matted and hardened, was rasping the tender, inflamed, and still oozing wounds. Very few of the wagons had even a layer of straw in them, and all were without springs. The road was rough and rocky from the heavy washings of the preceding day. The jolting was enough to have killed strong men, if long exposed to it. From nearly every wagon as the teams trotted on, urged by whip and shout, came such cries and shrieks as these:

"O God! Why can't I die."

"My God! Will no one have mercy and kill me?"

"Stop! Oh! For God's sake, stop just for one minute; take me out and leave me to die on the roadside."

"I am dying! I am dying! My poor wife, my dear children, what will become of you?"

Some were simply moaning; some were praying, and others uttering the most fearful oaths and execrations that despair and agony could wring from them; while a majority, with a stoicism sustained by sublime devotion to the cause they fought for, endured without complaint unspeakable tortures, and even had words of cheer and comfort to their unhappy comrades of less will or more acute nerves. . . . Except for drivers and the guards, all were wounded and utterly helpless in that vast procession of misery. During this one night I realized more of the horrors of war than I had in all the two preceding years.

So wrote Brigadier General John D. Imboden of the Confederate Army of Northern Virginia, to whom Robert E. Lee had assigned the wagon train of Confederate wounded after the Battle of Gettysburg, July 1–3, 1863.

Opposite: *A Vast Procession of Misery,* an undated drawing by A. C. Redwood, depicts a portion of the wagon train of Confederate wounded, a traveling nightmare seventeen miles long, as it rumbled slowly westward through driving rain during Lee's retreat from the battlefield at Gettysburg.

Amos Humiston (above) was celebrated throughout much of the North as Gettysburg's "unknown soldier." After the battle, his body was found near the foot of Cemetery Hill; he was clutching an ambrotype of three sad-eyed children (below), which was the only clue to his identity. Humiston's was only one of thousands of unidentified bodies at Gettysburg, but the poignance of his death struck a note with the public, and the story was reprinted in several Northern papers until he became a symbol of both the cost of the war and the nobility and personal sacrifice of those who fought.

That spring, the American Civil War had entered its third year. Few had expected it to last beyond a single summer. Back in the winter of 1860–61, when seven Southern states proclaimed their independence in the wake of Abraham Lincoln's election to the presidency, it had become clear that the sectional feuding over slavery and its future had finally boiled over into a full-fledged crisis. Not waiting to see what policies this "Black Republican" might propose, the seven seceded states amalgamated to form the Confederate States of America in February, and in April Lincoln's call for troops to suppress this "illegal assembly" after the firing on Fort Sumter provoked four more states to join the Confederacy. Even then, few anticipated what lay ahead.

In July of 1861 the armies of the two sides clashed along the banks of Bull Run Creek in northern Virginia in what some had expected—or at least hoped—would be the battle that decided the war. Instead, it provided only a glimpse of the carnage that would last four years and claim some 600,000 lives. Since that first engagement, armies from the two sides had met in Missouri, in Tennessee, in Kentucky, all across Virginia, and even in Maryland along the banks of Antietam Creek near Sharpsburg. Thousands had died; thousands more had been horribly wounded; even more had died of disease in the camps. And, despite this appalling sacrifice, the end seemed no nearer. Lincoln called for 300,000 volunteers, then 300,000 more. The Confederacy, with its smaller population, instituted a draft obligating all white males ages 18 to 35 to serve in the army. Then it raised the age limit to 45. Before the war was over, the draft would encompass all males ages 17 to 50.

Each side had underestimated the willingness of the other to sacrifice. But there were limits. The South would deplete its resources, or the North would exhaust its will. Some sense of that permeated both sides in the spring of 1863. In Mississippi a Confederate army under John C. Pemberton held a Union army under Ulysses S. Grant at bay outside Vicksburg; in Tennessee another Confederate army under Braxton Bragg vied with a Union army under William S. Rosecrans for control of that state; and in Virginia, where most of the political and international attention was focused, Robert E. Lee's Army of Northern Virginia faced a reinforced and revitalized Army of the Potomac along the banks of the Rappahannock River. Before the summer was out, Grant would have Vicksburg, Rosecrans would maneuver Bragg out of Tennessee, and the Army of the Potomac would win the most celebrated victory of the war near the small Pennsylvania town of Gettysburg.

These Union victories did not end the war, but they made it evident that the South could no longer hope to win the war on the battlefield. It would take a collapse of Northern will or outside intervention to conjure a Southern victory now. In that respect, the Union victories in the summer of 1863 were decisive, and none more so than the three-day Battle of Gettysburg in July 1863.

Fully a third of the 150,000 men who fought there became casualties. No one in the secession summer of 1861, even in his darkest nightmares, could have imagined such losses. None could have foreseen the moving horror that John D. Imboden encountered on July 5 when he rode out on Chambersburg Pike, along which the Southern army had advanced so confidently only five days before.

As heartbreaking as were the "cries and shrieks" of the wounded, they were deafened by the mute testimony of the thousands more who lay dead on the field. One of them was 33-year-old private Amos Humiston of Oswego, New York. Humiston had spent several years as a merchant seaman before marrying Philinda Ensworth, a 24-year-old widow, on the Fourth of July in 1854. Since then, they had had three children: a boy and two girls. Humiston had not enlisted in the first heady days after

Fort Sumter. He was, after all, a husband and a father. But in July 1862, in response to Lincoln's call for 300,000 volunteers in the wake of McClellan's failed campaign on the Virginia peninsula, Humiston joined a local company that became part of the 154th New York volunteers. Like most soldiers on both sides, he wrote home regularly to his wife, thus leaving a record of his experiences in the field. His homesickness was palpable. In December he wrote:

> I would give all most any thing if I could make you a good long visit and be back here again but that can not be but when I do come those red cheeks will get kissed more than once I can tel you. How I would like to be with you christmas and new years and [enjoy] one of your diners again and have the babies on my knee to hear them prattle as they used to. This war can not last for ever it does seem to me.

Two days after the Battle of Gettysburg, Amos Humiston's body was found near the town brickyard at the foot of Cemetery Hill. Soldiers wore no dog tags in those days, and the only clue to his identity was that in his hands he clutched a small ambrotype—a photograph—of three children. His sightless eyes gazed on that image, held tightly by fingers grown stiff in death. News of this heartrending tableau was printed in several Northern newspapers, but not until November, the same month that Abraham Lincoln traveled to Gettysburg to dedicate the National Cemetery, did Philinda see the story. Then she knew that she was a widow again.

Another who lay mute on the battlefield was Colonel Isaac Avery of North Carolina. Avery had come North as the temporary commander of what was generally

Colonel Isaac Avery (below left) exercised temporary command of Hoke's North Carolina brigade during the Gettysburg campaign. Leading his men in a twilight charge up Cemetery Hill on July 2, he was shot in the throat. Left behind in the growing darkness by the advancing line, unable to call out, and feeling his life slipping away, he committed his last words to paper in a scrawled note (below) to his second in command, Major Sam Tate: "Major, Tell my Father I died with my Face to the enemy. I. E. Avery."

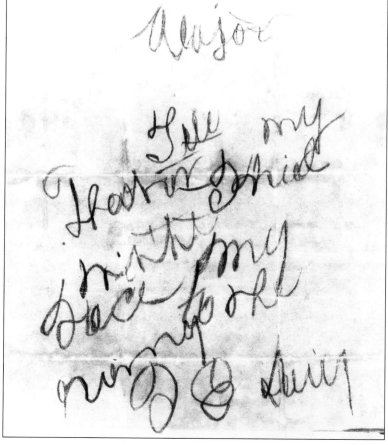

The 1885 photograph above depicts the juncture of two of ten roads that converged in Gettysburg. The road on the right is Emmitsburg Road, which John Reynolds's I Corps used in its approach to the battlefield. The road on the left is Baltimore Pike. The building between them is Snyder's Wagon Hotel.

Opposite: This bugle (top) is similar to ones used by Union troops at Gettysburg. Many buglers on both sides were boys, some of whom lied about their age in order to enlist. Their different bugle calls, which were the musical interpretations of commands to charge, retreat, etc., enabled an officer's orders to be heard by his men under all but the most extreme battlefield circumstances. In the 1884 photograph (bottom), tidy houses line Carlisle Road, which ran into Gettysburg from the north and along which elements of Richard S. Ewell's Confederate II Corps approached the town on July 1. Townspeople huddled together in their parlors or basements as Confederate troops occupied their town and the battle raged around them.

known as Hoke's brigade. Robert Hoke was still recovering from a wound when the Southern army went north into Pennsylvania, so Avery, as the senior colonel, assumed command. A big, bluff, sandy-haired man, Avery was imbued with the ideals and values of his time and place. For him, duty and honor were the indispensable elements of manhood. On the second day of the Battle of Gettysburg, he led his command in a twilight charge up Cemetery Hill. In the smoke and confusion of the charge, no one noticed when he fell from his horse, shot in the throat. The charge swept past him. Alone in the dark, he fumbled for a piece of paper and a pencil and, in the last action of his life, scribbled out a short note for his friend Major Sam Tate, "Major, Tell my Father I died with my Face to the enemy. I. E. Avery." He was still holding that note when his body was discovered less than a hundred yards from where Amos Humiston clutched the ambrotype of his children.

A modern visitor to the central square of Gettysburg—called the Diamond—requires no special vision or insight to note that the roads leading into that square come from all points of the compass. Those roads are identified today by their prosaic modern names (Route 15, Route 30, etc.), but in the nineteenth century they were known locally for the towns to which they led. Thus the residents of Gettysburg called the road stretching off to the north "Carlisle Road." It sprouted two branches only a few blocks away, one of them leading northwest to Mummasburg and the other northeast toward the state capital of Harrisburg. Three more roads led southward from that central square across the Mason-Dixon Line into Maryland toward the towns of

Emmitsburg, Taneytown, and Baltimore. Two roads led west to Chambersburg and Hagerstown; two more led east to York and Hanover. There were ten altogether.

In the summer of 1863, 150,000 armed men marched (like Humiston) or rode (like Avery) down those various roads, all aiming for the town of Gettysburg, population 2,400. Most of them were hardened veterans who had seen many battles, but few could have guessed that they were heading for a collision that would last three days, claim 50,000 casualties, and become celebrated as the largest military engagement in the history of the Western Hemisphere. It was not destiny that brought them to Gettysburg, nor, despite tradition, was it shoes. It was that network of roads so resembling a spider's web, with the town of Gettysburg at its very center.

CHAPTER ONE

Taken at the Flood

(May 1–June 2, 1863)

The sequence of events that led to the Battle of Gettysburg began in May in a 300-square-mile tangle of scrub and undergrowth in Virginia just south of where the Rapidan River flows into the Rappahannock, an area known locally as the Wilderness. Since the previous spring, when Confederate General Joseph E. Johnston had pulled back from his Manassas bivouac to settle in behind the protective barrier of the Rappahannock River, the Rapidan-Rappahannock line had constituted what one scholar has termed the "dare mark" of the Confederacy. Federal armies crossed that line at their peril. One—the so-called Army of Virginia under Major General John Pope—tried in the summer of 1862 only to scuttle back to Manassas where it was routed in the Second Battle of Bull Run. Another—this one under Ambrose Burnside—tried in December, assailing the heights behind Fredericksburg for most of a day before Burnside reluctantly but wisely gave up the effort. In May 1863 yet another Federal general—Joseph Hooker—accepted the dare.

Hooker's trespass across the dare mark was the most carefully planned and skillfully executed of the three. Holding Robert E. Lee's Army of Northern Virginia in place at Fredericksburg with two of his seven army corps, Hooker led the other five on a lengthy flank march upriver. They crossed the Rappahannock twenty miles upstream, then swung south and east across the Rapidan to take up a position ten miles behind Lee's army near a small Wilderness crossroads named for the Chancellor mansion and marked on the maps as Chancellorsville.

Hooker's maneuver was little short of brilliant. Indeed, it was so effective that Hooker himself was convinced that it would compel Lee to give up his position at Fredericksburg—indeed, give up the line of the Rappahannock altogether and fall back to the next logical defensive position, at the North Anna River. On May 1, Hooker halted his army in the wilderness area around the Chancellor mansion and waited for his enemy to retreat. When he received a report from his III Corps commander, Daniel Sickles, that a column of Confederate infantry was moving southwesterly across his front, Hooker accepted this as evidence that Lee was in fact retreating, and he resolved to let him go.

But Lee was not in retreat. True to his character as a commander who was willing to take long chances, Lee had dispatched his most trusted lieutenant, Thomas J.

Opposite: Generals Robert E. Lee and Stonewall Jackson are depicted in the 1869 painting *The Last Meeting of Lee and Jackson* by E. B. D. Julio. At the battle of Chancellorsville, in response to Lee's instructions, Jackson led his corps in a lengthy roundabout march to assail the Union army in its flank and rear. Though the attack was a tremendous success, it cost Jackson his life when he was struck by friendly fire in the confusion of a late-night battle in the tangled Wilderness.

"Fighting Joe" Hooker, in a wartime photo by Mathew Brady, commanded the Army of the Potomac in the spring of 1863. He restored the shattered spirit of the Northern army during the winter of 1862–63 by, among other things, approving a more liberal leave policy and issuing corps badges to encourage unit pride. A confident commander, Hooker was convinced that his detailed and elegant plan to outflank Lee's army at Fredericksburg would compel the Southern army to retreat.

"Stonewall" Jackson, on a maneuver at least as brilliant as Hooker's, and even more daring. Leaving himself with only about 15,000 men to face Hooker's main body, Lee sent Jackson's corps on a daylong twenty-mile march, first southwest, then northwest, to find the enemy rear. The column that Sickles's men had spied moving across a gap in the tree line was part of that movement. The flanker was about to be flanked.

At approximately five o'clock in the afternoon of May 2, the soldiers of Oliver O. Howard's XI Corps were gathered about their campfires cooking dinner when Jackson's Valley veterans smashed into their unprotected flank. Howard's men did not immediately break and flee despite later such charges. Division and brigade commanders scrambled to reorient their forces to face the onslaught; a few units made heroic stands, inflicting a thousand casualties on the attackers and buying the Union army valuable time. But the attackers had both numbers and momentum. When Howard's men finally gave way, the gray- and butternut-clad soldiers poured after them with Jackson driving them onward. True to his character, Jackson wanted not merely to defeat the Federal army but to annihilate it. "Press on! Press on!" he urged his subordinates. "Press the enemy until nightfall," he ordered one brigade commander.

But nightfall was the problem. Difficult as it was at any time to maneuver forces effectively in the uneven terrain and dense foliage of the Wilderness, it was impossible to do so in pitch darkness. Regardless of that, Jackson was determined to sustain his momentum, and at about nine o'clock he rode out ahead of his troops in the inky darkness hoping to discover some route by which he could cut the Yankees off from their line of retreat across the Rappahannock. Having discovered a secondary road that he thought might suit his purpose, Jackson was returning to his own lines when Confederate infantry mistook his group of mounted horsemen for Federal cavalry and opened fire. Jackson was hit three times. The wounds did not appear to be serious, but at the very least they removed Jackson's furious will from the battlefield. This fight, at least, would have to go on without him.

Hooker made good his "escape" across the Rappahannock. A bolder man might have tried a counterattack, for the Federals still had numerical superiority, but Hooker's nerve was shattered. Not only had the tactical situation become utterly unglued but he also experienced a personal brush with death the next morning when a Confederate artillery shell exploded against a column on the porch of the Chancellor mansion while he was leaning against it. Rather than attempt to recoup

Andrew J. Russell photographed soldiers of the Army of the Potomac in May 1863 as they patiently awaited orders in shallow trenches on the north side of the Rappahannock River. Having endured five changes in command in just over a year, the rank and file of the Northern army had developed a near fatalist outlook: they continued to do their duty, but often they did so without great confidence that their sacrifices would bring a swift end to the war.

An 1889 lithograph depicts the battle of Chancellorsville, in which Stonewall Jackson was felled at the moment of his greatest triumph—not by enemy fire, but at the hands of his own soldiers, who mistook his mounted group of staff officers for enemy cavalry. Initially it was believed that Jackson would survive his wound, though his left arm had to be amputated. Upon hearing the news, Lee is said to have remarked, "He has lost his left arm, but I have lost my right."

Opposite: In the spring of 1863, Hooker attempted to turn Lee's left flank along the line of the Rapidan–Rappahannock Rivers. Lee countered by sending Stonewall Jackson on a rapid and daring flank march that caught Union forces by surprise. Despite Jackson's mortal wound, Lee's stunning victory at Chancellorsville set the stage for his invasion of the North.

the situation, Hooker gave orders for the army to fall back. Once again a Federal army had crossed the dare mark and had suffered for it.

The Army of Northern Virginia had suffered as well. Jackson's wound necessitated the amputation of his left arm. Afterward, pneumonia set in, and he died a week after the battle. His death cast a pall over the South's celebration of yet another Confederate victory. But the mingled grief and joy obscured an important truth even more sobering than Jackson's death. In the fight at Chancellorsville, Lee's army had lost nearly 13,000 men out of an army that numbered barely 60,000. Though the Federals had suffered more casualties when counted in raw numbers (17,000), Union losses came to just under 15 percent of those engaged; Confederate losses were over 21 percent. A few more victories like Chancellorsville and the Southern army would be no more.

Increasingly, the war had become a numbers game. With a white population that was only about a quarter that of the Union states, the Confederacy had been forced to resort to the passage of a conscription law in the second year of the war. Before the war was over, the Confederacy would put some 900,000 men in uniform out of

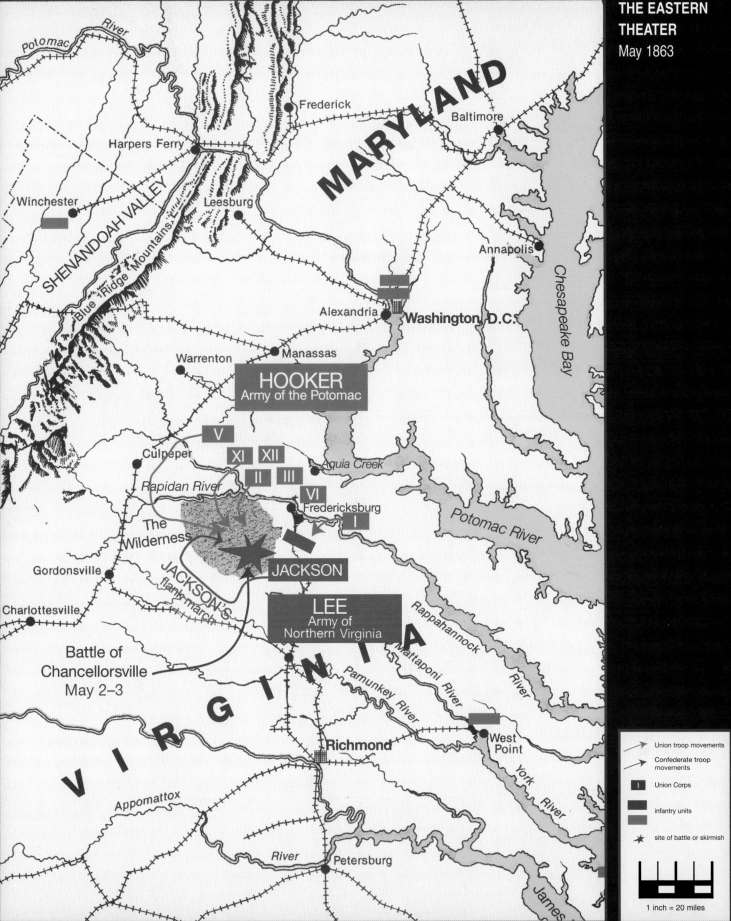

THE EASTERN
THEATER
May 1863

MARYLAND

Potomac River

Frederick

Baltimore

Harpers Ferry

Winchester

SHENANDOAH VALLEY

Leesburg

Annapolis

Blue Ridge Mountains

Chesapeake Bay

Alexandria

Washington, D.C.

Warrenton

Manassas

HOOKER
Army of the Potomac

V

Culpeper

XI XII

Aquia Creek

Rapidan River

II III

VI

Fredericksburg

I

The
Wilderness

Potomac River

Gordonsville

JACKSON'S
flank march

JACKSON

Charlottesville

LEE
Army of
Northern Virginia

Rappahannock River

Battle of
Chancellorsville
May 2–3

Mattaponi River

VIRGINIA

Pamunkey River

York River

West
Point

Richmond

Appomattox

River

Petersburg

James River

Union troop movements

Confederate troop
movements

I Union Corps

infantry units

site of battle or skirmish

1 inch = 20 miles

Jefferson Davis was a West Point graduate who had commanded a regiment in the war with Mexico and served as secretary of war under Franklin Pierce. Given those credentials, he was inclined to take an active hand in crafting Southern strategy as president of the Confederacy. He preferred a strategy of extended defense, hoping the North would wear itself out trying to reconquer the South. Nevertheless, Lee's great prestige after his several victories in Virginia led Davis to approve his successful general's request to take the war into enemy territory.

a white population of barely 5.5 million, a mobilization ratio that was unprecedented then and is unmatched since. Yet the North's armies were even larger—the Union would eventually put a total of 2 million men under arms. Then, too, the North could not only bring more men to the battlefield but it could sustain them more effectively because of its vast superiority in industry and transportation. The South made tremendous efforts to jury-rig a domestic industry to sustain the war effort, and it cannibalized less-used railroads to keep the main trunk lines open and even build new ones. But in spite of these efforts, in the spring of 1863 virtually all tangible indices of military power favored the Northern states, and the gap was widening.

These realities framed the debate as Southern strategists confronted the question of what to do next in the aftermath of the improbable Confederate victory at Chancellorsville. Among the myriad theoretical options, three commanded particular attention. One was, simply, to do nothing. The Confederate war aim, after all, was independence. To achieve it, all that was necessary was for the South to continue to repel Union initiatives until the Northern government or population tired of the effort and gave up the struggle. "All we ask is to be let alone," Davis had insisted at the war's outset, and his overall strategy of an extended defense was designed to convince the North that the South could not be conquered. Consistent with that goal, Lee's victorious army could remain undefeated behind the dare mark of the Rappahannock and Rapidan Rivers and defy the Yankees to try again . . . and again . . . until they stopped trying. This option would allow the South to bolster its defenses elsewhere, particularly along the Atlantic coast, where the U.S. Navy was consolidating its control of several key ports and threatening others. As president of a confederated government whose mantra was states' rights, Jefferson Davis felt keenly the pressure to assist the various communities that were appealing to him for military assistance.

Some of that pressure came from a group of Confederate congressmen and a handful of generals that historians have dubbed the western concentration bloc. Members of this group believed that a disproportionate amount of the South's military assets were tied up in the defense of Virginia while much of the West was feeling the burden of Federal occupation. They argued that a portion of Lee's army should be sent west to Tennessee or, more likely, to Mississippi where Ulysses S. Grant was threatening the Confederate citadel at Vicksburg. The fall of Vicksburg would mean the loss of the Mississippi River, which would sunder the Confederacy nearly in half and cut off three Confederate states, a devastating blow to Confederate unity. Then, too, Jefferson Davis had an emotional commitment to Vicksburg, for Mississippi was his home state, and his plantation, Briarfield, was only a few miles south of the city. Finally, the notion of using interior lines to shuttle troops from one threatened point to another was consistent with the president's advocacy of an extended defense.

Lee, however, opposed the idea of sending forces from Virginia to the western theater. For one thing, Lee was not convinced that the Yankee army in Virginia had been so weakened that it no longer constituted a threat. Hooker's well-planned maneuver had failed, but only because Lee's soldiers had overcome both numbers and position to wrest an unlikely victory from the invaders. Lee feared that if the Federal army were granted the luxury of a long period of unmolested preparation, its next effort would be even more daunting, and his soldiers might not be able to secure another victory against even longer odds. If he were required to send a portion of his army west, Lee believed he would be compelled to act on the defensive in Virginia, and very likely he would have to fall back to Richmond, thereby losing both a major

"I SHALL NEVER FORGET THE SCENE"

Seizing the initiative and taking the war into Pennsylvania was a high-risk strategy for the undermanned Confederacy, but Lee preferred the bold option to the more passive and reactive alternatives. In the third week of May 1863, President Jefferson Davis convened his cabinet for a lengthy discussion of military strategy. Lee did not attend this meeting, but his tremendous prestige and influence nevertheless permeated the room and doubtlessly affected the discussion. The Confederate postmaster general, John H. Reagan, later recalled the meeting in his memoirs. Like many postwar memoirs, Reagan's are self-serving in that he suggests that he alone, of all Davis's cabinet, had opposed the decision to invade the North. In the following passage, he recounts what he remembers about the arguments that won the day:

Early in the year 1863 the question of the invasion by our army of the country north of the Potomac was being discussed by the Cabinet and General Lee. One of the considerations favoring such a policy was that supplies for our army were much reduced—and these were abundant in the territory of the enemy. Another consideration was that a successful campaign in the territory adjacent to Washington, Baltimore, and Philadelphia might cause the withdrawal of the troops then menacing Vicksburg and Port Hudson. . . .

Our means of communication with western Louisiana, Arkansas, and Texas largely depended on our command of the Mississippi at those cities. It was apparent that their fall meant the bisecting of the Confederacy by the line of the Mississippi, in which event we should be deprived, in a large measure, of the men and supplies west of that river. As the lines came to be more and more tightly drawn, appeals from the civil and military authorities poured in for reinforcements for the army of General [John C.] Pemberton, who commanded before Vicksburg.

The President received a number of letters and telegrams from Governor Peters [John J. Pettus] of Mississippi, and others, advising him to dispatch reinforcements from General Lee's army to the defense of Vicksburg. These he read to the Cabinet and requested the members to meet him on the next day to consider the whole question of the campaign of 1863. We assembled early—it was Saturday—and remained in session in the anxious discussion of that campaign until after nightfall.

I shall never forget the scene. The President and members of the Cabinet fully realized the grave character of the question to be considered. General Lee did not meet with us on this occasion, though he often did so in his capacity as Military Adviser to the President, and latterly as general in the field. He was not a man of many words and when he spoke it was in the fullness of conviction. He had expressed his views on the subject of a campaign north of the Potomac. Every possible contingency was pointed out in our discussion, and it early became apparent to me that I stood almost alone. I urged that . . . we should . . . strengthen the defenses of Richmond, collect supplies for a six-month siege, and at the proper time dispatch 25,000 or 30,000 of General Lee's troops to Vicksburg. . . . I further contended that by sending a part of General Lee's army, and a part of the Army of Tennessee [under Braxton Bragg] confronting General Buell, and by directing General [Joseph E.] Johnston to collect and forward all the men and supplies he could from the Gulf States, General Grant might be crushed. . . .

It was urged in opposition to my view that the best way to protect Vicksburg was to put Washington and Baltimore in danger and thus cause the withdrawal of troops from Grant's army for their defense. To this I demurred. General Grant, I said, had reached a position which would prevent dealing with him in that way, and that what he was doing showed that he intended Vicksburg should fall if his army was not destroyed.

In the end it was determined that General Lee should cross the Potomac and put himself in a position to threaten Washington, Baltimore, and Philadelphia, and that General Johnston should get together such men and supplies as he could in the Gulf States and go to the relief of Pemberton.

SOURCE: John H. Reagan, *Memoirs with Special Reference to Secession and the Civil War* (New York: The Neale Publishing Company, 1906), pp. 150–52.

Thomas Kelly drew the Confederate cabinet for *Harper's Weekly* in 1861. Front row seated, from left to right: Attorney General Judah P. Benjamin, Secretary of Navy Stephen R. Mallory, Vice-President Alexander H. Stephens, President Jefferson Davis, Postmaster General John H. Reagan, Secretary of State Robert A. Toombs; back row standing, from left to right: Secretary of the Treasury Christopher G. Memminger and Secretary of War Leroy Pope Walker.

The strain of the war was clearly evident on Abraham Lincoln's face in this 1863 portrait by Mathew Brady. With Grant at an impasse at Vicksburg, two Union defeats at Fredericksburg and Chancellorsville, and facing a growing challenge from Peace Democrats to end the war, Lincoln remained resolute in his strategy to restore the South to the Union, but he knew he needed a major victory for that strategy to survive.

source of logistic support and his freedom of movement. Once his army was pinned up in the Richmond defenses, Lee believed, defeat would be inevitable.

Lee advocated a third option: taking his Army of Northern Virginia across the Potomac and into Pennsylvania. Lee was a dutiful subordinate, loath to provoke a confrontation with his political superior, but in the days after Chancellorsville, even as he prayed fervently for Stonewall Jackson's recovery, he sent Davis a series of earnest letters advising against any reduction of the Army of Northern Virginia. He urged instead that his army be reinforced by returning to him the two divisions under James Longstreet that had been engaged in an effort to recapture Suffolk, plus troops from the Shenandoah Valley and from North Carolina. On May 14, four days after Jackson's death, Davis asked Lee to come to Richmond to discuss the various strategic alternatives.

In a series of lengthy cabinet meetings held on the second floor of the Confederate White House on May 15 and 16, Lee laid out his case for keeping his army intact and using it to take the war into Pennsylvania. In his quiet but earnest way, he told Davis and the assembled cabinet officers that his soldiers suffered from dwindling supplies in war-worn Virginia. Moving the scene of war northward would open up new sources of supply for his men and also make the Northern population feel the effects of the war. He suggested that troops sent to the West could not arrive there in time to influence the ongoing campaigns in any case, and that even if they could, they could not be fed, supplies there being as scarce as they were in Virginia. Then Lee played his ace: a northward movement across the Potomac and into Pennsylvania, he argued, might compel the government in Washington to recall Grant from Mississippi, thus saving Vicksburg as well.

What Lee did not tell the cabinet officers was that he believed time was not on the side of the Confederacy. To remain where he was and await another, and then another, Federal initiative would eventually sap Confederate manpower and resources until the South had no resources left. Better, he believed, to shock Northern public opinion into acknowledging Southern independence by obtaining a victory on Northern soil than to remain on the defensive and hope that Northern will would eventually melt away after repeated disappointments on Southern soil. In other words, instead of reacting to the enemy's initiatives, Lee wanted to make the Federals react to his. Lee's prestige and dignity carried the day. After a lengthy conference, Davis and the cabinet agreed to let Lee conduct the offensive campaign he sought. Vicksburg would have to look out for itself.

Lee left Richmond on May 17, unaware that the day before Grant had defeated John C. Pemberton's Army of Mississippi in the Battle of Champion's Hill east of Vicksburg and forced the Confederates back into the city's defenses. It was now unlikely that Grant would be recalled from Mississippi no matter how successful Lee's foray into the North might prove. In reaction to the news, Davis convened another cabinet meeting to reconsider the wisdom of sending Lee north while Vicksburg was in such dire peril, but another lengthy meeting did not change the initial decision. Lee prepared to take his army northward, to cross the Potomac and put himself in a position to threaten Washington, Baltimore, and Philadelphia.

☙ ❧

Even before Davis and his cabinet approved an invasion of the North, Lee had begun to reorganize his army for an offensive campaign. The death of Stonewall Jackson on

Hooker placed part of the blame for his defeat in the Battle of Chancellorsville on his cavalry, and especially on its commander, Major General George Stoneman (above, in a Brady photograph). Hooker had ordered Stoneman to conduct a raid southward in the expectation that it would draw the Confederate cavalry away from the scene of action and open the way for a decisive flanking maneuver unhindered by rebel horsemen. Stoneman not only got a late start but he was also lethargic in his movements, and Stuart largely ignored him. After the battle, Hooker shuffled Stoneman off to an administrative post in Washington and replaced him with Alfred Pleasonton, who would command the Union cavalry during the Gettysburg campaign.

Lincoln not only had to fight a war against the rebellious South but he also had to contend with a fractious cabinet that included a number of so-called Radicals, such as Treasury Secretary Salmon P. Chase. Chase urged Lincoln to act more decisively against slavery and supported field generals who felt likewise. It was Chase and the other Radicals in Lincoln's cabinet who had persuaded him to appoint Hooker to command.

May 10 had made a restructuring of the high command necessary in any case, and the return of Longstreet's two divisions from Suffolk increased the size of the army to more than 70,000 men. Lee therefore deemed it advisable to reorder the army into three corps rather than two wings. But who would command these three corps? Longstreet was one obvious choice. The bearded, brooding Georgian, whom Lee called "my Old War Horse," was the surviving wing commander from the old organization, and Lee chose him to head the I Corps. The other two appointments were more problematic. Lee knew that picking the right men for these jobs was crucial to the army's success in the campaign he planned. He had unlimited confidence in the rank and file. "They will go anywhere and do anything if properly led," he wrote to one general officer. "But there is the difficulty—proper commanders—where can they be obtained?"

After much soul searching, Lee chose Richard Stoddert Ewell, who had lost a leg at the Battle of Groveton the previous August and who had been on convalescent leave ever since, to command the II Corps—Jackson's old command. Lee was less than enthusiastic about Ewell, whom he considered reliable rather than inspirational. But Ewell had served as Jackson's second in command in the Valley and was more likely than any other officer to be accepted by the men as Stonewall's successor. Lee wrote Davis that Ewell was "an honest, brave soldier, who has always done his duty well." Honest and brave he was, but Ewell was also a product of Jackson's authoritarian command style. Jackson had demanded unquestioning obedience and not only discouraged but actively punished independent thought. Lee's command style was quite different. As Ewell's biographer has noted, Ewell "had been taught to obey orders, not to interpret them. Discretionary orders like those issued by Lee made him uncomfortable."

To command the III Corps, Lee chose Ambrose Powell Hill, who had led the so-called light division in Jackson's old corps and who had distinguished himself at Antietam, Fredericksburg, and Chancellorsville. But Hill, too, had a critical flaw—his poor health. He suffered from prostatitus, a legacy of the gonorrhea he had contracted while on summer leave from West Point as a cadet. The disease was generally in remission, but it had a tendency to flare up unexpectedly. Moreover, Hill's personality even when he was healthy was perhaps more appropriate to division command, in which capacity he had often proven headstrong and impulsive, than to corps command, where his role would be more that of a chessmaster than a warrior. Nevertheless, Lee was relatively confident in recommending Hill for corps command. To Davis he wrote that Hill was "the best soldier of his grade with me."

One man who might have been disappointed by these appointments was the Confederate cavalry commander, James Ewell Brown Stuart, known by his initials as Jeb. Stuart had assumed command of Jackson's corps at Chancellorsville after Stonewall fell wounded, and he had performed well in that capacity, well enough, some thought, to justify his confirmation as permanent commander of the corps. But at age 30, Stuart was too young to be entrusted with such a command, and other than his interim service at Chancellorsville he had no experience as an infantry commander. Besides, Lee wanted Stuart in charge of the cavalry. As the army operated in enemy territory for only the second time in the war, Stuart's savvy assessment of enemy movements would be especially valuable. In lieu of giving Stuart a corps command, therefore, Lee doubled the size of the army's mounted force (from 5,000 to 10,000) by transferring units from the Valley and nominated him for promotion to lieutenant general and the command of what Lee labeled a "grand division" of cavalry.

By mid-June 1863, the Army of Northern Virginia had been both reorganized and reinforced. With a total of 73,000 men, mostly veterans, in three infantry corps and a grand division of cavalry, it carried with it a disproportionate amount of the Confederacy's military manpower as well as its hopes. Moreover, it was an army with an almost religious faith in itself. As Lee prepared to move north, his victorious and expanded army was full of confidence—in itself and in its commander.

North of the Rappahannock, Hooker had recovered from his disaster in the woods around Chancellorsville and was again exuding the brash confidence that was the hallmark of his personality. In his official report on the battle, he sought scapegoats for his defeat. He blamed his cavalry commander, George Stoneman, for failing to distract Stuart, and he blamed Oliver O. Howard whose mostly German soldiers had borne the brunt of Jackson's flanking attack. Hooker was aware that the history of the Army of the Potomac to date was one that suggested an unsuccessful general probably should be looking over his shoulder. Union armies in Virginia had already had five commanders (six, if one counted McClellan twice). Each had fought a single campaign, lost, and suffered the ignominy of replacement. Hooker himself had played a role in undermining his predecessor, Ambrose Burnside, and he surely suspected (correctly, as it turned out) that others were now working to unseat him. Moreover, Hooker knew that he had never been a particular favorite of the president. Lincoln had appointed "Fighting Joe" to command with great misgivings, alarmed by Hooker's incautious private statements about the need for a military dictatorship. The president had allowed Salmon P. Chase, the Radical secretary of the treasury and one of the more influential members of his cabinet, to talk him into giving Hooker his chance, but Lincoln had let Hooker know that he was on probation. "Only those generals who gain successes, can set up dictators," he had written to Hooker in his letter of appointment back in January. "What I ask of you is military success, and I will risk the dictatorship."

After Chancellorsville, Lincoln wrote Hooker again to enquire what he planned to do next, and Hooker replied that "I can only decide after an opportunity has been afforded to learn the feeling of the troops," a curious response that must have left Lincoln scratching his head. A few days later, the president visited the army and was distressed (but probably not surprised) when Darius N. Couch, commander of the II Corps, told him that Hooker was a disaster as army commander. Couch said that he would no longer serve under the man, and urged Lincoln in the strongest terms to replace Hooker with George G. Meade. Two other corps commanders supported Couch's assertions. But Lincoln was reluctant to make another command change so soon. For one thing, the president knew that the Radicals in his own party were not yet ready to give up on Hooker, and after all, the revolving door of command had to

Edwin Forbes's drawing depicts troops going into bivouac at night while, in the foreground, a soldier warms his hands beside a campfire. Soldiers in nineteenth-century armies had to carry with them all the accoutrements necessary for life in camp, including tents, blankets, cooking utensils, and, of course, food. Nevertheless, whenever the army stopped for the night, soldiers managed to discover what the local countryside could supply. Fence rails made excellent firewood, and one or more chickens might be "liberated" to supplement meager rations.

stop sometime. Disappointed by Lincoln's decision, Couch quit the army in disgust. To replace him, Hooker selected Winfield Scott Hancock, a choice that would prove in time to have been inspired.

The other Federal corps commanders were a mixed lot. John F. Reynolds was unquestionably the best of them. Recently the commandant of cadets at West Point, Reynolds was popular with officers and enlisted men alike. He effectively combined discipline with compassion and had made the I Corps a hard-hitting combat unit. Sometime in early June, Lincoln apparently offered him command of the army, but Reynolds turned it down when the president was unable to assure him that he could have a free hand. Another reliable officer was the V Corps' commander, George Gordon Meade, whom Couch had touted for the top job. A regular army officer (West Point, '35) Meade had effectively commanded a brigade in the Seven Days' Battles, a division at Antietam and Fredericksburg, and a corps at Chancellorsville. Known as the Old Snapping Turtle for his temper, he was an advocate of offensive action, a fact that endeared him to Lincoln. Among the others, Hancock was as yet untested, Daniel Sickles was a political general who owed his appointment to Tammany Hall, and Oliver O. Howard bore the burden of embarrassment for the rout of his corps at Chancellorsville.

In terms of raw strength, the Army of the Potomac had contracted since Chancellorsville even as Lee's Army of Northern Virginia had grown. From the 115,000 men that Hooker had commanded at Chancellorsville, the army had lost perhaps a fifth of its strength from combat casualties and expiring enlistments. Hooker now reported a total of about 80,000 infantry, plus some 8,000 cavalry. More importantly, the army's soul was damaged. The men would still fight despite their many disappointments, but their confidence had been shaken, and they had developed a kind of fatalism about their officers. The great Napoleon had once claimed that in warfare the morale is to the physical as three is to one. If so, the Army of the Potomac would embark on its next campaign against the Army of Northern Virginia seriously overmatched.

Although most Civil War regiments, from the North as well as the South, were identified by their state of origin (e.g., the 20th Maine or the 47th Alabama), the Union army also boasted a few regiments of U.S. Regulars. Here soldiers of the 8th U.S. Regulars pose outside Hooker's headquarters. Later in the war, some regiments of "U.S. Colored Troops" also carried a national designation, but in the spring and summer of 1863 there were no African-Americans yet serving with the Army of the Potomac.

ARMY ORGANIZATION

The basic organizational building block of nineteenth-century armies was the regiment. On paper, at least, regiments were composed of ten companies of 100 men each and thus went off to war numbering about 1,000 men. But as battle casualties and disease thinned the ranks, the numbers dropped, and those losses were almost never replaced. As a result, by the summer of 1863, few regiments had anywhere near their original strength. Those regiments that had been organized at the very beginning of the war (such as the 1st Minnesota) might have had no more than a few hundred men left in the ranks, while those organized much later (such as the 141st Pennsylvania) might have boasted 800 or more. The average regiment at Gettysburg numbered about 350 men. Regiments were generally commanded by a colonel.

Regiments were grouped into brigades, usually commanded by a brigadier general but occasionally commanded by a senior colonel. Brigades consisted of three to five regiments and therefore numbered about 1,400 men. Brigades in turn were grouped into divisions, each commanded by a major general. Federal divisions generally consisted of two or three brigades, while most Confederate divisions had four. As a result, Federal divisions might number 3,000 men while Confederate divisions could have twice that many.

Finally, divisions were grouped into corps (pronounced core), a term borrowed from the French and that had its roots in Latin (from *corpus,* for body). The Union army at Gettysburg was composed of seven corps, each numbering between 9,000 and 12,000 men. Lee divided his Army of Northern Virginia into three corps after Jackson's death and just prior to the start of the Gettysburg campaign. With 20,000 to 22,000 men in each Confederate corps, these units were each roughly twice as large as a Federal corps.

CONFEDERATE CORPS COMMANDERS

LIEUTENANT GENERAL JAMES LONGSTREET (I Corps) was the only non-Virginian among the corps commanders in the Army of Northern Virginia. Longstreet was also the most experienced of Lee's lieutenants, having held important commands in all the army's principal campaigns since the First Battle of Bull Run (or Manassas). At Second Manassas in August 1862 he launched the assault that drove the Federal army from the field, but he preferred fighting from cover, as he had in December of that year at Fredericksburg, where his troops had slaughtered the Federal attackers as they repeatedly attempted to assail Marye's Heights. Longstreet's deliberate command style and his abhorrence of the tactical offensive led him into conflict with his superior at Gettysburg and made him the most controversial of all the major players at Gettysburg.

RICHARD (DICK) S. EWELL (II Corps) had served in the Shenandoah Valley under Stonewall Jackson during the first year of the war. At first he had wondered if his eccentric commander was sane, but eventually he became a great admirer of Jackson, and his appointment to Jackson's old command derived at least in part from Lee's assumption that Jackson's men would welcome him as an appropriate replacement for the martyred Stonewall. Ewell had seen no action since Second Manassas due to a bad knee wound that had necessitated the amputation of his left leg, and during the Gettysburg campaign he wore a wooden prosthesis. Ewell's critics claim he missed a great opportunity on the first day of the battle at Gettysburg by declining to assail Cemetery Hill when he had the enemy on the run, and they assert that Jackson would not have hesitated to attack.

AMBROSE POWELL HILL (III Corps) was as impetuous as Longstreet was cautious. A year earlier, during the first of Lee's battles in the Seven Days', Hill had waited impatiently for orders to begin his attack, and finally had advanced without orders. Lee tended to be more forgiving of impetuosity than lethargy, however, and forgave Hill for exceeding his orders. Hill's "light division" subsequently earned a reputation as one of the hardest hitting units in the army in all the campaigns from Richmond to Chancellorsville. Hill's corps would be last in line as the Army of Northern Virginia struck northward across the Potomac into enemy territory, but it would be the first to arrive at Gettysburg, and his subordinates would initiate the battle.

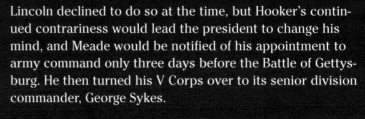

JOHN F. REYNOLDS (I Corps) was the beau ideal of a soldier. Tall, handsome, and-comfortable in the saddle, he completed a successful tour as the commandant of cadets at West Point just prior to the outbreak of war. A strict disciplinarian, he nevertheless managed to command volunteer soldiers without provoking their resentment or animosity. Lincoln offered Reynolds command of the army a month before the battle, but Reynolds declined when the president could not promise him a free hand. He would be the first Federal corps commander to arrive at Gettysburg.

WINFIELD SCOTT HANCOCK (II Corps), though new to command, would emerge as one of the heroes of the Battle of Gettysburg. Hancock (West Point, '44), a professional soldier like Reynolds, gained command of the II Corps only a month before the battle, when Darius Couch quit the army in disgust at Hooker's command leadership. At Gettysburg, Hancock would win accolades both for rallying the army on Cemetery Hill on July 1, and for his heroic defense of Cemetery Ridge on July 3.

DANIEL E. SICKLES (III Corps) was the only one of the Federal corps commanders who had not graduated from West Point. One of a number of so-called political generals in the Union army, he had been a New York congressman until 1861 and became a brigadier general by raising a brigade of New York infantry. Promoted to major general a year later, he was made a corps commander by his friend Joe Hooker. Notorious for his scandal-ridden private life, he was a strong-headed commander likely to rely more on his own judgement than on strict obedience to orders.

GEORGE GORDON MEADE (V Corps) lacked the charisma of Hancock and the panache of Sickles, but he was an experienced and competent commander. After the Chancellorsville fiasco, several officers urged Lincoln to make Meade the army commander in Hooker's place.

Lincoln declined to do so at the time, but Hooker's continued contrariness would lead the president to change his mind, and Meade would be notified of his appointment to army command only three days before the Battle of Gettysburg. He then turned his V Corps over to its senior division commander, George Sykes.

JOHN SEDGWICK (VI Corps), at age 60, was the oldest of the corps commanders who fought at Gettysburg. He had commanded a division in the Army of the Potomac until he was badly wounded at Antietam and was promoted to VI Corps command after recovering from his wounds. His principal contribution at Gettysburg was a successful forced march that brought his corps to the battlefield in time to shore up the Federal defensive line on July 2.

OLIVER OTIS HOWARD (XI Corps) was a brave and competent soldier who had been wounded twice and lost an arm in the battles outside Richmond in 1862. But Howard and his command were under a cloud. His men, mostly German immigrants, had suffered the ignominy of being routed by Jackson's flank attack at Chancellorsville, and they had not fully recovered from that experience by the time they arrived at Gettysburg. Howard nevertheless played a crucial role on the first day at Gettysburg, effectively commanding the army from 1 to 4 P.M. on July 1.

HENRY W. SLOCUM (XII Corps), at age 35, was the youngest of the Federal corps commanders at Gettysburg, but curiously he was also the most senior by date of rank, having been a major general since July 1862. An 1852 graduate of West Point, where he had roomed with Philip Sheridan, he was wounded in the First Battle of Bull Run but recovered in time to participate in the battles of Antietam and Chancellorsville. Slocum was competent and reliable but lacked the kind of magnetic personality that might have made him an inspirational leader. After the battle, some criticized his tardiness in getting his command to Gettysburg, and at least one insisted that he had lived up to his name: "slow come."

CHAPTER TWO

The Eyes and Ears of the Army

(June 3–June 28, 1863)

C ivil War army commanders depended on a variety of sources to keep track of their opponents. Sympathetic local farmers were often willing to recount what troops had passed by, and occasionally newspapers from the other side incautiously published the location, size, and disposition of military units. During the Peninsular campaign in 1862, McClellan had hired a detective (the subsequently famous Alan Pinkerton), and James Longstreet hired paid spies (or "scouts," as they were known) to gather information about the enemy. The most effective and reliable source of military intelligence for both sides, however, was the cavalry. The primary job of the mounted arm was to patrol the countryside and bring information about enemy strength and movements, and simultaneously to screen its own army from the prying eyes of enemy cavalry. So far in the war, the South had been more effective at this than the North. Hooker had been disgusted by the inefficiency of the Union cavalry during the Chancellorsville campaign, though in part, at least, its failure was his own fault. He had ordered his cavalry commander, George Stoneman, on an extended raid south of the Wilderness in the expectation that Stuart's rebel cavalry would follow him. Instead, Stuart had stayed with the Confederate main body and had played a crucial role in the Southern victory. Hooker nevertheless dispatched Stoneman to a desk job in Washington and replaced him in the field with Alfred Pleasonton, who, at 39, was a decade older than his Confederate counterpart. In the four weeks preceding the Battle of Gettysburg, the cavalry of both sides scoured the countryside, each seeking intelligence about the other's army. Their successes, and their failures, would affect the campaign in important ways.

Lee's army began moving early on the morning of June 3. Two of Longstreet's divisions (those of John Bell Hood and Lafayette McLaws) pulled out of their bivouacs near the fords across the Rappahannock and began tramping westward toward Culpeper, halfway between the Virginia Wilderness and the Blue Ridge. From there,

Opposite: Jeb Stuart is portrayed as the dashing cavalier in *Seasons of the Confederacy—Autumn*, a mural by Charles Hoffbauer that captures the aura of glamour that surrounded the mounted arm, especially in the Southern armies. But the real business of the cavalry had less to do with bold raids and dramatic charges than it did with the more mundane tasks of gathering information and providing assessments for the army commander.

Lee could either move farther west into the Shenandoah Valley, the scene of Jackson's victories in the 1862 campaign, or he could head north along the Orange & Alexandria Railroad to Manassas, the scene of two other famous Confederate victories. Later that same morning, Ewell's corps also pulled out of camp and marched west following Longstreet. A. P. Hill's corps remained in place near Fredericksburg, opposite the Federal pickets on the north bank.

Hooker learned of the movement almost at once and assumed it was preliminary to yet another rebel campaign in the direction of Manassas Junction. He telegraphed Lincoln about Lee's move and urged that he be allowed "to pitch into his rear"—that is, to attack Hill's isolated corps at Fredericksburg—though he acknowledged that doing so would mean that Lee's lead elements might well reach Warrenton, two-thirds of the way to Manassas, before Hooker could complete his victory.

Lincoln was not pleased by the prospect of Hooker committing his army to a battle south of the Rappahannock while two-thirds of Lee's army was moving north toward Washington, and through his chief of staff, Major General Henry Wager Halleck, he suggested a different strategy. "Would it not be more advisable to fight his movable column first," Halleck wired, "instead of attacking his intrenchments?" In that same telegram, Halleck reminded Hooker that the defenses of Washington were unlikely to stand up to a serious attack by Lee's main army and that it was therefore "perilous" for Hooker "to permit Lee's main force to move upon the Potomac while your army is attacking an intrenched position on the other side of the Rappahannock." Just in case Hooker missed the point, Lincoln wrote him a private letter the same day that showed both Lincoln's instinctive grasp of strategy and also his characteristic use of colorful images. "In case you find Lee coming to the North of the Rappahannock," Lincoln wrote, "I would by no means cross to the South of it. If he should leave a rear force at Fredericksburg, tempting you to fall upon it, it would fight in intrenchments, and have you at disadvantage, and so, man for man, worst you at that point, while his main force would in some way be getting an advantage of you northward. In one word, I would not take any risk of being entangled upon the river, like an ox jumped half over a fence, and liable to be torn by dogs, front and rear, without a fair chance to gore one way or kick the other." It was just the kind of backwoods analogy that used to provoke George McClellan's scorn, and perhaps Hooker, too, was less appreciative of the advice than he ought to have been.

Denied his preferred strategy, Hooker sought to obtain information about Lee's intentions. Was he planning to slip farther west into the Valley or advance northward along the Orange & Alexandria to the old battleground at Manassas? To find out, and to throw Lee off his stroke, Hooker ordered his new cavalry commander to conduct a reconnaissance in force. He instructed Pleasonton to take three divisions of cavalry (about 8,000 troopers), reinforced by two brigades of infantry, a total of some 11,000 men, and probe the growing enemy campsite north of Culpeper at a railroad siding known as

In May 1864, a well-equipped mobile telegraph station was captured by photographer David Knox in Petersburg, Virginia. The Civil War was the first large-scale conflict to make wide use of telegraphic communication. Even when the armies were on maneuver, mobile telegraphic stations such as this one kept army commanders in touch with their political masters. Lincoln often spent many long hours in the telegraph office in Washington awaiting news from the front, and he used the telegraph to maintain contact with his field commanders.

J. E. B. STUART

James Ewell Brown Stuart was only 30 years old during the Gettysburg campaign. He may have grown his luxuriant beard, in part at least, to conceal his youth. Another motive may have been a determination to cover an uninspiring physiognomy. When clean shaven, Stuart's features were so plain that his West Point classmates had sarcastically nicknamed him Beauty. Graduating thirteenth out of forty-six in the West Point class of 1854, Stuart spent most of the rest of the decade on cavalry service in "Bleeding Kansas." In 1855 he married Flora Cooke, the daughter of future Union general Philip St. George Cooke.

Resigning immediately after Fort Sumter, Stuart made his way to Virginia, where Lee made him a lieutenant colonel of cavalry in the forces of Virginia. Stuart idolized Lee, whom he had first met as a cadet at West Point when Lee was superintendent. And Lee as well came to rely on Stuart, whom he treated almost as a son. Stuart was promoted to brigadier general after the Battle of Bull Run, but his emergence as a national hero occurred in the spring of 1862, when he conducted his famous Ride Around McClellan during the Peninsular campaign. Stuart's escapade helped lift the gloom off the Confederacy after a dismal winter and spring, and his bold dash

J. E. B. Stuart by John Adams Elder

achieved heroic proportions in the Richmond press, which took great glee in pointing out that Stuart had made a fool of his own father-in-law, General Cooke, who had fruitlessly pursued him for most of four days. Stuart's boldness seemed to personify the spirit of the revolutionary South, and he became "Jeb," the dashing cavalier, the "bold dragoon." Almost as if determined to live up to this portrait of himself, he took to wearing a scarlet-lined cape, a bright yellow sash, highly polished boots, and a cavalry hat dominated by a large ostrich plume.

But Stuart was not merely a military fop. Along with having a popular image, he was also a professional soldier who took his responsibilities seriously. Lee trusted him more than any of his cavalry officers, and when he reorganized the army after Chancellorsville, he made Stuart the commanding officer of a "grand division" of 10,000 men. Lee necessarily sought officers whose discretion he could trust, for he tended to give his officers a lot of leeway. Stuart's critics argue that during the Gettysburg campaign, Stuart took advantage of that tendency by behaving irresponsibly, even childishly: leading three brigades of his "grand division" on an extended raid near the national capital instead of guarding the van of the army as it entered Pennsylvania.

Brandy Station, where Stuart's cavalry corps was all but flaunting itself by holding reviews and parades.

One such review took place on June 5, and it was an impressive spectacle. Stuart's long line of 9,536 mounted troopers stretched for more than a mile end to end. Three bands played martial airs while Stuart reviewed the troops, and then the whole grand division passed in review, first at a walk, then a gallop. Afterward the men participated in a mock battle as the cavalry charged the horse artillery, which fired blank cartridges. With the troopers whooping and hollering, the artillery firing blank rounds, and the smoke from the black powder filling the air, it made a grand display, and the ladies who had come out to watch cheered and clapped enthusiastically. That night the officers attended a ball held in their honor. Stuart was pleased with the review, but he was disappointed that Lee had not been present. When the commanding gen-

John Buford (seated, posing with his staff) was arguably the most talented of the Federal cavalry officers. Passed over for command of the cavalry arm after Stoneman's dismissal because he was junior to Alfred Pleasonton by eleven days, Buford was nevertheless a critical player in the Gettysburg campaign. He led the initial charge at Brandy Station, and he was the first Federal general officer to arrive at Gettysburg.

eral did arrive three days later, on June 8, Stuart put on another review for his entertainment. Once again the corps passed by in review. But there was no mock battle this time. Lee wanted Stuart to be ready for an early start the next morning.

Stuart might be forgiven for assuming that he had little to fear from Union cavalry. In two years of warfare he had never encountered a mounted Yankee force that could match his own. Exactly one year before, during the Peninsular campaign in June 1862, Stuart had won his first public notice by leading 1,200 troopers on a scouting raid beyond the Federal right flank, then circling completely around behind the Federal army, cutting telegraph wires and burning bridges as he rode. Stuart and his men were pursued by a force that was easily three times larger than Stuart's own (ironically commanded by his own father-in-law), Stuart's men stayed in the saddle for three days and returned safely to Richmond only after riding completely around the Federal army. To the residents of the imperiled rebel capital, it was just the tonic needed to boost morale. It was as if Stuart had participated in a grand game of "capture the flag" and had come home waving the enemy banner. Stuart duplicated this feat in the fall, when he led another raiding party around McClellan's army in the aftermath of the Antietam campaign. Now that he commanded a unified cavalry corps, it was barely imaginable that the bluecoats would attempt to molest him.

Yet even as Stuart's troopers bedded down on June 8 after their second grand review in four days, two of Pleasonton's cavalry divisions were gathering on the north bank of the Rappahannock at Kelly's Ford, less than five miles away, and a third was approaching Beverly Ford, only three miles away. The division at Beverly Ford was commanded by Brigadier General John Buford, a dark-eyed professional soldier who might very well have been tapped for command of the corps but for the fact that Pleasonton was a mere eleven days his senior in rank. At just past 2 A.M. on June 9, Buford awakened his troopers, and by 4:30 they were splashing across the Rappahannock in a dense early-morning fog. His men quickly overcame the rebel pickets on the south bank and drove deep into the Confederate campsite fending off rebel troopers from the 7th Virginia, some of whom were still in their nightshirts. This brash assault attracted the attention of the bulk of Stuart's command, including Stuart himself, and soon Buford found himself outnumbered and forced to go on the defensive.

Buford's bold sally had stalled, but it had also cleared the way for the other two divisions in this Federal pincer movement, those of David McMurtrie Gregg and Alfred N. Duffie, as well as the two brigades of infantry, all advancing from Kelly's Ford. Stuart had anticipated that any enemy threat to his position was likely to come from both river crossings, so before he joined the fight against Buford, he sent a

Allen Carter Redwood's 1863 woodcut portrays the charge of Buford's command in the Battle of Brandy Station on June 9. Buford's bold assault caught the Confederates by surprise, though Stuart's men soon rallied and fought the Federal horsemen to a standstill. Even so, the fight marked the emergence of a new sense of pride within the Union cavalry and may have also contributed to Stuart's decision making in the critical days before the Battle of Gettysburg.

brigade under Beverly Robertson to block the road from Kelly's Ford. But the Federals who crossed there not only started late but they failed to take the direct road west toward Fleetwood Hill where Stuart made his headquarters. Instead they rode south for a mile before turning west, and in doing so they inadvertently bypassed Robertson's brigade, which was lying in wait for them on the wrong road. Thus it was that Stuart was shocked at midmorning to learn that even as he fought Buford's outnumbered division to a standstill, other enemy forces had swept around him and were threatening Fleetwood Hill, the capture of which would force him to give up the battlefield. It was a sobering, not to say shocking, moment.

It was also a moment of great opportunity for both Gregg and Duffie, but so

Confederate Brigadier General Beverly H. Robertson had briefly commanded Stonewall Jackson's cavalry in the Shenandoah Valley, and had served successfully in North Carolina, but Stuart never fully trusted him. Stuart called him "by far the most troublesome man I have to deal with," though his antipathy may have been derived in part from the fact that Robertson was also a former suitor of Stuart's wife, Flora.

If Stuart represented the stereotype of the dashing Southern cavalry officer, Alfred Pleasonton very likely represented (to Southern eyes at least) the stereotype of the conniving Yankee. He even sported the kind of pointed waxed mustache (the tips of which extended nearly to his ears) often associated with vaudeville villains. Pleasonton's officers thought him a posturing dissembler. Perhaps the most devastating testimony came from Charles Francis Adams Jr., scion of a famous Massachusetts family whose father was the U.S. ambassador to Britain. The younger Adams wrote home to his mother that Pleasonton "is pure and simple a newspaper humbug. You always see his name in the papers, but to us who have served under him he is notorious as a bully and a toady." Nor was Adams alone in such views. Charles Russell Lowell concluded that Pleasonton's promotion to command the Union cavalry was the product of "systematic lying."

Hooker gave Pleasonton the command of all Union cavalry because he was determined to rid himself of George Stoneman, whose cautious (Hooker would have said timorous) leadership of the cavalry during the Chancellorsville campaign he found wanting. Pleasonton was the next senior

Major General Alfred Pleasonton

officer and had ingratiated himself at headquarters. Hooker briefly considered giving John Buford the command (which hindsight suggests would have been a better decision), but Pleasonton was eleven days senior in rank to Buford, and rather than provoke another controversy, Hooker gave the job to Pleasonton on May 22.

Pleasonton directed the Union raid on Brandy Station on June 9, which brought the much criticized Federal cavalry new credibility and greatly embarrassed Jeb Stuart. As a reward for this action, Hooker recommended Pleasonton's promotion to major general effective June 22, the day after the Battle of Upperville. In spite of these limited successes, however, Pleasonton's cavalry failed to penetrate Stuart's screen to discover the location or movements of Lee's infantry. The blue troopers fought their gray counterparts almost to a standstill throughout much of June— at Aldie, Middleburg, Upperville, and elsewhere—but they failed to gain the critical intelligence that Hooker (and later Meade) needed to make timely decisions. As a result, the Federal army moved northward from the Rappahannock into Maryland and finally into Pennsylvania, uncertain where Lee was or where he was going.

unaccustomed were they to having the upper hand over their rebel counterparts that they failed to take advantage of it. Instead of charging up and over Fleetwood Hill and winning the day, they paused, deterred by the presence of a single piece of rebel artillery atop the hill. Their hesitation gave Stuart the chance he needed to reinforce the threatened position. After that, the battle at Brandy Station deteriorated into a wild melee: mounted troopers on both sides wheeled about with drawn sabers to slash at one another; dust roiled up from 10,000 hooves making visibility difficult and rendering the battlefield even more confusing. One member of the 1st Pennsylvania regiment, part of Gregg's division, recalled "an indescribable clashing and slashing, banging and yelling. . . . We were now so mixed up with the rebels that every man was fighting desperately." After several hours, the Federals gradually found their way back to the Rappahannock and withdrew in good order to the north bank of the river.

A Cavalry Charge by Edwin Forbes depicts a Federal cavalry advance against Confederate artillery. The Battle of Brandy Station was the first, and largest, true cavalry battle in the Civil War. It was also the engagement where Federal cavalry finally demonstrated it could fight Stuart's horsemen on even terms.

Technically Brandy Station was a drawn battle. The Federals had surprised Stuart's cavalry, but they had not defeated it. Neither had they managed to penetrate Stuart's screen to discover the strength and location of Lee's infantry, which was the reason for which Hooker had dispatched them. Moreover, the Federal attackers had suffered more casualties (484 to 433), and they had lost an additional 372 captured. But emotionally Brandy Station was a tremendous morale boost for the Federal troopers. They had caught Stuart by surprise and had fought him to a standstill, withdrawing from the field at their leisure. They insisted the battle proved that Union cavalry was now on a par with its Confederate foe. For his part, Stuart claimed a victory and he noted—accurately—that it was Southern cavalry that held the field at the end of the day. But he could not disguise the fact that he had been embarrassed. More than one student of the Gettysburg campaign has suggested that Stuart's humiliation at being caught by surprise at Brandy Station was instrumental in his subsequent decision making during the ensuing days and weeks.

Brandy Station was not a great battle. With fewer than a thousand casualties, it barely ranked as a serious skirmish in the long list of bloody Civil War battles, and Lee did not let it interfere with his timetable. The very next morning, his infantry was up and on the road early, marching west toward the Blue Ridge. Ewell's corps was in the lead this time; the veterans of the Valley campaign were returning to the scene of their greatest victories. They passed through Sperryville and turned north toward Chester Gap, snaking up the side of the Blue Ridge, through the pass, and then down its western face to Front Royal on the Shenandoah River. Longstreet and Hill remained in place at Culpeper.

It seemed to Hooker that his best opportunity in these circumstances was to again ignore Ewell and strike southward. He even proposed to Lincoln that he avoid Lee's army altogether and make a "rapid advance on Richmond." "I now have two bridges over the Rappahannock," he wired the president on June 10, "ready to spring over the river below Fredericksburg." He suggested that "a sufficiency of troops" could be scraped together to deal with whatever emergency Lee's movements might provoke in the North while he struck out for the rebel capital. "Will it not promote the true interest of the cause for me to march to Richmond at once?" he queried.

Once again Lincoln had to turn his general around and show him what was important. "*Lee's* army and not *Richmond*, is your true objective point," the president wrote patiently to his field general, underscoring the key words. "If he comes toward the upper Potomac, follow him on his flank, and on the inside track, shortening your lines while he lengthens his. Fight him when opportunity offers. If he stays where he is fret him and fret him."

Hooker's engineers had constructed these two pontoon bridges over the Rappahannock (as seen in Timothy O'Sullivan's May 1863 photo). As Ewell's corps moved northward through the Valley toward the crossings of the Potomac, Hooker wired Washington asking permission to ignore the rebel column and strike southward. Hooker announced that he was ready "to spring over the river" and make a "rapid advance on Richmond," but Lincoln ordered him to concentrate instead on Lee's marching column.

The Federal cavalry again proved its mettle on June 21, when Pleasonton's troopers drove Stuart's men from Upperville, Virginia. In Edwin Forbes's illustration of that battle, Federal horsemen chase rebel cavalry toward the Blue Ridge Mountains in the near distance. The Federal cavalry pursued them but halted when they encountered Confederate infantry. A member of the 7th South Carolina infantry recalled that "a courier arrived from the rear saying Stuart's cavalry was heavily pressed by the enemy. We were put under arms & by 3 pm ordered back across this river [the Shenandoah], marched three miles, drew up in line of battle . . . up on the mountain. Here we allowed the cavalry to pass to our rear, & we waited for the enemy. . . . As soon as they discovered we had infantry they turned [back] toward Manassas."

Again disappointed, Hooker fell back from the Rappahannock and moved northward along the Orange & Alexandria toward Manassas, which kept him between Lee's army and Washington. As soon as he began to fall back, Hill's corps broke camp and followed Ewell westward into the Valley. Longstreet's corps took a different route. His men marched northward out of Culpeper, staying east of the Blue Ridge as far as Ashby's Gap, well north of the Manassas Gap Railroad, before turning west and disappearing over the ridge line. Once all three of Lee's corps had disappeared behind the gray curtain of the Blue Ridge, Hooker both figuratively and literally lost sight of them. Unless and until his own cavalry could penetrate Stuart's screen to bring back reports from the Valley, he could only guess at what was happening on the other side of the mountains.

It would not have improved his mood if he had known. The advanced elements of Ewell's II Corps reached Winchester on June 14, the same day that Hooker began to fall back from the Rappahannock. At Winchester, a Union garrison of some 6,900 men under Major General Robert H. Milroy was acting as a kind of advance guard for Harpers Ferry at the foot of the Valley. Despite warnings from Washington that he was too exposed, Milroy had remained at Winchester, and only now did he try to extricate himself. It was too late. Acting with the kind of speed and decisiveness that would have drawn the approval of Stonewall Jackson, Ewell coordinated an enveloping movement, and his men descended on Winchester from three directions at once. Milroy tried to fight his way out, but Ewell caught him and routed him in the early-morning hours of June 15 in what has gone down in history as the Second Battle of Winchester. Ewell's men inflicted some 450 casualties and took nearly 4,000 prisoners as well as twenty-three cannons and 300 wagons. It was a spectacular little victory, and it cleared the way for Lee's continuing advance down the Valley to the crossings over the Potomac.

Meanwhile, in an effort to obtain some hard information about Lee's location and movement, Hooker ordered Pleasonton to send three brigades of cavalry to investigate the passes through the Blue Ridge from Ashby's Gap to Snicker's Gap, eight miles farther north. The road to both gaps ran through the little town of Aldie, Virginia, which nestled in a pass through the Bull Run Mountains a dozen miles east of the Blue Ridge. Judson Kilpatrick's was the first Federal cavalry brigade to arrive at

The beautiful rolling Piedmont of Virginia, as seen in this 1985 photograph, was the scene of a series of cavalry clashes in mid-June 1863, as the two armies moved northward on opposite sides of the Blue Ridge (seen in the distance). Despite a series of small successes, the Union troopers failed to penetrate the passes of the Blue Ridge to discover where Lee's infantry was and where it was going.

Aldie on June 17, and his men found it held by elements of Stuart's command. Never the contemplative type, Kilpatrick ordered an immediate charge that swept past the first line of rebel defenders, but then almost at once he found himself the target of a powerful counterattack. After a fight that lasted several hours, Kilpatrick managed to drive the rebel cavalry from the town, but he failed to get beyond it to the Blue Ridge, and he learned nothing of Lee's dispositions.

Virtually the same scenario played itself out at Middleburg, five miles to the west. Alfred Duffie, demoted to regimental command after his tardiness at Brandy Station, swept aside a small Confederate picket at Middleburg but then found himself attacked by a much larger force and had to give up his position and fall back.

The Federal cavalry made other efforts to push through Stuart's troopers, none of them successful. On June 18, they captured Middleburg, and on June 21, in the biggest cavalry confrontation since Brandy Station, Pleasonton attacked Stuart's dismounted troopers at Upperville. In this fight, the Federals were reinforced by an infantry brigade—one of the best in the army—commanded by Colonel Strong Vincent, who had turned 26 just four days earlier. Vincent's brigade of infantry flushed Stuart's men from their positions with a series of flanking maneuvers, and the Federal cavalry pursued them all the way to Ashby's Gap, which was being held by the Confederate division of Lafayette McLaws. Satisfied with this tactical victory, Pleasonton withdrew.

A victory it may have been, but except for gaining the information that a rebel infantry division held Ashby's Gap, Hooker was no better informed about Lee's dispositions after Upperville than he had been before. Although the Federal cavalry had once again proved its mettle, and Strong Vincent had shown evidence of things to come, Stuart could rightfully claim that he had fulfilled his mission: he had kept the prying eyes of the Federal cavalry east of the Blue Ridge, and Lee's northward movement could continue not only unhindered but unobserved.

Now it was Stuart's turn to consider his alternatives. On June 22, the day after the fight at Upperville, he wrote to Longstreet, the nearest corps commander, to ask about the next phase of the campaign. Ewell's corps was by now safely through the Valley (on June 22, his men were closing in on Chambersburg, Pennsylvania). Hill's corps was not far behind, though Longstreet's men remained in the lower Valley. Hooker's army was still bivouacked on the east side of the Bull Run Mountains near Manassas. One option was for Stuart to remain on Longstreet's flank and rear to fend off further Federal cavalry probes. To do this, he might parallel Longstreet's advance, riding northward along the eastern side of the Blue Ridge, until the whole army was north of the Potomac. A second possibility was to move to the front of the column and screen Ewell's advance into Pennsylvania. Ewell did have one brigade of cavalry with him as he moved into enemy territory, but that was not enough for an army moving in unfamiliar terrain. A third possibility was for Stuart to divide up his command (he had five brigades) and attempt to accomplish both tasks. Stuart asked Longstreet to determine which of these alternatives was most desirable.

Longstreet took Stuart's letter to Lee, and they responded by suggesting that Stuart divide his "grand division" not quite in half, leaving two brigades to guard the flank and rear of Longstreet's corps, while he led the other three north to screen Ewell's advance. Characteristically, Lee's response left Stuart a lot of latitude:

If you find that he [Hooker] is moving northward, and that two brigades can guard the Blue Ridge & take care of your rear, you can move with the other three into Maryland & take position on General Ewell's right, place yourself in communication with him, guard his flank, keep him informed of the enemy's movements & collect all the supplies you can for the use of the army.

Lee did not suggest a route by which Stuart might "move . . . into Maryland." It was not part of Lee's command style to micromanage his subordinates, and he trusted Stuart's judgment. It is not unreasonable to speculate, however, that Lee presumed that Stuart would move northward either through the Valley or parallel to it east of the Blue Ridge, thus continuing to screen the army, until he reached Ewell's right flank somewhere in Pennsylvania. But Longstreet's note, which Stuart received the same day, suggested another possibility. Longstreet wrote that Stuart should follow Hooker as the Federal army moved north, crossing the Potomac in the enemy's rear. Moreover, he implied that Lee concurred in this suggestion.

Longstreet's proposal was more in line with what Stuart wanted to do. When John Singleton Mosby rode into camp the next day (June 23) and told Stuart that it would be possible to pass through the rear of Hooker's army and swing around *behind* it before continuing north, Stuart dispatched a messenger to Lee to ask if such a course would be acceptable. Lee replied with conditional approval. "You will . . . be able to judge whether you can pass around their army without hindrance," he wrote. But he also made it clear that screening the advance was Stuart's first priority. "The sooner you cross into Maryland, after tomorrow, the better," he wrote. Then, almost as an afterthought, he added: "Be watchful and circumspect in all your movements."

Stuart was delighted. He interpreted Lee's letter as permission to ride around Hooker's army to the east, crossing the Potomac between Hooker and Washington before turning west for an eventual linkup with Ewell. Such a movement would disrupt Federal communications, it would send a shock wave through the national capital, and it would provide many more opportunities for collecting supplies for the army. Not incidentally, it would also reestablish the superiority of the Confederate cavalry after the embarrassment of Brandy Station.

Stuart's decision to ride around the Federal army was certainly bold enough (though hardly "circumspect"), but almost as important was the decision he made about how to divide his command. Of his five brigadiers, there were two whom he did not fully trust. One was Beverly Robertson, who had waited passively on the road

A Federal horse artillery fires in support of the Federal cavalry at Upperville on June 21 as Stuart's horsemen retreat toward Ashby's Gap in this drawing by Alfred Waud. Even more than Brandy Station, the Battle of Upperville, in Virginia's beautiful horse country, proved that the Federal cavalry had become a match for their gray-clad counterparts.

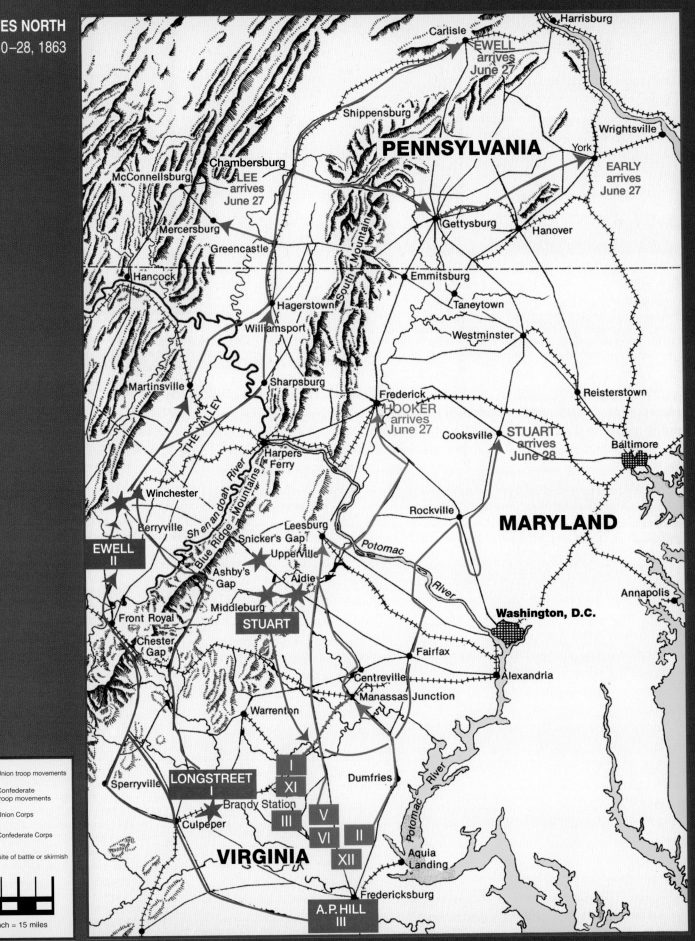

LEE MOVES NORTH
June 10–28, 1863

PENNSYLVANIA

Harrisburg
Carlisle
EWELL arrives June 27
Shippensburg
Wrightsville
York
McConnellsburg
Chambersburg
LEE arrives June 27
EARLY arrives June 27
Mercersburg
Greencastle
Gettysburg
Hanover
Hancock
Emmitsburg
Taneytown
Hagerstown
Williamsport
Westminster
Martinsville
Sharpsburg
Frederick
HOOKER arrives June 27
Reisterstown
THE VALLEY
Harpers Ferry
Cooksville
STUART arrives June 28
Baltimore
Winchester
MARYLAND
Berryville
Rockville
Snicker's Gap
Leesburg
EWELL II
Upperville
Potomac
Ashby's Gap
Aldie
River
Annapolis
Middleburg
STUART
Washington, D.C.
Front Royal
Chester Gap
Fairfax
Centreville
Alexandria
Warrenton
Manassas Junction
Sperryville
Dumfries
Potomac River
LONGSTREET I
I
XI
Brandy Station
V
Culpeper
III
II
VI
Aquia Landing
VIRGINIA
XII
Fredericksburg
A.P. HILL III

→ Union troop movements
→ Confederate troop movements
I   Union Corps
EWELL II   Confederate Corps
★   site of battle or skirmish

1 inch = 15 miles

from Kelly's Ford during the Battle of Brandy Station, a passivity that suggested a lack of imagination, if not worse. Stuart thought Robertson could perform routine duties well enough but did not trust him to make important decisions. The other was William E. "Grumble" Jones, a successful raider who was much loved by his own troopers but who was also the near opposite of Stuart in personal characteristics. Jones was careless in his appearance, even sloppy, and he was both profane and cantankerous. Stuart simply did not like him. In making his dispositions, therefore, Stuart detailed Robertson and Jones to remain with the army, with Robertson in command, while he took the other three brigades—those of Wade Hampton, John Chambliss, and Fitzhugh Lee, the 28-year-old nephew of the commanding general—for an extended ride around

Hooker's army. In doing so, not only did he take three-fifths of his command but he took his three best subordinate generals as well. Stuart expected that the raid would last three, perhaps four, days. Instead it lasted seven. Meanwhile, Lee's infantry, if not quite "blind" (the word often used by Stuart's critics), was nevertheless deprived of its best cavalry commanders, a circumstance that limited the quality, as well as the quantity, of information that flowed into Lee's headquarters as the army moved north into Pennsylvania.

Stuart departed on his raid on June 25, and he ran into trouble almost at once. A Federal infantry division occupied the road that he had planned to use from Aldie to Fairfax. He therefore swung southward, thus extending his route, to avoid a direct confrontation. His gray troopers rode southeast to Bristoe Station, where they bivouacked on June 26, then turned northeast for Fairfax and a crossing of the Potomac at Rowser's Ford, twenty miles upriver from Washington, early on the morning of June 28. Across the river that same day, his videttes (mounted sentinels) discovered a cavalryman's dream: a long train of fully loaded wagons headed for Washington on the Rockville Pike. Unable to ignore this prize, Stuart's troopers galloped after it and captured 125 wagons, but the chase took up much of the day, and Stuart's further advance would now be slowed by his determination to bring these wagons with him. That night he camped at Cooksville in central Maryland. He had already been on the road for four days, and the Federals still lay between him and the main body of the Confederate army. Indeed, by now Stuart could not have said for sure where the Confederate army was.

British artist Frank Vizetelly, who covered the Civil War for England's *Illustrated London News*, sketched Stuart in camp talking with his subordinates. After successfully defending the passes through the Blue Ridge, Stuart considered several alternatives for the next phase of the campaign. In the end he decided (characteristically) on the boldest option: to take his three best brigades and ride completely around the Union army before rejoining the Confederate army somewhere in Pennsylvania.

Opposite: In June, Lee sent his three corps marching first west over the Blue Ridge Mountains, then north through the Shenandoah Valley into Maryland and Pennsylvania. Hooker wanted to plunge south toward Richmond, but Lincoln ordered him to keep his army between Lee and Washington. After guarding the passes through the ridge, Confederate cavalry commander J. E. B. Stuart embarked on a lengthy raid behind enemy lines.

Stuart's cavalry marches near the Culpeper courthouse, as illustrated by Vizetelly. The three brigades of cavalry Stuart took with him on his lengthy raid through Maryland covered more than 220 miles in seven days. Though he captured a wagon train of Federal supplies and caused panic in a number of Northern cities, he was out of touch with the Confederate infantry for most of a week, which dramatically limited the amount and the quality of information Lee and his subordinates had on which to base their decisions.

That same night, twenty miles west of Stuart's position at Cooksville, the Army of the Potomac was bivouacked around Frederick, Maryland, where it had arrived the day before having crossed the Potomac at Edward's Ferry on June 25 and 26. Hooker was in a foul mood. All week he had quarreled with his masters in Washington. Though the cables came from Halleck, Hooker knew it was Lincoln's voice he was hearing. And he did not like what he heard. On June 27, with his army safely bivouacked around Frederick, Hooker visited Harpers Ferry, which the Confederates had bypassed on their way into Pennsylvania. He believed that the outpost had lost its usefulness in the campaign, and was in any case vulnerable to being plucked like a ripe peach by an enemy force that occupied the high ground around it. Rather than await such an eventuality, he argued that the post should be abandoned and its garrison added to his field army. Lincoln (through Halleck) told him no. Hold Harpers Ferry as long as possible, Halleck told him. For Hooker, this was the last straw. Expecting to shock Lincoln and Halleck into acquiescence, he submitted his resignation.

Three hours past midnight, a courier from Washington arrived in the Federal camp at Frederick and found George Gordon Meade asleep in his tent. The courier, Colonel James A. Hardie, told Meade that he was the bearer of "trouble" for the general. Meade's sense of humor was never very acute even at the best of times, and he was not quite sure what to make of Hardie's ominous declaration until the colonel

handed Meade the dispatch that made him commanding general of the army. Once again the Federal army would go into battle with a new hand at the helm.

If, instead of depending on their cavalry, either of the opposing army commanders on the morning of June 28 could somehow have applied twenty-first century technology and ordered a global positioning satellite to pinpoint the disposition of all military units within a fifty-mile radius of Gettysburg, he would have seen a curious phenomenon. The Federal Army of the Potomac, now under its fourth commander in eight months, was encamped around Frederick, Maryland, thirty miles south of Gettysburg. Lee's infantry, the *Southern* army, was spread out well *north* of the Federal army in a wide semicircle across south-central Pennsylvania: the men of Ewell's corps were split between York, fifty miles north of Baltimore, and Carlisle, thirty miles north of Gettysburg; Hill's corps was west of Gettysburg nearing the passes through South Mountain (as the Blue Ridge was called in Pennsylvania); and Longstreet was behind him in a long column from Chambersburg south toward Greencastle. Near the bottom of our satellite map, twenty miles south of Hooker's army at Frederick, and some

C. O. Bostwick's photograph of Harpers Ferry during the Civil War, taken from the Maryland side of the Potomac River, makes it evident that the security of the small town (and its armory), which was nestled in a crook of the Shenandoah and Potomac Rivers, was entirely at the mercy of any forces that might occupy the high ground around it. The high ground right behind the town is Bolivar Heights.

George Gordon Meade, in a painting by Daniel Ridgway Knight, became the fifth commander of the Union army in the eastern theater on June 28. Surprised by his appointment, Meade was also less than thrilled to be ordered to take command literally in the midst of an ongoing campaign. A normally taciturn individual, he was prone to bursts of anger when frustrated and thus earned the nickname Old Snapping Turtle.

A 1996 photograph of Harpers Ferry looks over the town from Bolivar Heights to Maryland Heights on the other side of the Potomac. After Lee crossed into Pennsylvania, Hooker argued with his superiors President Lincoln and General Henry Halleck that the town's vulnerable location made it useless and that it should be abandoned so that its garrison could be added to the Army of the Potomac. Lincoln and Halleck turned him down. Hooker, aware that he had lost their confidence, used that as a reason to resign, and Lincoln appointed Meade to command the army.

eighty miles south of Ewell's troops at Carlisle, were Stuart's three cavalry brigades, which only at dawn on June 28 were splashing across the Potomac at Rowser's Ford. Even with a new commander in charge, the Federal army at the center of this strategic map had a chance to inflict a mortal wound on its enemy if Meade could concentrate most of his strength against one or two of the widely separated elements of the rebel host.

Of course he had to find them first. Although Stuart had left Lee bereft of his most trusted source of information, Meade had even less information about the whereabouts of Lee's army. Both army commanders groped forward like men in a darkened room with their arms outstretched. Eventually they would bump into each other, but when . . . and where?

CHAPTER THREE

Invasion

(June 21–June 30, 1863)

When Ewell's corps crossed the Mason-Dixon Line into Pennsylvania, it marked the first invasion of enemy territory by a Confederate army during the war. Lee had crossed the Potomac into Maryland in the fall of 1862, but the Confederate government had advertised that move not as aggression against an enemy but, rather, as the liberation of an occupied and subjugated neighbor. Maryland, after all, was a slave state, and many Southerners believed—or at least they hoped—that given the chance its residents would renounce their ties to Lincoln's brand of Unionism and join their Southern brethren in the Confederacy. There was no such pretense about the move into Pennsylvania, which was indisputably enemy territory.

On one level the Confederate invasion of Pennsylvania was a clash of cultures. Both the invaders and the invaded found many of their prejudices confirmed and yet also found reasons to be surprised. The most common reaction of the Pennsylvania citizens was shock at the ragged and emaciated look of the invaders. They were, as one Pennsylvanian noted, "a queer lot to look at." For their part, the soldiers were astonished by the apparent prosperity of the land through which they passed. They were especially impressed by the huge stone barns, the function of which was a mystery to them. They were much less impressed by the people. Major General William D. (Dorsey) Pender, commanding a division in Hill's corps, wrote home that "Their dwelling houses are large & comfortable looking . . . but such louts that live in them."

On another level, the residents of Pennsylvania hardly knew what to expect from these tattered soldiers of the slavocracy. To many it seemed not unlikely that Lee's ragged veterans would steal everything of value, burn whatever was left, and likely commit rape and murder in the process. And, indeed, many Southern soldiers looked upon their invasion of the North as an opportunity for retribution. More than one shared the view of a Virginia soldier who wrote home that "We will try & pay them for what they have been doing to the innocent & helpless in our good southern land." To rein in such impulses, Lee issued General Order No. 72 on June 21. "While in the enemy's country," he wrote, "the following regulations for procuring supplies will be strictly observed." What followed was a list of do's and don'ts for the army's officers and men. In general Lee forbade any destruction of private property, and he required that all "requisitions upon the local authorities" be paid for with Confederate scrip. If payment was refused (Confederate money being virtually worthless in

Opposite: Elements of Lee's cavalry screen, probably part of Albert Gallatin Jenkins's brigade, cross the Potomac into Maryland in a sketch by George Law. The northward march of the rebel army brought panic to cities as distant as Baltimore and Philadelphia.

An illustration by George Law shows Lee's army crossing the Potomac on its June 11 trek to Gettysburg. Some Maryland citizens welcomed the invaders, but as Lee's army moved north, Governor Andrew Curtin of Pennsylvania issued a proclamation calling for the citizens of the Keystone State to defend "their own homes, firesides, and property." In the end, however, relations between the Southern army and Northern civilians were less confrontational than such a declaration implied, and while each side thought the other strange, there was little violence by either.

Pennsylvania), officers were authorized to requisition the stores anyway and give the supplier a receipt—essentially a promissory note. Of course such notes were equally worthless unless the South won the war and made good on its pledge of payment. In short, commissary officers could appropriate what they needed from the citizens of Pennsylvania, but they would acknowledge their appropriations. According to Lee's General Orders, only if and when a citizen tried to conceal his goods from requisition by hiding them or spiriting them away, could the army simply seize those goods without acknowledgment or compensation.

The first town to feel the burden of Southern occupation was Chambersburg. The cavalry of Brigadier General Albert Gallatin Jenkins, screening Ewell's advance, rode into Chambersburg ahead of the infantry on June 15. Jenkins's command was a recent addition to the Army of Northern Virginia, and the men lacked the training and experience of Stuart's troopers. Nevertheless, Jenkins's conduct as an occupying invader set something of a pattern for Confederate behavior during the campaign. First he ordered all the citizens of Chambersburg to surrender their personal firearms, warning them that if they refused he would authorize a house-to-house search. The threat yielded a cache of arms, and Jenkins was satisfied that the townspeople had been largely disarmed. Next he ordered the merchants of the town to open their stores to his men, who then went on a shopping spree, spending their Confederate money (as well as local bank notes and even scrawled IOUs) to buy all sorts of goods not generally available in the Confederacy: buttons, gloves, factory-made cloth and thread, coffee, and other such delights. So relieved were the local merchants not to be simply robbed at gunpoint—or shot dead, for that matter—that they uncomplainingly accepted whatever paper they were offered in exchange.

A few days after Jenkins's cavalry moved on, the first of Ewell's infantry came up the road, and they too wanted to go shopping. As unit after unit came up from the South and passed through town, the shelves of the Chambersburg merchants were literally swept clean, leaving them with nothing to show for it but a drawer full of Confederate money. In addition to these private shopping sprees, Ewell's commissary officers handed the town fathers a long list of goods ranging from saddles to sauerkraut that the town was expected to provide. Ewell then "paid" for the goods with more promissory notes. In a few communities, Confederate officers demanded a cash indemnity, warning that a failure to pay would result in the destruction of the town. Generally the ransom was paid. In York the city fathers insisted they could collect only $28,600 of the $100,000 that Jubal Early demanded, and Early accepted their

A cartoon that appeared in Northern newspapers depicts a group of Confederate soldiers "buying" anything in sight including, apparently, hoop skirts. Though Lee enjoined his soldiers to behave themselves and to refrain from looting during their occupation of Northern territory, rebel soldiers took advantage of the opportunity to "shop" for goods not available in Virginia, paying for them with Confederate scrip. Intimidated shopkeepers were reluctant to complain and often accepted whatever paper the soldiers shoved at them.

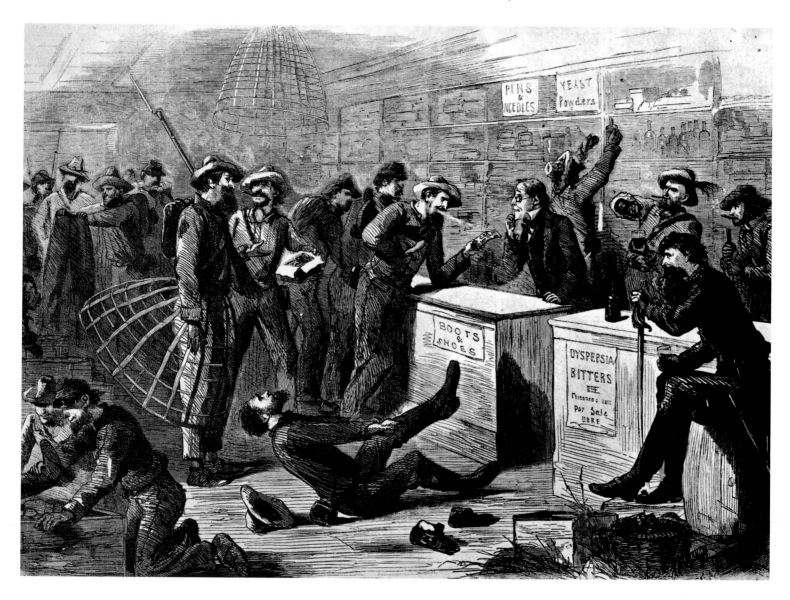

Chambersburg, shown in an 1860s photograph, was the first major town north of the Mason–Dixon Line to suffer the consequences of enemy occupation. Over a period of nearly two weeks, as unit after unit of the rebel army passed through its streets, Chambersburg was all but stripped of whatever commodities occupied the shelves of its merchants, though the city itself was spared. In the end, however, the war claimed Chambersburg after all. Just over a year later, during a raid toward Washington in July 1864, Confederate general John McCausland demanded a ransom of $500,000 from the town. When the citizens refused to pay it, Confederates set the town afire. The ensuing blaze destroyed some four hundred buildings, including the courthouse and the town hall.

explanation that fearful bankers had sent their cash reserves away in anticipation of his arrival.

There were more than a few cases of both theft and vandalism. As soldiers in enemy territory will do, the invading rebels "liberated" chickens, eggs, pigs, and almost anything potable with an alcoholic content; fences and outbuildings became material for campfires. In general, however, the invaders were less destructive than the citizens of Pennsylvania had feared. As one Virginia officer admitted in a letter home, "There was, in short, a good deal of lawlessness, but not so much as might have been expected under the circumstances." The most notorious violation of Lee's prohibition against the deliberate destruction of private property was Early's decision to burn the Caledonia Iron Works, which belonged to Republican Congressman Thaddeus Stevens, one of the most Radical members of the Northern Congress. Early was careful to note for the record that "This I did on my own responsibility," and Lee later expressed his unhappiness with the fact that Early's men destroyed not only the workshops but the workers' houses as well, though Early was never disciplined for exceeding his orders.

As might have been expected, the invaders encountered hostility from the local population in their passage through Pennsylvania, though seldom did it manifest itself in anything more threatening than bitter looks or the occasional surly remark. Ewell noted that "The people look as sour as vinegar and, I have no doubt, would gladly send us all to Kingdom come if they could." Occasionally some bold soul would flaunt an American flag. One woman with an ample bosom challengingly wore the flag pinned to her chest, provoking one Southern soldier to call out: "Take care, madam, for Hood's boys are great at storming breastworks when the Yankee colors is on them." Not all such confrontations ended humorously. One elderly citizen, ordered to turn his horses over to a Confederate requisitioning agent, adamantly refused, and when the rebel officer prepared to take them anyway, the man grabbed a rifle and began shooting. He managed to kill five rebel soldiers before he was himself shot down.

The most disgraceful activity undertaken by the invaders was their seizure of some two score Northern blacks, a few of them escaped slaves but most of them free persons of color, including at least some who had been free born, and sending them South into slavery under guard. For many Southern officers, such behavior was justified by the long record of Northern noncompliance with the Federal Fugitive Slave

News that Lee's army was marching through Pennsylvania provoked near panic among some citizens in border states, as shown in an 1863 drawing of Baltimore. On June 28, when the vanguard of Lee's army reached York, citizens of Baltimore began barricading the streets of their city. Some seem to be carrying muskets as well, as if they were prepared to man the barricades personally.

Farmers wait impatiently to cross to the eastern bank of the Susquehanna River in this drawing from *Frank Leslie's Illustrated Newspaper* (right). Some residents of south-central Pennsylvania fled before the Southern army arrived. When rebel forces reached the river, they found the railroad bridge at Wrightsville in flames. The Susquehanna marked the farthest advance by the Southern army.

F. H. Bellew's engraving (below) shows the citizens of Harrisburg digging field entrenchments in the expectation of the imminent arrival of Lee's veterans. The Pennsylvania state capital, Harrisburg, was the initial objective of Lee's movement into Pennsylvania. News that the Federal army had come north of the Potomac, however, convinced Lee to call off the advance to Harrisburg and instead concentrate his army near Gettysburg.

Brigadier General Albert Gallatin Jenkins (left) and his cavalry brigade led the advance of Lee's Army of Northern Virginia into Pennsylvania. A graduate of Harvard Law School and a former member of both the Federal and Confederate congresses, Jenkins enjoined his men to respect private property, which for the most part they did. Nevertheless, their arrival often sent Northern civilians fleeing for the countryside.

J. L. Schicks's Dry Goods Store (below) stood in the heart of central Gettysburg, adjoining the town square. Like many merchants in town, Schick shipped most of his inventory to Philadelphia when he learned of the approaching rebel army. During the fighting in the streets, he hid in the basement of this building and later claimed that he had been so nervous that he smoked twenty-one cigars.

"THEY WERE A RUDE SET"

The citizens of Pennsylvania reacted in various ways to the rebel invaders. Some fled; a few offered a tentative welcome; most reacted with sullen defiance. A representative response is captured in this excerpt from memoirs by a young girl who recalls the passage of Confederate troops through Gettysburg on June 26. The galloping cavalry described herein belonged to Brigadier General Albert Jenkins's brigade, and the infantry to John Gordon's brigade of Jubal Early's division:

There they were, human beings (!) clad almost in rags, covered with dust, riding wildly, pell-mell down the hill toward our home (!) shouting, yelling most unearthly, cursing, brandishing their revolvers, and firing right and left. Soon the town was filled with infantry, and then the searching and ransacking began in earnest.

They wanted horses, clothing, anything and almost everything they could conveniently carry away.

Nor were they particular about asking. Whatever suited them they took. They did, however, make a formal demand of the town authorities, for a large supply of flour, meat, groceries, shoes, hats, and (doubtless not least in their estimation), ten barrels of whiskey; or, in lieu of all this, five thousand dollars. . . .

I have often thought what a laughable spectacle this wing of southern chivalry would have presented on dress parade, had they obtained and donned the variety of hats generally found upon the shelves of a village store. But they were reduced to extremity and doubtless were not particular.

Upon the report of, and just previous to this raid, the citizens had sent their horses out the Baltimore Pike, as far as the Cemetery. There they were to be kept until those having the care of them were signaled that the enemy was about, when they were to hasten as fast as possible in the direction of Baltimore. Along with this party Father sent our own horse. . . . I was very much attached to the animal, for she was gentle and very pretty. I had often ridden her.

The [Confederate] cavalry . . . overtook the boys with the horses, captured, and brought them all back to town. . . . Mother and I began to plead for the horse. As I stood there begging and weeping, I was so shocked and insulted, I shall never forget it. One impudent and coarse Confederate said to me:

"Sissy, what are you crying about? Go in the house and mind your business."

I felt so indignant at his treatment I only wished I could have had some manner of revenge on the fellow. They left, however, without giving satisfaction.

About one-half hour after this some of these same raiders came back, and, stopping at the kitchen door, asked Mother for something to eat. She replied:

"Yes, you ought to come back and ask for something to eat after taking a person's horse." She nevertheless gave them some food, for Mother always had a kind and noble heart even toward her enemies.

Their manner of eating was shocking in the extreme. As I stood in a doorway and saw them laughing and joking at their deeds of the day, they threw the apple butter in all directions while spreading their bread. I was heartily glad when they left, for they were a rude set.

While they were still in the kitchen, my mother pleaded earnestly for our horse, so they told her that if we would go to Colonel [E. V.] White, their commander, we might, perhaps, get the horse back.

Father went with them; but when he got before Colonel White, he was informed by that officer that he understood father was "A Black Abolitionist; so black, that he was turning black;" also, that he understood that he had two sons in the Union Army, whom he supposed had taken as much from the South as they were now taking from him. So my father returned without the horse.

SOURCE: **Mrs. Tillie (Pierce) Alleman,** *At Gettysburg: or What a Girl Saw and Heard of the Battle* (New York: W. Lake Borland, 1889), pp. 22–26.

This photo of Mississippi infantrymen was taken in 1861. Most Gettysburg citizens were taken aback by the uncouth manners and haggard appearance of their Confederate invaders.

Law. But for Pennsylvanians, such barbaric actions only verified their assumption that Lee's invading host was the army of slavery. News of this practice spread ahead of the invaders, and free blacks living in the path of their advance fled, including most of the 190 black residents of Gettysburg.

From Chambersburg, Ewell divided his corps into three unequal parts, sending one brigade west to requisition supplies from Mercersburg and dispatching Jubal Early's division due east through Cashtown and Gettysburg to York to cut off the Northern Central Railroad from Baltimore to Harrisburg. Ewell led the largest element of his corps northward toward Carlisle, the site of the U.S. Army's cavalry school and a post where many Confederate and Union officers had served together in happier days. Upon their arrival there, Confederate officers decided that the capture of the Carlisle Barracks was such a milestone that it should be marked by some sort of ceremony. A handful of general officers, including Ewell himself, made short speeches in honor of the moment, and the rebel battle flag was hoisted to the top of the Carlisle Barracks. It proved to be the northernmost penetration of the North by the Confederate army during the war.

While Ewell's men commemorated the capture of Carlisle, the men of Jubal Early's division marched westward (burning the Caledonia Iron Works en route) through Cashtown toward Gettysburg. Just outside Gettysburg they encountered a brand new regiment of Pennsylvania volunteer militia, which, perhaps predictably, bolted at the sight of the Valley veterans, and that night (June 26) Early's men bivouacked in Gettysburg. As they slept, none of them could have imagined how hard they would have to fight to reenter that town five days later.

They were up and on the road early the next morning, and after an all-day march, they entered York, which sat astride the railroad from Harrisburg to Baltimore. Early's lead brigade was under the command of Major General William Smith (known as Extra Billy Smith because of a reputation for having charged a little "extra" as manager of a mail service). As Smith's soldiers entered York, the townspeople at first manifested the same look of mingled scorn and fear that the rebels had seen all day. But Smith, a former governor of Virginia who had recently been reelected to that position in absentia, decided to put on something of a show. He ordered the fife-and-drum band to play "Yankee Doodle," and he rode out in front of his marching column waving to the crowd. By the time he reached the town square, the citizens' expressions were less hostile and more curious. Adapting himself to this mood, Smith ordered his column to halt and stack arms, and assuming a speaker's pose, he began to declaim. He was just warming up when Jubal Early arrived and demanded to know what Smith meant by stopping the whole column to give a speech! Old Jube, who was known to color the air with pungent language when provoked, got Smith's brigade out of the town square and sent another brigade, that of John B. Gordon, onward toward Wrightsville to secure the bridge over the Susquehanna River, though when Gordon's men reached the river, the bridge was in flames.

Fifty miles and two days' march behind Gordon, Robert E. Lee entered Chambersburg that same day (June 27). From there he issued orders for Ewell to continue his

Confederate Major General William "Extra Billy" Smith led the column of Confederate soldiers that entered York on June 28. A former congressman and past and future governor of Virginia, Smith was as much a politician as he was a soldier, and he halted his column in the town square to offer the local citizens a speech until Jubal Early arrived to put an end to such nonsense, pushing the Confederate forces on to the next objective.

A nineteenth-century drawing by Louis Miller depicts the arrival of Jubal Early's brigade in York on June 28. Early demanded that the town provide him with 2,000 pairs of shoes, foodstuffs, and $100,000 in cash, warning that otherwise he would burn the town. The townspeople managed to come up with only 1,500 pairs of shoes and $28,600 in cash. Satisfied with their explanation that the banks had sent the rest of their money away, Early accepted what was offered and spared the town, even posting a provost guard to protect private property.

June 28th 1863. The Rebels in York.

advance toward the Pennsylvania state capital at Harrisburg, and he also issued General Order No. 73 essentially reiterating the cautions and proscriptions of his earlier General Order. "We make war only upon armed men," he wrote. "The commanding general therefore earnestly exhorts the troops to abstain with most scrupulous care from unnecessary or wanton injury to private property." But Lee had more to worry about than the behavior of the troops, for he still did not know the location of the Federal army.

The next day brought a partial answer. At around ten o'clock on the night of June

Early. & Gorden.

L. Miller.

28, a staff officer reported to Lee that a paid spy in the employ of James Longstreet had brought word that the Federal army had crossed the Potomac the day before and was in the vicinity of Frederick, Maryland. He also reported that Meade had replaced Hooker in command. Lee personally questioned the spy, a man named James Harrison. Lee was loath to accept this information as face value. The man was a spy, after all—a "scout," in the parlance of the day—who worked for money. Even though Longstreet said the man could be trusted, Lee put his faith in professional soldiers. If the Federal army was as close as Frederick, why had he not heard this information

In a drawing from a soldier's letter home, Union infantrymen slog northward in pursuit of Lee's force. The sketch artist was Charles W. Reed, the bugler of the 9th Massachusetts battery, who would win the Medal of Honor at Gettysburg. With Meade now in command, the Army of the Potomac moved northward to find Lee and interpose itself between the rebel army and its objective—whatever that might be.

Opposite: The Lutheran Seminary (bottom) at Gettysburg offered a clear view of the approaching Confederate army. From its cupola Buford surveyed the area (top) and decided that the grounds were well suited for a defense. He thereupon took it upon himself to defend the town until he was either driven off by the enemy or relieved by the Federal infantry. The gentle fold of ground on which the seminary building still stands was soon to be the scene of bloody conflict and is known to history as Seminary Ridge.

from Stuart? Still, to ignore this scout would be perilous indeed, for Lee's army was widely scattered and operating in enemy territory. He could not take the chance. He decided to cancel Ewell's orders to advance toward Harrisburg and order him instead to hasten back in order to concentrate the army. At first he instructed Ewell to head for Chambersburg, but early the next morning he changed his mind and directed him to move south to Gettysburg. There he could link up with Early, who would be coming from the east, and with Hill, who would arrive from the west.

As Lee issued orders for the army to concentrate, Stuart's mounted troopers were still attempting to get around the Federal army. On June 29 they were approaching Hanover, where they encountered Judson Kilpatrick's Federal cavalry brigade. Stuart attacked, but the Federals were there in strength, and a furious Union counterattack caught most of Stuart's men in a column instead of deployed for a fight. The lead regiment in Stuart's column bolted for the rear, and Stuart, accompanied only by his personal staff, found himself facing an entire Federal brigade. There was nothing to do but flee. With the enemy hard on his heels, Stuart jumped his mare over a fifteen-foot gully at a full gallop and thus saved himself from the ignominy of capture. Eventually the rebel cavalry regrouped and drove off the Union horsemen. Even so, the encounter meant still more delay as Stuart had to round up his tired men and their nearly exhausted horses, and get them back on the road, taking yet another detour eastward around Hanover. As he did so, he might well have asked himself why units of the Federal cavalry were operating this far north.

They were looking for Lee's army. Kilpatrick's force was one of three cavalry probes that Meade had sent out in different directions to look for the rebel infantry. Kilpatrick had been assigned to the middle quadrant, going northeast toward Littleton and Hanover, where he ran into Stuart; off to the east, beyond Kilpatrick's right, two more Federal cavalry brigades under David M. Gregg probed toward Westminster, Maryland; and off to the west, on Kilpatrick's left, were two more under John Buford. As Stuart's column detoured to the east to get around Kilpatrick and Ewell reoriented his troops for a march south from Carlisle to comply with Lee's new orders, Buford's troopers were feeling their way northward along Hagerstown Road toward Gettysburg.

Buford was the first Union officer to enter the borough of Gettysburg. He trotted his horse into town at about 10:30 in the morning on June 30. Behind him more than two thousand horsemen made up a column more than a mile long. They had traveled a hard road. For three weeks—ever since Brandy Station—they had attempted (unsuccessfully) to fight their way through the rebel cavalry screen along the Blue Ridge to find out where Lee's infantry was going. By the time they arrived in Gettysburg, they had been in the saddle for as many as twenty of every twenty-four hours for several days in a row. Buford reported to Pleasonton that his men were "fagged out" (tired).

The farm of Edward McPherson, a mile west of Gettysburg, marked the site of the first important fighting at Gettysburg. The McPherson farmhouse in on the right and the McPherson barn, which still stands, is on the left. John Buford deployed two brigades of Union cavalry

along this ridgeline with the intention of holding it until the infantry
came up to support him. The dark-coated gentleman in this image is
the famous photographer Mathew Brady, whose team took the photo
on July 15, 1863, two weeks after the battle.

Thomas Devin was the son of Irish immigrants and a bold leader of the Union cavalry. At Gettysburg, Buford placed Devin's brigade atop McPherson's Ridge with orders to hold on until relieved, warning him that "you will have to fight like the devil."

But Gettysburg was no place for an extended rest, for there Buford finally found the information he had been seeking. The people of the town crowded around him, gesturing both east and west and talking, it seemed, all at once. They were, Buford reported, "in a terrible state of excitement." They told him that a Confederate division had passed through town only four days earlier heading east and that more enemy soldiers were even then approaching from the west. The alarmed citizens estimated enemy strength in the tens of thousands, and though Buford tended to discount such panicky estimates, he sent a patrol out Chambersburg Road to reconnoiter. It returned with the news that there was indeed rebel infantry on Chambersburg Road west of town. The rebels had retreated westward when they had seen Buford's videttes, but local farmers said the men were from A. P. Hill's Confederate corps, the main body of which, more than 20,000 strong, was only nine miles to the west, near Cashtown. Other reports, which Buford could not yet confirm, placed a second enemy corps to the north approaching Gettysburg along Carlisle Road. If these reports were accurate, Buford's two brigades of worn-out cavalry were at the convergence point of perhaps 50,000 enemy infantry.

That night, Buford sat down to report what he had found, dispatching a courier to carry the news back to Meade. He sent a copy of the report to John Reynolds, commander of the Federal I Corps which was the nearest friendly infantry, six miles to the south. After that, Buford had to look out for his own command. His men and horses were tired, and they were nearly out of supplies. In particular the horses needed reshoeing, but the men of Jubal Early's division had taken every shoe and nail they could find when they had passed through Gettysburg on June 26, and Buford's mounts would have to do without new shoes. Worse yet, the closest friendly infantry, Reynolds's corps, was not significantly closer than either of the enemy corps that were converging on the town. Discretion suggested that now was the time for Buford to escape from the closing vice. After all, it was not part of Buford's assignment to select a site for an engagement with the enemy; he was supposed to gather information and report. If he had evacuated the town in the face of such odds, few would have found fault.

But Buford never considered leaving. As he took note of the converging road network in Gettysburg and surveyed the rolling farmland north and west of town, he decided that the road hub was worth holding, at least for a while. He deployed his men athwart Chambersburg Road a mile west of town on a slight rise of ground known as McPherson's Ridge after a local farm and set up a picket line a mile farther west along another rise known as Herr's Ridge after a local tavern. By the time he had made these dispositions, it was nightfall.

Buford was up late that night seeing to the disposition of his troopers. At about eleven o'clock, he rode to the headquarters tent of Thomas Devin, one of his two brigade commanders. He told Devin that the morning would almost certainly bring with it an enemy assault, and that it might be some time before friendly infantry arrived to support him. Devin, perhaps wishing to demonstrate confidence before his commander, told Buford that his men could handle whatever the enemy had to throw at them. But Buford did not want any false bravado—he wanted Devin to know the odds against him. When Devin said his men would easily prevail, Buford shot back, "No you won't! They will attack you in the morning and will come booming, skirmishers three deep. You will have to fight like the devil to hold your own. . . . The enemy must know the importance of this position and will strain every nerve to secure it, and if we are able to hold it, we will do well." Under any circumstances, two brigades of cavalry could not hold out for long against a determined assault by rebel infantry in division strength or greater. Buford's bold decision to hold the hub of the road network would be meaningless if Federal infantry did not march to support him.

That decision belonged to George Gordon Meade, the brand new commander of the Army of the Potomac. Meade received Buford's message about the presence of enemy infantry near Gettysburg at his Taneytown, Maryland, headquarters late on the evening of June 30. He also received a note from Reynolds, who suggested that the army should set up a defensive position just north of Emmitsburg near the Maryland-Pennsylvania border. Finally, Meade heard from Pleasonton about Kilpatrick's brush with Stuart near Hanover the day before. He now knew Lee's army was east of South Mountain, that it seemed to be congregating at Gettysburg, and that Stuart's cavalry was operating somewhere to the east. But he was not yet sure what to do about it. If the rebel army was still moving toward the Susquehanna, which Stuart's presence at Hanover suggested, Meade's plan was to strike northward toward Gettysburg in order to draw enemy forces away from the state capital at Harrisburg. If, on the other hand, it appeared that Lee was instead concentrating his army—which Meade estimated to number some 92,000 men—at Gettysburg, then Meade planned to fall back to a defensive position behind Pipe's Creek near Westminster, Maryland. He even drafted a general order—ever since known as the Pipe's Creek Circular—for the army to fall back. He had been in command of the army for less than forty-eight hours, and he had to make a decision on which the fate of the country might hang. For now, he simply replied to Reynolds that "so soon as I can make up any positive opinion as to their position, I will move again." In the meantime, he wrote, "Please get all the information you can."

That night, Meade discovered just how lonely command could be. As he turned the alternatives over in his mind, he took the time to write a private letter to his wife in which he confessed that he was "much oppressed with a sense of responsibility and the magnitude of the great interests entrusted [to] me." In the end, Meade decided to keep his options open. In order to adapt quickly to either alternative, he decided to keep his headquarters at Taneytown, but to order all seven of his infantry corps to move northward on four different roads to positions that would allow them to adjust to whatever news the day might bring. He endowed Reynolds with the command of the III and XI Corps as well as his own, making him effectively a wing commander, and ordered him to advance up Emmitsburg Road toward Gettysburg to be close enough to support Buford if necessary.

Reynolds received the order at 4 A.M. Dawn was less than an hour away. Meade had ordered him to conduct a reconnaissance in force toward Gettysburg to support Buford, but his instructions did not seem to suggest any particular need for haste. Reynolds therefore issued orders for the men to be roused at sunrise, which would put them on the road to Gettysburg by eight. He could not have known that even as he gave the order, the Confederate infantry at Cashtown was already beginning its march to Gettysburg. In the race to control the hub of the road network, the rebels would have a three-hour head start.

SHOULDER ARMS AND INFANTRY TACTICS

For more than a hundred years before the Civil War, the shoulder arms of infantry soldiers had changed little. They consisted of muzzle-loading, smooth-bore muskets that used black powder to fire a round lead ball. Setting the musket butt first on the ground, the soldier loaded it by pouring a measured amount of power into the muzzle, dropping a lead ball on top of it, stuffing in some wadding (usually paper), and ramming it all into place with a ramrod. To fire, he then brought the musket to port arms (chest height), drew back the hammer to half cock, fitted a percussion cap filled with fulminate of mercury onto the nipple above the breech, brought the musket to his shoulder, pulled the hammer to full cock, and pulled the trigger. (If the weapon went off at half cock, it might not fire, hence the old expression about "going off half-cocked.")

Because bullets were often made by hand, they could seldom be molded with enough precision to fit the muzzle exactly. Instead, they were made just a little smaller to ensure that they dropped easily down the muzzle. That is also why wadding was necessary: to ensure that the bullet didn't roll back out the barrel. But because of this indifferent fit, bullets exited the muzzle with an uncertain trajectory. A man-size target more than a hundred yards away was fairly safe from such a projectile, except by chance. As a result, infantry tactics in the years before the Civil War called for soldiers to advance toward the enemy in tight, disciplined blocks up to within effective range (fifty to sixty yards), fire a concentrated volley, then charge with the bayonet before the enemy had time to reload.

There was a way to make shoulder arms more accurate, and it was no secret. If arms manufacturers cut grooves in a corkscrew pattern inside the musket barrel, this put a spin on the bullet that dramatically improved its accuracy over distance. This was called rifling and any weapon so modified was a rifle. Rifles had existed as far back as the American Revolution; Daniel Boone had claimed to be able to shoot the eye out of a squirrel with one. But the problem with rifles before the 1850s was that they took so long to load. In order for the bullet to engage the rifling, the fit had to be exact. The bullet itself not only had to be smoothed

into a perfect sphere by hand but also had to be literally pounded down into the barrel to be seated snugly against the black powder charge. This could take several minutes. To use a rifle, therefore, meant that the rate of fire was diminished almost in precise proportion to the increase in range.

Then in the 1840s a French army officer named Claude-Etienne Minié designed a special bullet that allowed rifles to be loaded and fired as fast as smooth-bores. Called a minié ball in testment to its inventor, it was conical (that is, bullet shaped) rather than spherical and had a hollow base so that when the black powder ignited, the rim of the bullet expanded outward to engage the rifled grooves inside the barrel. Now, for the first time, it became possible to load a shoulder arm quickly (twenty to thirty seconds) and fire it accurately over distances of up to half a mile, though three hundred yards was more realistic. Troops in the Civil War generally used rifled muskets that fired a .58-caliber minié ball. (Union minié balls had three rings around the base, Confederate minié balls generally had two, but each side could use the other's bullets.)

Obviously, this had profound implications on tactics. Whereas before, troops could march toward an enemy line with some confidence that they were beyond effective range until they got to within sixty to eighty yards, now they would begin taking fire at several hundred yards. Given the ability of veteran soldiers to get off three rounds in a minute, frontal charges therefore became highly risky affairs. Civil War officers knew this, of course, which was why they generally tried to avoid frontal assaults in favor of turning a flank.

Breech loading was another recent innovation. A conventional musket was best loaded from a standing position, which made it difficult (though not impossible) for infantrymen to fight from a prone or even a seated position. There were some breech-loading weapons available by 1863, but only in limited numbers, and in recognition of the fact that it was all but impossible to reload a conventional musket from horseback, nearly all of them were entrusted to the cavalry rather than the infantry. Even more desirable for cavalry was the much shorter rifled carbine, which was only twenty-two inches long and therefore much easier to handle from horseback than the almost-five-foot-long shoulder musket. Armed with the breech-loading Sharps carbine, John Buford's Federal cavalry at Gettysburg could fire as many as eight to ten shots a minute rather than the two or three shots per minute fired by infantrymen with muzzle loaders.

The revolution in arms technology in the half decade before the outbreak of war affected both tactics and casualties and was one of the factors that made the Civil War the bloodiest war in American history.

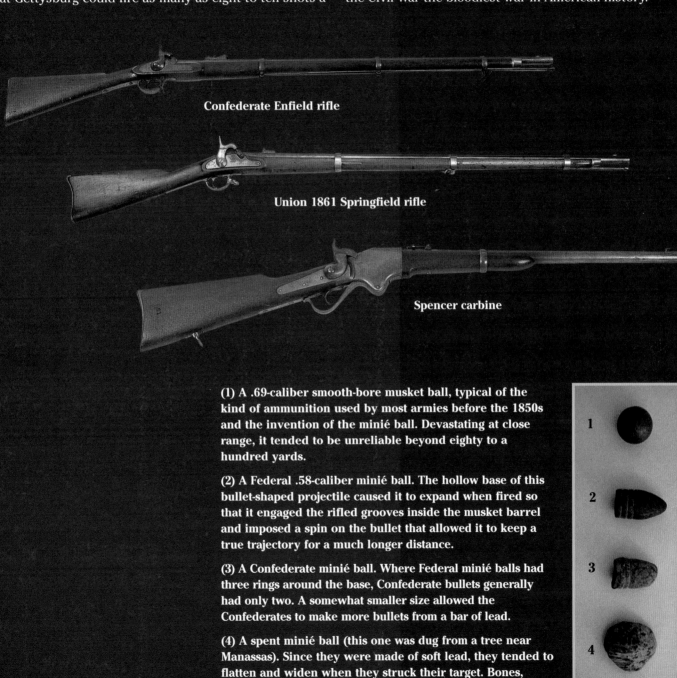

Confederate Enfield rifle

Union 1861 Springfield rifle

Spencer carbine

(1) A .69-caliber smooth-bore musket ball, typical of the kind of ammunition used by most armies before the 1850s and the invention of the minié ball. Devastating at close range, it tended to be unreliable beyond eighty to a hundred yards.

(2) A Federal .58-caliber minié ball. The hollow base of this bullet-shaped projectile caused it to expand when fired so that it engaged the rifled grooves inside the musket barrel and imposed a spin on the bullet that allowed it to keep a true trajectory for a much longer distance.

(3) A Confederate minié ball. Where Federal minié balls had three rings around the base, Confederate bullets generally had only two. A somewhat smaller size allowed the Confederates to make more bullets from a bar of lead.

(4) A spent minié ball (this one was dug from a tree near Manassas). Since they were made of soft lead, they tended to flatten and widen when they struck their target. Bones, instead of breaking, tended to shatter.

CHAPTER FOUR

McPherson's Ridge

(5 A.M.–Noon, July 1, 1863)

The rebel infantry that Buford's scouts had spotted on Chambersburg Road west of Gettysburg belonged to James J. Pettigrew's brigade of North Carolinians, part of A. P. Hill's corps, the main body of which was at Cashtown, eight miles to the west. Pettigrew's division commander, Major General Henry Heth (pronounced Heath), had ordered him to Gettysburg primarily to see what supplies might be had there. In particular, Heth was hopeful that Gettysburg could provide his barefoot soldiers with some shoes, though he ought to have guessed that Early's passage through the town four days earlier had effectively stripped it of whatever shoes there might have been. Even so, Pettigrew's 2,400 men were on what amounted to a large-scale commissary raid when they approached Gettysburg early on the afternoon of June 30 and spotted the patrol that Buford had sent out to investigate the rumors of approaching rebel infantry. Pettigrew had learned of Buford's presence in Gettysburg from a local citizen who was sympathetic to the Southern cause, and because he was under orders to avoid an engagement, he directed his brigade to countermarch back to Cashtown as soon as his skirmishers spotted the Yankee troopers on the pike. It must have caused some grumbling in the ranks to back off from Yankee cavalry, for not only did it keep them from entering the town and helping themselves to whatever desirable commodities might have lined the shelves of its merchants (including shoes), but in addition infantry tended to be scornful of cavalry. Pettigrew's men no doubt felt they could easily sweep aside this gaggle of horse soldiers and march into town. Still, orders were orders, and so they turned around and marched slowly back to Cashtown, leaving Gettysburg to Buford and his blue-clad troopers.

Back in Cashtown, Pettigrew reported to Heth that he had seen Yankee cavalry in Gettysburg, that they were in at least brigade strength, and that from the look of them, they were not home-guard forces but Army of the Potomac veterans. Heth dutifully repeated all this to Hill, but the corps commander was reluctant to believe it. At most, Hill suggested, the Yankees in Gettysburg were probably part of a detached "squadron of observation" sent out from the main body, which would still be miles away. In that, of course, he was correct. Less accurately, Hill also assumed that such a detached squadron would not make a fight of it against a determined push by a division of infantry. And a determined push was just what Harry Heth had in mind. Heth was still thinking in terms of a commissary raid when he asked Hill if he had any

Opposite: Private Charles P. Keeler of Company B, 6th Wisconsin regiment, the Iron Brigade, borrowed $15 against his pay to buy a new uniform, including a brand-new Hardee-model black hat, the symbol of the Iron Brigade. Keeler cleared his debts on June 29, and two days later he participated in the hard fighting for McPherson's Ridge and was shot in both legs.

A Confederate's-eye view of Gettysburg from Seminary Ridge, taken by Mathew Brady a few weeks after the battle, shows the ground between the railroad cut (left) and Chambersburg Road (right) north and west of Gettysburg. The height of Culp's Hill can be seen looming beyond the town in the upper right corner.

James Johnston Pettigrew (in an 1866 painting by William Browne), who was commonly called by his middle name, commanded the 1st brigade of Harry Heth's Confederate division. A man with a scholarly bent, he had served as a professor at the Naval Observatory in Washington, D.C., before traveling to Germany to study Roman law. Fate and circumstance placed his command at the head of Lee's marching column in the last week of June, and it was his brigade that first approached Gettysburg along Chambersburg Road on June 30.

objection to his taking his whole division back to Gettysburg in the morning to "get those shoes." "None in the world," Hill replied.

Heth started early. He had his men up before dawn on July 1 (a "blood red dawn," according to one poetic witness), and they were on the road by 5 A.M., while Reynolds's men at Emmitsburg were still boiling their coffee. This time Heth did not rely on a single brigade; he ordered out his whole division, and by six, a long column of more than seven thousand men was marching eastward along Chambersburg Pike. The morning was overcast and the air heavy with the promise of rain, but the weather cleared as the sun rose, and the marching men pulled their slouch hats low on their foreheads to shield their eyes from the sun that was rising in their faces. About halfway to Gettysburg at Marsh Creek, they spotted the first of the Yankee horsemen: videttes of the 8th Illinois cavalry stationed on the road by Buford to give early warning of a rebel advance. James J. Archer, in command of Heth's lead brigade, deployed skirmishers out to the right and left and sent them forward to drive off the impertinent cavalry. The horsemen exchanged a few long-range shots with these skirmishers, then mounted and rode eastward to carry the news to their commander. Heth's column resumed its march. Two miles from Gettysburg they struck Herr's Ridge and the first serious obstacle to their raid.

The defenders of Herr's Ridge were several squadrons of Colonel William Gamble's cavalry brigade. They faced daunting odds, especially since a quarter of them had to be detailed to hold the horses behind the ridge, but they had several advantages: they had the high ground, they were armed with breech-loading Sharps carbines that gave them a faster rate of fire than their foes, and they knew their job was not to defeat this host of infantry, but only to delay it. They did delay it—but not for long. The rebel infantry overlapped both of Gamble's flanks and soon drove the Yankee horsemen from the ridge. Gamble's men retreated back to Buford's main defense line on McPherson's Ridge, where they joined their comrades and prepared to make another stand.

Heth's lead brigades hit this second, much stronger, line and began to appreciate that what was supposed to be a relatively easy assertion of the superiority of infantry over cavalry was likely to turn into a stiff little fight; Buford's troopers showed no sign of a willingness to yield. Heth deployed the brigade of Joseph R. Davis (the Confederate president's nephew) north of the road and Archer's brigade south of it, about 2,700 men altogether. By the time both brigades were ready to advance with seriousness of purpose, it was nearly ten o'clock.

At about that time, John Reynolds rode up to Buford's headquarters at the Lutheran Seminary, a quarter mile behind the troopers crouching on McPherson's Ridge. Reynolds had been riding at the head of his marching infantry on Emmitsburg Road when a courier had galloped up, saluted, and handed him a note from Buford, who reported that he was engaged with the enemy west of Gettysburg and in need of support. Reynolds immediately put the spur to his mount and galloped ahead to see for himself. Like many officers on both sides, Reynolds and Buford had served together in the "Old Army" (as veterans referred to the U.S. Army in its prewar days). Buford

Harry Heth, Pettigrew's division commander, was anything but a scholar. He readily acknowledged having graduated last in the celebrated West Point class of 1847. Personally brave and quick to act, he possessed an open and candid personality and treated others with a frankness and lack of pretense that made him well liked by both officers and enlisted men. It was Heth who asked for permission to return to Gettysburg, in spite of the cavalry forces there, in order to "get those shoes."

In Allen Carter Redwood's nineteenth-century drawing, Confederate infantry attack up Chambersburg Road past the McPherson barn toward the ridgeline held by Buford's troopers. A wounded rebel lies in the road, and another makes for the rear with a hand wound. Other Confederates pause to reload. The woods in the background are McPherson's Woods. Note the missing rails from the fence, perhaps thrown down by the attackers to speed their advance or gathered up by the defenders to make a low barricade.

had taught at West Point while Reynolds had been a commandant, and the two men had developed a relationship that was as intimate as the formalities of rank allowed. As he reined up at Buford's headquarters, Reynolds called out to him, "What's the matter, John?" To which Buford replied, "There's the devil to pay." Buford quickly sketched out for Reynolds the circumstances of the ongoing fight. Reynolds could see for himself the strategic importance of holding the hub of the road network in Gettysburg, and he could see, too, that Buford had selected a good defensive position. He took it upon himself to make a decision with profound consequences: telling Buford that the infantry was only a few miles away, he urged him to hold on until they arrived. Then he headed back toward Emmitsburg Road to expedite the advance of the infantry. En route, he ordered the members of his staff to tear down the fences between the road and McPherson's Ridge so his troops could take a direct route across country to get into the fight.

The lead unit in that column of marching infantry was the division of Brigadier General James S. Wadsworth. Wadsworth himself had seen relatively little combat. A handsome, blue-eyed, Harvard-educated lawyer, he had been the unsuccessful Republican candidate for governor of New York the year before, and the only service he had seen was at Chancellorsville, where his command had been largely inactive. But such a record belied the hitting power of Wadsworth's command. Though it contained only two brigades, they were among the best in the army, and their timely arrival would dramatically change the tide of battle.

Lysander Cutler's brigade of mostly New York troops was the first to arrive, the men sloughing off their packs without breaking stride and cutting across the open fields at the double-quick. Reynolds took personal charge of placing the troops. He sent three of Cutler's five regiments north of Chambersburg Road, where Davis's

Buford's dismounted cavalry holds McPherson's Ridge against the initial thrust of the Confederate infantry, as shown in this undated engraving. Under most circumstances, cavalry did not expect to have to stand up to a determined infantry assault, and infantrymen tended to be scornful of the mounted arm. "Whoever saw a dead cavalryman?" was their frequent jibe. But Buford's men, armed with rapid-firing Sharps and Burnside carbines, fought determinedly, and they held the ridge long enough for the Union infantry to arrive.

The Hardee-model hat was worn by members of Solomon Meredith's Iron Brigade. The insignia on the crown identifies the wearer as belonging to Company C of the 2nd Wisconsin volunteer infantry. This particular hat belonged to Sergeant Philander Wright, the regimental color bearer, who was wounded during the brigade's charge into McPherson's Woods.

Confederates were deploying, and he led the other two out the road to support the six-gun Maine battery of Captain James A. Hall, which he placed alongside the road on the forward slope of the ridge. It was an extremely exposed position, but from it Hall's gunners could engage the Confederate artillery on Herr's Ridge.

A mile behind Cutler's men, the Iron Brigade was approaching Gettysburg. It was the only brigade in the eastern army that was composed entirely of soldiers from western states: three regiments from Wisconsin plus the 24th Michigan and the 19th Indiana. The brigade had won its nickname at the Battle of South Mountain, and to distinguish itself further, the men of this midwestern outfit wore the 1858 model Hardee hat: a black, broad-brimmed affair topped with a black plume and often decorated with a brass regimental emblem. But this was no parade-ground unit. The men took great pride in their combat reputation, which they had won fairly on every battlefield since Groveton, where they had fought stubbornly and suffered 33 percent casualties. Even the rebels had learned to look out for what they called the "Black Hat boys." If the hats alone did not mark them out on the battlefield, their commander would: he was six-foot-seven-inch Solomon Meredith, whom the soldiers appropriately called Long Sol.

Cutler's men were already engaged when the men of the Iron Brigade came up at a run, their canteens clinking and jangling, and the men gasping for air in the morning humidity. Reynolds directed them into the fight south of the road opposite a clump of woods atop the ridge. The regiments deployed quickly from column into line and then advanced at the double-quick, loading as they ran. They charged across an open field, passed through the ranks of the exhausted cavalrymen who were already beginning to fall back, and crashed into the woods from the east just as Archer's Confederate brigade entered the same woods from the west. The usually calm Reynolds excitedly waved them on, calling out, "Forward, men! Forward, for God's sake. . . ." They were practically the last words he ever spoke. As he urged them onward, his head suddenly jerked backward, and he reeled from his horse, falling heavily to the ground. His staff members leapt to his aid and carried him to a nearby tree, leaning him against its trunk. But it was in vain, for he was already dead, killed, some said later, by a sniper in McPherson's barn, but more likely the victim of an overshot from the fighting that was already welling up in McPherson's Woods.★

Reynolds's death was a devastating blow to Union fortunes, for he commanded not only the troops on the field, and indeed the whole I Corps, the rest of which was still coming up Emmitsburg Road, but also the III and XI Corps—very nearly half the army. Just before he fell, Reynolds had ordered a courier to get word to General Howard to bring his XI Corps up to Gettysburg as quickly as possible. But Reynolds's loss meant that decision making on the battlefield would devolve on the officers already engaged. It was one of the rare moments in the annals of military history when a commanding general became a mortal casualty of the fight he was directing.

For everyone else the battle continued. The Alabama and Tennessee soldiers of Archer's brigade had not expected to encounter infantry at all, and in particular not the hardened veterans of the Iron Brigade. As the two sides engaged in McPherson's Woods, one Wisconsin soldier heard a rebel call out, "Hell, those are not raw militia, they are those 'Black Hat devils!' " The fighting in the woods was fierce, but the Fed-

★The wood lot near the McPherson Farm was actually known as Herbst's Woods, but most contemporary and historical accounts refer to it as McPherson's Woods, a practice which will be followed here.

erals had the advantage of surprise, and their left flank overlapped Archer's right. The Confederates began to get the worst of it, and soon they gave way, the men of the Iron Brigade pursuing them and scooping up nearly a hundred prisoners (General Archer among them) as the rebels attempted to scramble over a rail fence near Willoughby Run. As the disconsolate Archer was being escorted to the rear, he passed Major General Abner Doubleday, who had succeeded to command of the I Corps upon Reynolds's death. Doubleday and Archer had been friends in the Old Army, and Doubleday's face lit up when he saw him. "Good morning, Archer," he called out cheerfully. "How are you? I am glad to see you." Archer's response was more suited to the moment: "Well, I am not glad to see you, by a damn sight, Doubleday."

The triumph of the Iron Brigade in McPherson's Woods did not end the fighting on McPherson's Ridge, for three of Lysander Cutler's regiments were still slugging it out with Joe Davis's Confederate brigade north of the road. Without benefit of any kind of cover, the two sides simply stood and shot at one another from close range atop a gentle fold of Pennsylvania farmland. The casualties were horrific. The 76th New York regiment had 45 percent of its men killed and wounded in about half an hour.

Alfred Waud's drawing shows Major General John Reynolds at the moment he was struck by the bullet that took his life. Waud, an English-born sketch artist who accompanied the Union army to many of its battlefields, produced a number of vivid sketches of war scenes from Bull Run to Appomattox.

Overleaf: *Attack at Seminary Ridge, Gettysburg,* **by an unknown artist, shows Union forces in the foreground, in precision alignment, as they rush forward to meet the attack by Confederate infantry on the horizon.**

The men of Hall's battery fire a round down Chambersburg Road toward the approaching rebel infantry. As the Federal I Corps rushed into action on McPherson's Ridge, the four-gun battery of Captain James Hall galloped down Chambersburg Road directly in the path of the advancing rebels.

As Davis's troops enveloped their right, Wadsworth ordered Cutler to fall back. Two of Cutler's regiments retreated eastward, toward town, and essentially out of the fight. The 147th New York didn't receive the order and stood by Hall's battery, which was still firing as fast as the gunners could load. The rest of Cutler's brigade changed front to face north rather than west and looked about for help. The only help at hand was the 6th Wisconsin of the Iron Brigade, which Doubleday had held back as a division reserve. Now he committed it. He sent a staff officer galloping to the unit's commander, Colonel Rufus Dawes, and ordered him to "move to the right" and "go like hell."

Dawes pivoted his regiment of some 450 men to face northward and marched them across the swale of low ground between McPherson's Ridge and the Lutheran Seminary. He could see the guns of Hall's battery being hauled rapidly to the rear, retreating, finally, from their exposed position. The 147th New York was falling back as well. Dawes halted his men at a fence line along Chambersburg Road to fire a volley into Davis's Mississippi and North Carolina regiments that were now advancing southward. The Southern troops looked about for cover, and there in front of them, as if providentially placed, was a ready-made trench: the bed of an unfinished railroad that ran parallel to Chambersburg Road about 150 yards north of it. Without hesitation, they clambered into the cut. To the astonished Wisconsin boys, it seemed that the whole rebel line that had been advancing toward them suddenly disappeared into the earth. The Confederates were now naturally positioned to fend off any Union counterattack—or so it seemed.

Colonel Dawes found the commanding officer of the 95th New York regiment, Major Edward Pye. "Let's go for them, Major!" Dawes shouted at him. "We are with you!" Pye shouted back. With that, Dawes ordered his regiment forward. The 14th Brooklyn joined the assault, and the whole line, perhaps a thousand men altogether, moved northward across Chambersburg Road and straight on toward the railroad cut. They encountered a hail of rifle fire, and instinctively they ducked their heads and leaned forward as they advanced, as if bucking a strong wind, while the bullets zipped past them. But not all the defenders in the railroad cut were firing. What had seemed a haven to Davis's soldiers when they had first clambered into it now proved to be a trap. Though the rebel colors could be seen flying above it, parts of the cut were too deep to allow the defenders to fire at the oncoming Yankee infantry. Despite their losses, the attackers covered the 150 yards to the cut in a matter of a few minutes and to their own astonishment, found themselves looking down on the Mississippi and North Carolina troops in the deepest part of the cut. Some of the Wisconsin troops occupied a shallow portion of the cut on the Confederate left where the ground fell away to a level grade, and they fired down the length of the cut. Others crossed to the northern side and subjected the Confederates to a deadly cross fire.

The Wisconsin boys saw at once the advantage they had gained, and they called upon the rebels to throw down their arms. The circumstances were self-evident. Those rebels who could fled westward out of the cut, eventually finding their way back to the relative safety of Herr's Ridge. The rest dropped their muskets and raised their hands. The Wisconsinites took more than two hundred prisoners. Dawes found

When Reynolds fell mortally wounded from his horse, his staff officers immediately carried him from the field in a blanket and attempted to revive him. But he was already dead. The "Reynolds Tree" (below left), located near where he fell, was uprooted in a storm in 1987. A monument (below) now stands nearby.

The nineteenth-century photograph above shows the railroad cut east of Gettysburg as it appeared just after the war; the photo at right, taken in 2000, shows the bridge over the middle cut. In 1863, the rails of the Gettysburg & Hanover Railroad ended at the station in town, but the route west of town had been graded for a continuation of the railroad. The area where the roadbed cut through McPherson's Ridge seemed to offer security for Davis's troops advancing southward toward Chambersburg Road. Instead it became their trap.

Opposite: Fighting began on July 1 along McPherson's Ridge, a low rise of ground west of town. Buford's cavalry held off Heth's division long enough for Reynolds's I Corps to arrive. Buford then pulled back, leaving Gamble's brigade behind. Reynolds was killed early in the fight, but the Union held the ridgeline.

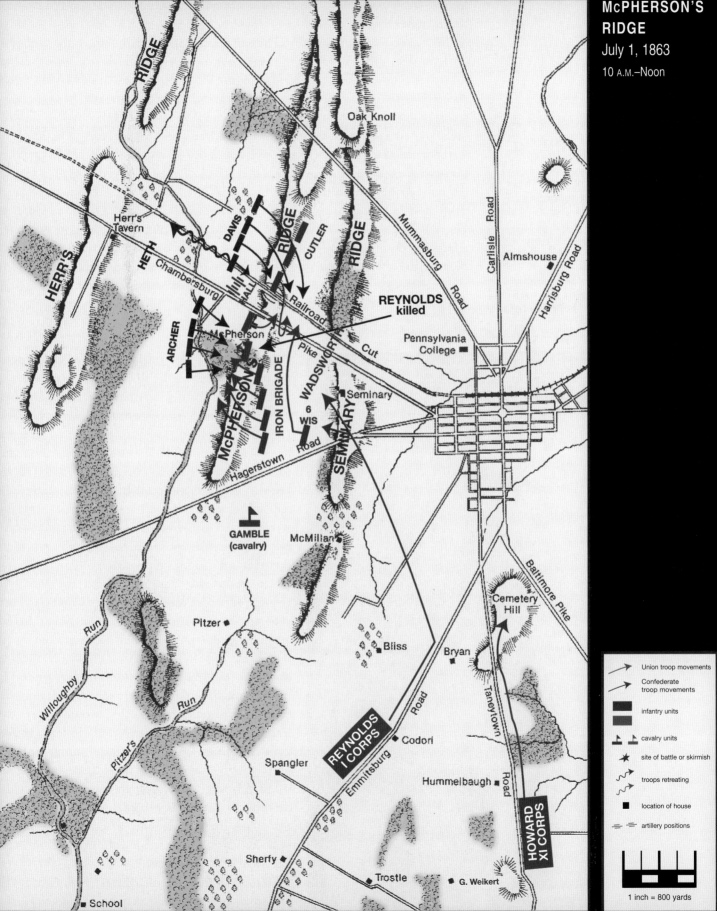

McPHERSON'S RIDGE

July 1, 1863

10 A.M.–Noon

RIDGE

Oak Knoll

Mummasburg Road

Carlisle Road

Almshouse

Harrisburg Road

Herr's Tavern

DAVIS

RIDGE

CUTLER

HETH

Chambersburg

HALL

Railroad

RIDGE

REYNOLDS
killed

HERR'S

ARCHER

McPherson

Pike

Cut

Pennsylvania
College

Railroad

IRON BRIGADE

WADSWORTH

Seminary

6
WIS

McPHERSON'S

Hagerstown

Road

SEMINARY

GAMBLE
(cavalry)

McMillan

Pitzer

Willoughby Run

Pitzer's Run

Bliss

Bryan

Cemetery
Hill

Baltimore Pike

REYNOLDS
I CORPS

Codori

Taneytown

Spangler

Emmitsburg Road

Hummelbaugh

Road

HOWARD
XI CORPS

Sherfy

Trostle

G. Weikert

School

Union troop movements

Confederate
troop movements

infantry units

cavalry units

site of battle or skirmish

troops retreating

location of house

artillery positions

1 inch = 800 yards

himself encumbered with a half dozen surrendered swords. It was a sweet moment that he never forgot.

By eleven the fighting on McPherson's Ridge had ended, though the artillerists on both sides carried on a long-range duel for several more hours. Taking shelter from the cannonade on the reverse slope, the victorious but exhausted Union troops rested on their arms and took stock. The day had become oppressively hot. Temperatures had climbed to near eighty, and the humidity remained high as well so that soldiers in their issue wool uniforms perspired freely and thirsted for water. Even the warm water in their canteens was welcome since in biting off the paper cartridges they had used to load their weapons, they inevitably had managed to get black powder on their lips and in their mouths, and its acrid taste was hard to purge. Few of them thought the fighting was over. Heth's wounded division had fallen back only to Herr's Ridge, less than a mile away, and other Confederate troops were even then advancing toward the battlefield. Of course Union troops were en route as well. From the west, the north, and the south, other pieces of a complicated military mosaic were clicking into place as elements from both armies converged on Gettysburg.

One element of that mosaic was the XI Corps of Oliver Otis Howard, whose men still wore a metaphorical albatross around their necks for their poor showing at Chancellorsville. Howard arrived in Gettysburg at about eleven o'clock, just as the fighting on McPherson's Ridge was dying out. He dispatched an aide to find Reynolds in order to get instructions for the placement of his corps. Instead a staff officer returned with the news that Reynolds was dead, and that Howard was now the ranking officer on the field. Howard had lost his right arm at the Battle of Seven Pines the year before, an action for which he would later be awarded the Medal of Honor. He was an intelligent officer who had earned a degree from Bowdoin College in Maine before attending West Point, where he had graduated fourth in the class of 1854. He was also a devoutly religious man who did not drink, smoke, or play cards. His critics thought him too contemplative and not sufficiently energetic. (Sherman would later say scathingly that he "ought to have been born in petticoats.") But he was now the man on the spot, and necessarily he had to bring order to the existing situation. He later wrote that the news of Reynolds's death rocked him: "Is it confessing weakness to say that when the responsibility of my position flashed upon me I was penetrated with an emotion never experienced before or since?"

Howard rode back to Cemetery Hill, a gentle rise just south of Gettysburg that he had noted on his

Oliver Otis Howard arrived at Gettysburg bearing the scars of two wounds. His empty right sleeve was the consequence of a wound he had received in the Battle of Seven Pines outside Richmond in 1862, an action for which he would subsequently be awarded the Medal of Honor. The other scar was psychological: Howard and his command had not fully recovered from their catastrophic rout at Chancellorsville two months before. It was therefore a shock to him when he arrived at Gettysburg to learn that Reynolds had been killed and that he was now the senior Federal officer on the battlefield.

Abner Doubleday (third from right), sitting with his staff, succeeded to the command of the I Corps at Gettysburg upon Reynolds's death, and he supervised the Union defense of McPherson's Ridge and Seminary Ridge on July 1. Meade was unsure of Doubleday's ability to command a corps, however, and that night he replaced him with Doubleday's West Point classmate John Newton, a decision that Doubleday resented for the rest of his life.

Overleaf: The nineteenth-century artist Peter Frederick Rothermel attempted to condense all the action on McPherson's Ridge into his 1868 painting *The Death of General Reynolds.* The McPherson barn stands at the center of the painting, with McPherson's Woods just to the left. Heth's Confederate division attacks from the right while I Corps reinforcements arrive from the left. At the bottom center, stretcher bearers carry off the body of John Reynolds.

"SURRENDER OR I WILL FIRE"

Rufus Dawes, the Ohio native who commanded the 6th Wisconsin infantry at Gettysburg, was one of many Civil War veterans who wrote his memoirs after the war. In the following passage from those memoirs, he describes the famous charge by his regiment that reversed the tide of battle on McPherson's Ridge on the morning of July 1.

In the field, beyond the turnpike, a long line of yelling Confederates could be seen running forward and firing, and our troops of Cutler's brigade were running back in disorder. The fire of our carefully aimed muskets, resting on the fence rails, striking their flank, soon checked the rebels in their headlong pursuit. The rebel line swayed and bent, and suddenly stopped firing and the men ran into the railroad cut, parallel to the Cashtown [Chambersburg] Turnpike. I ordered my men to climb over the turnpike fences and advance. . . .

The only commands I gave, as we advanced, were, "Align on the colors! Close up on the colors! Close up on the colors!" The regiment was being so broken up that this order alone could hold the body together. Meanwhile the colors fell upon the ground several times, but were raised again by the heroes of the color guard. Four hundred and twenty men started in the regiment from the turnpike fence, of whom about two hundred and forty reached the railroad cut. . . .

Colonel Rufus Dawes

Running forward through our line of men, I found myself face to face with hundreds of rebels, whom I looked down upon in the railroad cut, which was, where I stood, four feet deep. Adjutant [Edward P.] Brooks, equal to the emergency, quickly placed about twenty men across the cut in position to fire through it. I have always congratulated myself upon getting the first word. I shouted: "Where is the colonel of this regiment?" An officer in gray, with stars on his collar, who stood among the men in the cut, said: "Who are you?" I said: "I command this regiment. Surrender or I will fire." The officer replied not a word, but promptly handed me his sword, and his men, who still held them, threw down their muskets. The coolness, self-possession, and discipline which held back our men from pouring in a general volley saved a hundred lives of the enemy, and as my mind goes back to the fearful excitement of the moment, I marvel at it. The fighting around the rebel colors had not ceased when this surrender took place. I took the sword. It would have been the handsome thing to say, "Keep your sword, sir," but I was new to such occasions, and when six other officers came up and handed me their swords, I took them also.

SOURCE: Rufus R. Dawes, *Service with the Sixth Wisconsin Volunteers* (Marietta, Ohio: E. R. Alderman & Sons, 1890), pp. 167–69.

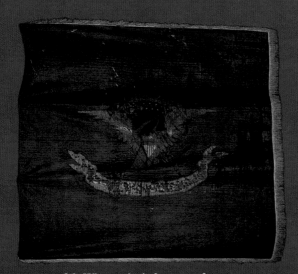

6th Wisconsin infantry colors

2nd Mississippi infantry flag

way into town, and set up a headquarters there. As commanding general on the field, he turned his own corps over to the German-born Carl Schurz, a lean, bespectacled individual who looked more like an academic than a general, and gave him orders to take two of the corps's three divisions to extend Doubleday's right to cover Mummasburg Road. Howard planned to keep the third division, that of Adolph von Steinwehr (which was still en route), on Cemetery Hill as a reserve.

Howard had barely issued these orders when the ever vigilant John Buford reported that a large body of Confederate infantry was approaching Gettysburg from the north. This, of course, was the van of Ewell's corps moving to Gettysburg in response to Lee's order of the day before. The timing of his arrival was largely coincidental since Ewell (like Heth) was moving forward without a cavalry screen, but his appearance at just this moment effectively turned Howard's position. Forced by these circumstances to change his dispositions, Howard ordered Schurz to deploy his six thousand men in an east-west line north of town connecting his left to Doubleday's right to form a lazy L with Doubleday's corps facing west and Schurz's two divisions facing north. The task assigned to Schurz was daunting. There was no natural cover north of town for the defenders. The ridgelines in south-central Pennsylvania all ran north-south, and Schurz's men would be stretched out in an east-west line across a broad, open valley. Nor was there any time for them to prepare fieldworks, for Schurz's men barely arrived before the first Confederates appeared on their front. Those Confederate troops, moreover, were from the same rebel units that had crashed into the flank of the XI Corps two months before, almost to the day.

Carl Schurz immigrated to the United States from Germany (via France) in 1852. An intelligent and articulate man who had served as a lieutenant in the Prussian army, he quickly became a leader in the German-American community and an activist in the antislavery movement. Named ambassador to Spain by Abraham Lincoln in 1861, he returned to the United States a year later and received a commission as a brigadier general of volunteers. His appointment pleased the many German immigrants in the ranks of the Union army. At Gettysburg he commanded a division in Howard's mostly German XI Corps.

By noon on July 1, it was evident that the Federals had won the first round at Gettysburg. A bold decision by Buford to hold the ridgeline west of town, the cavalier attitude of Heth, who committed only two relatively inexperienced brigades to the fight, and the timely arrival of Wadsworth's division had given the men in blue a victory on McPherson's Ridge. But the appearance of Ewell's corps north of town dramatically changed the tactical picture. For once in the war, the Confederates had numerical superiority over their foe, a foe that was exposed, unentrenched, and still bearing the psychological scars of the last confrontation. The Army of Northern Virginia confronted a splendid opportunity of a kind not likely to be repeated.

CHAPTER FIVE

The Shadow of Stonewall

(1 P.M. – 8 P.M., July 1, 1863)

Of all the controversies that surround the Battle of Gettysburg, one of the most persistent concerns the role of Lieutenant General Richard Stoddert Ewell, "Old Bald Head," the commander of the Confederate II Corps, whose troops showed up north of town an hour past noon. The principal charge against Ewell is that he was not Stonewall Jackson. On the afternoon and evening of July 1, his critics claim, Ewell fumbled away an opportunity to win the Battle of Gettysburg, and perhaps the war, by not seizing the moment and pressing the fight with the kind of Old Testament ferocity that had been the hallmark of the martyred Jackson.

The controversy about Ewell grew out of several factors, the most prominent of which was a postwar effort by Lee's admirers to absolve their beloved commander of any blame for the disappointing outcome of the battle. Defying the adage that defeat is an orphan, Lee's staunch defenders identified a numerous patrimony for Gettysburg: there was Stuart, whose irresponsible "joyriding" left Lee "blind" in Pennsylvania; there was Hill, who precipitately and thoughtlessly committed the army to a battle that Lee did not want; and there was Ewell, who failed to win the victory that circumstance offered to him by showing a cautious streak at the most inopportune moment. Other potential scapegoats would make their appearance in due course. But one controversy at a time.

Ewell was 46 years old in the summer of 1863. A West Point graduate (class of 1840), he had begun the war as a lieutenant colonel in the forces of Virginia. Promoted to brigadier general in the Confederate army, he commanded a brigade in the Battle of Manassas (or Bull Run, as the Yankees called it), but he first obtained wide notice as Jackson's second in command during the Shenandoah Valley campaign in 1862. Ewell hardly knew what to make of Jackson. "Old Jack" gave orders without explanation and expected literal adherence to them regardless of changing circumstances. For a time Ewell wondered if his commanding officer was insane, but before long he began to see Stonewall's eccentricities as evidence of genius rather than madness, and he

Opposite: Richard Stoddert Ewell was the central figure in the drama that unfolded north of Gettysburg in the late afternoon and evening of July 1. His decisions and actions (or inaction) that day would affect both his place in the army and his historical reputation and would make him a centerpiece in the debate about Confederate decision making at Gettysburg.

became Jackson's stalwart advocate and acolyte. In August 1862, Ewell was severely wounded in the knee at the Battle at Groveton, the opening phase of the Confederate victory at Second Manassas. The wound led to the amputation of his left leg, and Ewell went on convalescent leave.

He was nursed to recovery by his cousin, Lizinka Brown, with whom he had been in love more or less all his life. In late May 1863, literally the day before he rejoined the army sporting a new wooden leg and only a week before the army started north for Pennsylvania, he and Brown were married. Later some of Ewell's detractors would whisper that his new status as a married man bred caution in the formerly spirited leader, as if marriage had somehow unmanned him. At the time, however, Ewell's appointment to the II Corps was popular with the troops, and during the first few weeks of his tenure his performance seemed to validate Lee's good judgement in selecting him for the post. So impressive was his conduct of operations in the Shenandoah Valley that in his classic study, *Lee's Lieutenants*, Douglas Southall Freeman titled his chapter on the Battle at Winchester "As If a Second Jackson Had Come."

But Ewell was not a second Jackson nor should anyone who knew the two men have expected that he would be. One problem, ironically, was that Jackson had never endowed his subordinates with the kind of discretion that Lee had routinely bestowed on him. In effect, service under Jackson was a poor school for any officer who aspired to become a second Jackson. Nevertheless, Ewell appeared to be in confident command of the situation as he marched his corps through Maryland and into Pennsylvania. Then, at Carlisle on the night of June 28, he received Lee's order instructing him to forsake Harrisburg and turn west to join the rest of the army. The order directed him "to proceed to Cashtown or Gettysburg, as circumstances might dictate." Ewell may have been discomfited by what he called Lee's "indefinite phraseology." According to Isaac Trimble (one of Ewell's critics), Old Bald Head read the order aloud several times, then sputtered, "Why can't a Commanding General have someone on his staff who can write an intelligible order?" To Trimble's eye, Ewell was already beginning to crack under the pressure of having to make independent decisions.

Ewell decided to send his divisions southward from Carlisle by different roads, which would not only allow faster movement but also postpone the moment when he would have to choose between Cashtown and Gettysburg as a destination. Before he had covered half the distance, he received a note from Hill that the III Corps was engaged near Gettysburg, and (Jackson-like) Ewell at once moved to support him.

The first of Ewell's three divisions to reach the battlefield belonged to Robert Emmett Rodes, a talented, young (34) officer with pale blue eyes, coarse dark hair, and a walrus mustache. Popular with the men he led (one soldier described his command style as "firmness tempered with kindness"), Rodes had been in the thick of most of the fighting in the eastern theater since First Bull Run. It was Rodes's brigade that had defended the Bloody Lane at Antietam, and it was Rodes's division that had led the flank attack at Chancellorsville only two months back. Indeed, Rodes must have been reminded of that assault at Chancellorsville when he arrived at Gettysburg atop a tree-covered knoll north of town and saw Doubleday's open right flank in front of him. But even as he surveyed the ground, he espied Schurz's XI Corps soldiers coming out of town to cover that flank. The sight spurred him to action—perhaps precipitately. In a hurry to seize the opportunity, Rodes sent his two lead brigades forward on either side of the Mummasburg Road to attack Doubleday's flank before Schurz's men arrived on the scene.

Robert Emmett Rodes was an 1848 graduate of the Virginia Military Institute, and at the outbreak of war was an instructor there. At Chancellorsville, his division had led Jackson's flank attack with such ferocity that Jackson, literally on his deathbed, recommended Rodes's promotion to major general.

It was too little, too soon. The Alabama brigade of Colonel Edward A. O'Neal advanced with only three of its five regiments, and it did so without O'Neal, who remained behind. Its attack was effectively broken before Rodes's other brigade got started. That brigade suffered an even worse fate: the four North Carolina regiments of Brigadier General Alfred Iverson (who also failed to accompany his command in the attack) were caught in deadly flanking fire that all but annihilated the Tarheels. "When we were in point-blank range," one of the survivors recalled, "the dense line of the enemy rose from its protected lair and poured into us a withering fire." Most of the attackers fell where they stood; one observer later counted seventy-nine of them lying in a straight line—all dead. The rest carried on a brief, unequal contest before most of them were taken prisoner.

This is the view of Gettysburg that met Rodes's soldiers when they reached Oak Hill, north of town. Carlisle Road runs into Gettysburg on the left. The large building on the right is Pennsylvania College, and just behind it is Culp's Hill. The arrival of Ewell's lead divisions effectively turned the Union right flank, which would have been off to the right in this photo.

Watching all this from Herr's Ridge west of town was a trio of Confederate generals: a somewhat chastened Harry Heth, an ailing Powell Hill, and an increasingly concerned Robert E. Lee. The outcome of the battle on McPherson's Ridge had stunned Heth. He still had six to seven thousand men deployed in a line of battle on Herr's Ridge, plus the twenty-gun battalion of Major William (Willie) Pegram that was banging away at the bluecoats on McPherson's Ridge. With such a force he might yet carry the enemy position opposite him, especially if he were supported by Dorsey Pender's division, which was just behind him. Watching Rodes go into action north of town, he sought permission from Lee to renew his advance. "Rodes is heavily engaged," he said to Lee. "Had I not better attack?"

Lee had never intended to fight a battle with only part of his army, and already that morning he had ridden up to Herr's Ridge to find Heth's division repulsed from an engagement west of Gettysburg, and now he watched as Rodes was apparently about to suffer a similar fate north of town. He was not about to commit his army further, especially since he did not know just how many enemy troops there were in Gettysburg. Lee turned Heth down with a shake of his head. "I am not prepared to bring on a general engagement today," he told him. "Longstreet is not up."

At age 31, John B. Gordon (above) was a rising star in the Confederate army. He had earned his reputation as a fierce fighter at Antietam, where he had suffered no fewer than five wounds while his regiment defended Bloody Lane from a series of determined Federal assaults. For his heroism, Gordon was promoted to brigadier general, and his brigade of Georgians led the advance of Early's division that turned the Federals north of town out of position.

Nineteen-year-old lieutenant Bayard Wilkeson, shown in a watercolor sketch by Alfred Waud, directs the fire of his battery on Barlow's Knoll alongside Harrisburg Road in a vain attempt to slow down the advance of Gordon's brigade. When Wilkeson's right leg was all but severed by counterbattery fire, he used his sash to make a tourniquet, then amputated the wreckage of the limb himself with his own pocketknife. He did not survive the day.

Then fate lent a hand. Only a few minutes after this conversation, the sound of heavy gunfire from the northeast reached Lee's ears. It was John B. Gordon's brigade of Georgia troops, the lead element of Jubal Early's division, coming down Harrisburg Road. Though entirely coincidental, its arrival at that precise place and time could not have been deliberately calculated to have greater impact, and Gordon was just the man to make the most of it. One of Gordon's admiring soldiers insisted that Gordon was "most the prettiest thing you ever did see on a field of fight. It'ud put fight into a whipped chicken just to look at him!" Early deployed his entire division athwart Harrisburg Road and sent it forward crashing into the Federal division of Francis C. Barlow. On his own authority, Barlow had pushed his division out to an exposed knoll alongside Harrisburg Road (ever after called Barlow's Knoll). Now Gordon's men, joined by Doles's brigade from Rodes's division, assailed the knoll, while the brigades of Harry Hays and Isaac Avery (with Hoke's brigade) swept around Barlow's unprotected right. Outflanked and outnumbered, Barlow's men clung desperately to the knoll, while all around them the Federal line wavered and threatened to collapse. From his vantage point on Herr's Ridge, Lee could see enemy units pulling out from his front and moving north to face Rodes. Lee knew an opportunity when he saw one.

"ARE YOU THE MAN WHO KILLED ME?"

Brigadier General Francis Barlow

**Brigadier General
John B. Gordon**

As John B. Gordon's brigade swept over the crest of Barlow's Knoll on the afternoon of July 1, Francis Barlow (left) was struck by a minié ball that passed through his torso and exited out his back very near his spine. He fell to the ground paralyzed in all four limbs. As his troops were forced to evacuate the knoll, he could not be moved and had to be left behind. When Gordon rode to the top of the knoll, he noticed Barlow lying among the scattered Union corpses. Gordon stopped and dismounted. Gently lifting Barlow's head, he offered the apparently dying man a drink of water from his canteen. Barlow thanked him and asked Gordon if he could send word to his wife that he had died doing his duty, and Gordon promised to do so. Barlow was then carried to the Confederate rear on a litter believing that he would not last the night. As promised, Gordon sent a message to Mrs. Barlow assuring her of her late husband's heroic performance in battle.

But Barlow did not die. He slowly recovered and was eventually exchanged. A year later, after one of the many battles during the Overland campaign in Virginia, he read in the papers about the death of General J. B. Gordon of the Confederate army and assumed, not unreasonably, that it was the man who had shared his water at Gettysburg. In fact, it was a distant relative of John B. Gordon. Thus, as Gordon recalled in his memoirs, "To me, Barlow was dead; to Barlow I was dead." And so both men believed for fifteen years. Gordon tells the rest of the story in his book:

During my second term in the United States Senate, the Hon. Clarkson Potter, of New York, was a member of the House of Representatives. He invited me to dinner in Washington to meet a General Barlow who had served in the Union army. Potter knew nothing of the Gettysburg incident. I had heard that there was another Barlow in the Union army, and supposed, of course, that it was this Barlow with whom I was to dine. Barlow had a similar reflection as to the Gordon he was to meet. Seated at Clarkson's table, I asked Barlow: "General, are you related to the Barlow who was killed at Gettysburg?" He replied: "Why, I am the man, sir. Are you related to the Gordon who killed me?" "I am the man sir," I responded. No words of mine can convey any conception of the emotions awakened by those startling announcements. Nothing short of an actual resurrection from the dead could have amazed either of us more. Thenceforward, until his untimely death in 1896, the friendship between us which was born amidst the thunders of Gettysburg was greatly cherished by both.

SOURCE: John B. Gordon, *Reminiscences of the Civil War* (New York: Charles Scribner's Sons, 1903), pp. 152–53.

He reversed his earlier decision and ordered Heth to recommit his division, and he sent Dorsey Pender's division in after it. Four rebel divisions—nearly 25,000 men—swept forward on two fronts against 15,000 defenders.

The attack was irresistible. North of Gettysburg, Barlow's men were driven from the knoll, leaving their wounded commander on the field to be taken prisoner. Led now by 27-year-old Adelbert Ames, they attempted to rally near an almshouse on the

The German-born Federal Brigadier General Alexander Schimmelfennig (above) owed his commission, in part at least, to his spectacular name. Presented with a list of possible candidates for promotion, and sensitive to the army's many German-born soldiers, Lincoln selected Schimmelfennig even after it was suggested to him that others were equally qualified. Alas, though he was a competent general, Schimmelfennig did not cover himself with glory at Gettysburg. Forced to flee with the rest of his command from the advancing Confederates, he took refuge in the yard of a local family where livestock was kept, giving rise to the longstanding tale that he spent the battle hiding in a pigsty. An engraving by Allen Carter Redwood (above right) shows soldiers of the XI Corps fleeing in near panic during the Battle of Chancellorsville in May. Despite its determination to wash away that stain on its record, the XI Corps was broken again at Gettysburg by the convergence of two Confederate divisions arriving from the north.

outskirts of town. A Georgia soldier praised their determination: "They were harder to drive than we had ever known them before," he wrote. "Their officers were cheering their men and behaving like heroes." But both numbers and momentum were against them. To many, it was Chancellorsville all over again as the men of the XI Corps fled for the protection of the town. They fell back through the streets of Gettysburg, stopping to fire at moments of opportunity but losing unity and cohesion because of the narrow streets and the confusion of the moment.

The story was much the same west of town. Pettigrew's fresh brigade of North Carolinians spearheaded the renewed attack on McPherson's Ridge, assailing the Iron Brigade south of the woods the midwesterners had captured only that morning. Though much reduced by casualties from the morning's fight, the Black Hat boys fought furiously, and they inflicted heavy casualties on Pettigrew's men. But once again numbers and momentum prevailed, and when Dorsey Pender's division joined the fight, the Federals on McPherson's Ridge began to fall back. The small brigade of Colonel Roy Stone, composed of three Pennsylvania regiments, held on near the McPherson farm until it was all but surrounded before it finally gave way, conducting a fighting retreat back to Seminary Ridge.

There the Federals took cover behind a stone wall and some light breastworks and prepared to make another stand. The Confederates attacked across the open ground on a broad front, their colors held aloft in parade-ground style, and though they suffered terrible casualties, they burst through the undermanned Federal line just south of the seminary building. After that, the I Corps survivors had to fall back into the town. There, as with the men of the XI Corps, their unit cohesion was broken up by the grid of streets.

It was not quite a rout. The Federals retired grudgingly, fighting street to street as the terrified residents cowered in their basements, a rare case of urban warfare in the Civil War. One of the retreating Federal soldiers later wrote home that "The enemy were pouring into town on two if not three sides, and sweeping the streets with a

For the citizens of Gettysburg, July 1 was a terrifying day. They cheered and waved their handkerchiefs when the men of the XI Corps marched past in the morning to take up their defensive positions north of town, then they feared for their lives when those same soldiers retreated back through town only a few hours later with the dreaded rebels hard on their heels. Albertus McCreary was only a boy at the time, but in the following excerpt from his memoirs, he recalls with vivid clarity the events and the emotions of that hot summer afternoon:

It was about noon, and we sat down to our dinner as usual; but before we were through there was so much noise and racket in the street that we all left the table and went to the doors to see what was going on.

The street was full of Union soldiers, running and pushing each other, sweaty and black from powder and dust. They called to us for water. It was a hot July day. We got great buckets of water and tin dippers, and supplied them as fast as we could from the porch at the side of the house off the main street. Many were the hearty thanks we received. Hundreds thus got a refreshing drink as they fled in full retreat through the town. . . .

We kept right on distributing water until an officer rode his horse up on the pavement among the soldiers and said, "All you good people go down in your cellars or you will all be killed." We obeyed him at once. Several neighboring families had sought our house, for it was large and well built, with strong walls of stone.

Hardly were we all down in the cellar, when we heard fighting all around the house, over the porch where a few moments before we had been handing out water, and over the cellar doors in the pavement. I heard a voice say, "Shoot that fellow going over the fence." The order was obeyed, and a shot rang out just by the cellar window. There were several small windows in the walls and their light cast shadows on the opposite wall, of men rushing back and forth; those shadows filled all of us with horror. There was more and more shooting, until the sound was one continuous racket. I peeped out of one of the windows just in time to see a cannon unlimbered and fired down the street. What a noise it made, and how the dust did fly!

After a time the noise grew less and less, and farther and farther away. We were all

suddenly the outer cellar doors were pulled open, and five Confederate soldiers jumped down among us. We thought our last day had come. Some of the women cried, while others, with hands clasped, stood rooted to the spot with fear. Father stepped forward and asked what they wanted and begged them not to harm his people.

One fellow—I can see him yet—with a red face covered with freckles, and very red hair, dirty, and sweaty, with his gun in his hand said, "We are looking for Union soldiers." "There are none here," Father answered. But the soldier said he would have to search, and that we could go upstairs, as the danger was over for a time.

From that time on we had no fear of harm from individual soldiers. We all went upstairs, and the searchers found thirteen of our men hiding in all parts of the house, some under the beds, and one under the piano, and others in the closets. The prisoners were brought into the dining-room, where the officer in charge took their names.

I well remember my father as he said, "Gentlemen, won't you have something to eat?"

The table was just as we had left it such a short time before. They were only too glad to accept the invitation. While all were eating, I went around and took down the names of the prisoners, telling them I would write to their friends. Now that they had stopped fighting, both sides seemed to be on the best of terms, and laughed and chatted like old comrades.

SOURCE: Albertus McCreary, "Gettysburg: A Boy's Experience of the Battle," *McClure's Magazine* (July 1909), 33: pp. 244–46.

A photograph by Alexander Gardner, taken in 1865, shows Baltimore Street in

The brick archway at Evergreen Cemetery was the dominant landmark atop Cemetery Hill. Erected in 1855, it served as both a gateway to the cemetery and the residence for the supervisor. During the battle, the gatehouse stood within Federal lines and was used as an observation post. This photograph, taken a few days after the battle, shows surprisingly little battle damage beyond a few broken windows. The archway still stands today.

terrific cross fire of musketry, while the solid shot tore the buildings and ploughed through the living mass, the shell screeched through the air scattering deadly missiles as thick as hail." The 6th Wisconsin, which had captured most of the 2nd Mississippi regiment in the railroad cut that morning, tried to hold together as it made its way through town. At one point its commander directed his men to crawl one by one through a hole in a backyard fence to get from one street to another. Eventually those of the I and XI Corps who had not fallen or been captured made their way back to Cemetery Hill south of town where Howard had established his headquarters at eleven that morning. There they were cheered by the sight of the army's reserve in battle formation backed by artillery, and they took up defensive positions facing north and west as they prepared to defend the heights. It was approximately four o'clock in the afternoon.

The arrival of Ewell's corps had reversed the course of battle and secured a spectacular victory for Confederate arms. Both north and west of town, the Federal army had been broken. Nearly four thousand Federal soldiers had been taken prisoner, most of them from the unlucky XI Corps on Ewell's front. Ewell rode over to congratulate John Gordon for the role his troops had played in the victory. In his postwar memoirs, Gordon claimed that he responded by urging Ewell to seize the moment and continue the attack: to pass through town and assail the high ground of Cemetery Hill that could be seen beyond the spires of Gettysburg's churches. Ewell did not turn him down; in fact, he said nothing at all. Eighty years later, the historian D. S. Freeman explained Ewell's silence as a failure of character. "Inwardly," Freeman wrote, "something had happened to the will of Richard Ewell. In place of his usual chatter, there was silence. While some of the most fateful seconds in American history ticked past, he waited." Of course, enigmatic silence had been Stonewall Jackson's most salient personality characteristic. It may well be that Ewell was simply taking a lesson from his departed mentor.

Most likely Ewell was recalling that just before Early's attack he had received an order from Lee reminding him *not* to bring on a general action until the army was unified. When he had received that order, Rodes was already engaged and Gordon

A nineteenth-century photo of Culp's Hill by C. J. Tyson shows the kind of terrain that made the height such a daunting obstacle. The view is from the base of East Cemetery Hill, and the road in the foreground is Baltimore Pike. Ewell's men would have had to cross this ground to assault the Federal defensive lines on July 1.

was preparing to attack. Ewell decided that the action was too advanced to recall it, and he had pressed the attack vigorously despite Lee's order. Though the results had more than justified his decision, he had defied a direct order to achieve them. To renew the attack now, in continued disregard of those orders, would be more than bold; it would be insubordinate. When a cavalry officer rode up to report that Ewell's 3rd division, that of Edward "Allegheny" Johnson, was approaching the battlefield, Ewell sent orders for Johnson to halt and await orders.

Many years later, long after Ewell's death in 1872, a number of individuals who claimed to have heard those orders testified that they were both shocked and disappointed. Henry Kyd Douglas, who brought Ewell the news of Johnson's approach, was one such witness. Writing in 1899, he asserted that Ewell's chief of staff, Colonel Alexander (Sandy) Pendleton, muttered aloud, "Oh, for the presence and inspiration of Old Jack for just one hour!" Similarly, another of Ewell's young staff officers claimed in 1905 that one of their number (he did not say which one) said sadly and meaningfully, "Jackson is not here." Such after-the-fact testimonials are suspect. Thirty years after the battle, at the height of "Lost Cause" revisionism, Southerners looked back to Gettysburg as the high-water mark of Southern fortunes. By then it was evident to them that Ewell *should* have attacked, and with the benefit of three decades of hindsight, they recalled that they had known it even at the time.

With his supposedly disappointed staffers trailing him, Ewell rode into Gettysburg, though the town was not yet completely secured. Earlier in the afternoon Ewell had had a horse shot out from under him. Now a minié ball struck him in the leg. "Are you hurt, sir?" Gordon asked anxiously. "No, no, I'm not hurt," Ewell replied, chuckling. "It don't hurt a bit to be shot in a wooden leg." In town, Ewell dismounted in the central square where the roads from ten directions converged. He was there when Walter Taylor, Lee's aide, arrived with new orders from the commanding general. Having watched the retreat of the XI Corps through Gettysburg, Lee now asked Ewell to press the enemy and attack the hill south of town if he "could do so to advantage." Thus released from the earlier cautionary order to avoid a general engagement, Ewell sent for Early and Rodes to plan a coordinated assault.

Both division commanders were eager to renew the fight. Their forces had passed through the town and were even then not far from the foot of Cemetery Hill. But those forces had also become disorganized, and Rodes in particular had suffered heavy casualties. Both generals asserted that they would need support from A. P. Hill's corps on their right. Could Hill cooperate? Ewell sent an aide galloping back toward Seminary Ridge, where Lee had set up his field headquarters, to find out. Meanwhile the three generals rode forward to observe the objective. Beyond Buford's cavalry at the foot of the hill, they could see solid ranks of blue infantry near the crest supported by forty pieces of artillery. That artillery would command the ground where Ewell would have to deploy his forces: Rodes's division had lost nearly 2,900 men in the fighting on Oak Knoll and was badly disorganized; half of Early's division had been dispatched to watch York Road, along which rumor had more Yankees arriving; Johnson's division was still a few miles away and would have to maneuver either through town or around it and then deploy before it could attack. It would be dicey, but it might be possible. Then the courier returned with news from Lee. Hill's corps would be unable to offer any support, the courier reported; if Ewell attacked Cemetery Hill, he would have to do it alone. Moreover, Lee reiterated his earlier caution not to bring on a general engagement. In other words, Ewell should attack if he perceived that the enemy was disorganized and vulnerable, but he should not attack if doing so would provoke a full-scale battle.

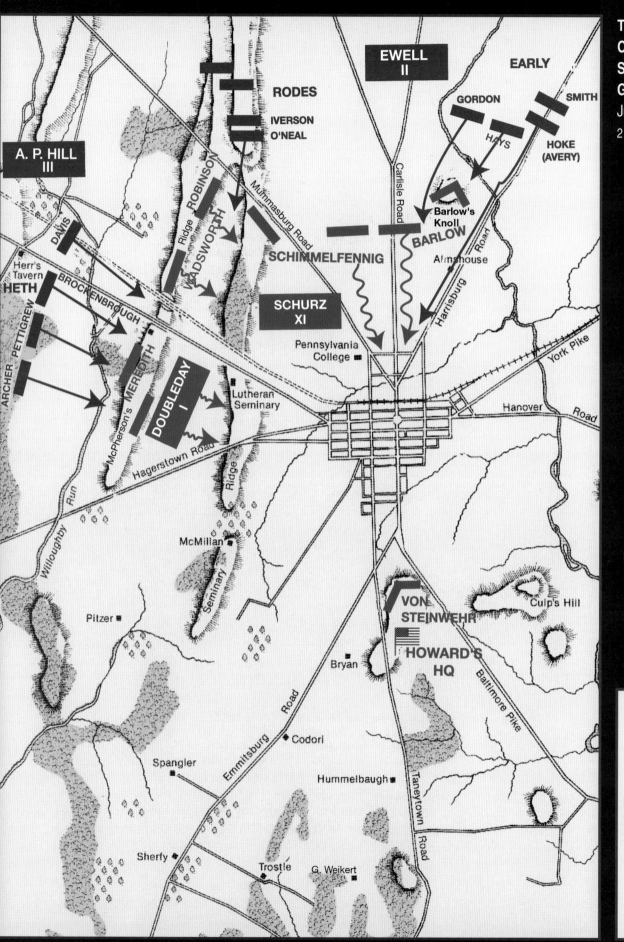

THE
CONFEDERATES
SEIZE
GETTYSBURG

July 1, 1863

2 P.M.– 5 P.M.

EWELL
II

EARLY

RODES

GORDON
SMITH

IVERSON
O'NEAL

HAYS

HOKE
(AVERY)

A. P. HILL
III

ROBINSON

Carlisle Road

Barlow's
Knoll

DAVIS

Mummasburg Road

BARLOW

Herr's
Tavern

BROCKENBROUGH

SCHIMMELFENNIG

Almshouse

HETH

Ridge

WADSWORTH

Harrisburg Road

ARCHER
PETTIGREW

MEREDITH

SCHURZ
XI

DOUBLEDAY
I

Pennsylvania
College

York Pike

McPherson's

Lutheran
Seminary

Hagerstown Road

Hanover   Road

Willoughby Run

Ridge

McMillan

Seminary

Culp's Hill

Pitzer

VON
STEINWEHR

Bryan

HOWARD'S
HQ

Baltimore Pike

Road

Emmitsburg

Codori

Taneytown Road

Spangler

Hummelbaugh

Sherfy

Trostle

G. Weikert

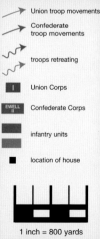

→ Union troop movements

→ Confederate
troop movements

〜 troops retreating

I Union Corps

EWELL II Confederate Corps

▬ infantry units

▪ location of house

1 inch = 800 yards

Here, then, is the crux of the controversy about Ewell at Gettysburg. Lee gave his II Corps commander the discretionary authority to attack if he thought it advisable. If he took the hill he might win the battle. If he were repulsed he might forfeit the gains of the afternoon. If he did not attack at all he might lose a priceless opportunity. Was there no other alternative?

In fact, there was. Just to the east of Cemetery Hill, now bristling with cannons, was another eminence, even higher in elevation and covered with trees. It was Culp's Hill. If Ewell could seize that hill it would effectively turn the Federals out of their position on Cemetery Hill. Absent the promise of support, Ewell shelved his plan to attack Cemetery Hill and decided to focus instead on the more lightly defended Culp's Hill. He offered the opportunity to Rodes, but that officer said his men were too used up, and, besides, Rodes said, they were guarding several thousand Union prisoners. Ewell made the same offer to Early, but Old Jube suggested that Allegheny Johnson's fresh division, just then arriving, was a more suitable weapon.

Johnson arrived ahead of his division sometime around 6 P.M., with sunset about an hour away. At about the same time, Ewell received a report (incorrect, as it would prove) that Culp's Hill was still unoccupied. Ewell passed this information on to his subordinate and ordered him to move his division up to occupy the hill. It would take another hour or so for Johnson's men to get into position, but since it would not be fully dark until around eight, that should not have been a problem. Isaac Trimble, a 61-year-old major general who had come north without a command hoping that something would turn up, pressed Ewell not to delay. If Ewell would give him a

A photograph, taken in midafternoon in 2000 from the base of Culp's Hill, shows the kind of terrain that Confederate attackers would have faced in attempting to secure a foothold there. The thick foliage, uneven footing, and steep ascent all made it difficult to determine if the hill was held by enemy forces. By late afternoon, darkness would have been an additional impediment.

"IT WAS A CRITICAL MOMENT FOR US"

Isaac Trimble was a Confederate raised in Maryland who, like Ewell, had been wounded prior to the Gettysburg campaign but, unlike Ewell, did not recover in time to obtain a command in Lee's reorganized army. Unwilling to miss the action, he went north with the army anyway as a "volunteer officer" and attached himself to Ewell's command. Disappointed by Ewell's failure to seize the high ground south of Gettysburg during the afternoon and evening of July 1, he was extremely critical of Ewell in his postwar comments, portraying him as confused and indecisive. The following is from an address that Trimble gave to a Veterans Association meeting after the war, that was subsequently published in the *Southern Historical Society Papers*.

Major General Isaac Trimble

About 2 P.M. Hill and Rodes had driven the enemy on our right, and General Early, having reached the field on our extreme left, encountered a heavy body of the enemy, who were sent to turn our left, and drove them back in confusion with heavy loss.

From the position I was in [on Oak Knoll], I could command a view a mile and a half in extent from one flank to the other, and noticed that the whole space in open fields was covered with Union soldiers retreating in broken masses towards the town from our own and General Hill's front.

This was about 2.30 P.M. Soon after General Ewell rode to the town, passing a numerous body of prisoners. I said to a [Federal] officer: "Fortune is against you to-day." He replied: "We have been worse whipped than ever."

At this time, about 3, the firing had ceased entirely, save occasional discharges of artillery from the hill above the town. The battle was over and we had won it handsomely. General Ewell moved about uneasily, a good deal excited, and seemed to me to be undecided what to do next. I

approached him and said: "Well, General, we have had a grand success; are you not going to follow it up and push our advantage?"

He replied that "General Lee had instructed him not to bring on a general engagement without orders, and that he would wait for them."

I said, that hardly applies to the present state of things, as we have fought a hard battle already, and should secure the advantage gained. He made no rejoinder, but was far from composure. I was deeply impressed with the conviction that it was a critical moment for us and made a remark to that effect.

As no movement seemed immediate, I rode off to our left, north of the town, to reconnoitre, and noticed conspicuously the wooded hill northeast of Gettysburg [Culp's], and a half mile distant, and of an elevation to command the country for miles each way, and overlooking Cemetery Hill above the town. Returning to see General Ewell, who was still under much embarrassment, I said: "General, there," pointing to Culp's Hill, "is an eminence of commanding position, and not now occupied, as it ought to be by us or the enemy soon. I advise you to send a brigade and hold it if we are to remain here." He said: "Are you sure it commands the town?" "Certainly it does, as you can see, and it ought to be held by us at once." General Ewell made some impatient reply, and the conversation dropped.

By night [it was then about 3:30], that hill—Culp's—the key of the position around Gettysburg was occupied by part of the XII Corps, Slocum's, and reinforced the next day.

SOURCE: Isaac Trimble, "The Battle and Campaign of Gettysburg," *Southern Historical Society Papers* (1898), vol. 26, pp. 122–24.

In an 1864 photo, Major General Winfield Scott Hancock sits surrounded by his division officers, each of whom played crucial roles in the Battle of Gettysburg. They are (from left to right): Brigadier General Francis Barlow of the XI Corps, who was wounded (mortally, it was believed at the time) on what is still called Barlow's Knoll north of Gettysburg on July 1; Major General David Birney, who took over command of the III Corps after Daniel Sickles was wounded on July 2; and Brigadier General John Gibbon, whose II Corps division defended the center of the Union line during the grand assault on Cemetery Ridge on July 3.

brigade, he asserted, he would take the hill at once. When Ewell did not reply, Trimble pressed him: "Give me a good *regiment* and I will do it!" Without a command of his own, Trimble had plenty of time to offer advice, and Ewell was beginning to weary of it. He turned to Trimble and said, "When I need advice from a junior officer, I generally ask for it." Furious, Trimble yanked his horse's head around and rode away, obtaining his revenge years later in the pages of the *Southern Historical Society Papers.*

On the Federal side of the line, Cemetery Hill at four o'clock was a roiling summit of men, horses, guns, and confusion. As the defeated elements of the I and XI Corps streamed back through town, Howard stationed staff officers at the foot of the hill to direct them into position. The I Corps survivors occupied the western slope of the hill facing Seminary Ridge, while the mostly German soldiers of the XI Corps,

humiliated at having been twice routed in two months, took up positions along the hill's northern face overlooking the town. At least some of the I Corps veterans now filing into place believed that the XI Corps had once again let them down. The collapse of the XI Corps, they reasoned, had uncovered their own right and compelled their retirement from McPherson's Ridge. Passing a staff officer who was directing foot traffic to the right and left, one I Corps soldier mocked his instructions by calling out, "The I Corps go to the right, and the XI Corps can go to hell."

At around 4:30, Major General Winfield Scott Hancock rode up onto Cemetery Hill. Learning of Reynolds's death at one that afternoon, and unwilling to leave Howard in command of the battlefield, Meade had ordered Hancock to Gettysburg with instructions to take command of the field and determine if the army should fight a battle there. Hancock began his journey riding in an army ambulance, but impatient with the slow progress, he called for his horse and rode ahead of the wagons to Cemetery Hill. He arrived just as Howard was patching together his defensive line.

The XI Corps commander was not happy to see him. Indeed, Howard seemed to have trouble absorbing the information that Meade wanted Hancock to take command; it was inconceivable to him that the commanding general had so little confidence in his leadership as to send a junior officer to take charge. Howard reminded

In *The Runaway Limber* by W. H. Shelton, the brick gatehouse of the cemetery is visible amid the smoke in the upper left corner as a team of horses reacts to the explosion of an artillery shell nearby. Just beyond, Federal gunners attempt to unlimber their pieces to resist the expected Confederate onslaught. Confusion was king on top of Cemetery Hill on the late afternoon of July 1.

Overleaf: The great tactical opportunity for the Confederate army is evident in James Walker's panoramic view of the battlefield from McPherson's Ridge. As Heth's division sweeps over McPherson's Ridge, driving back the Pennsylvania soldiers of Stone's brigade, Ewell's two divisions are arriving from the north. The Confederate soldier in the right foreground holds the captured colors of the 143rd Pennsylvania. Culp's Hill, the object of so much postwar discussion, is at left, and the Round Tops are at the right center.

Hancock that he was senior. "I am aware of that, General," Hancock replied, "but I have written orders in my pocket from General Meade which I will show you if you wish to see them." That would not be necessary, Howard replied glumly. He agreed that this was "no time for talking," and both men threw themselves into the job of preparing the army to defend its new position.

Meade had asked Hancock to assess the army's circumstances to determine if Gettysburg was a good place to fight a battle. Looking about himself on Cemetery Hill, Hancock complimented Howard on his selection of a defensive site, declaring that "this is the strongest position by nature upon which to fight a battle that I ever saw." Howard agreed, and Hancock thereupon announced, "Very well, sir, I select this as the battlefield." After that, Hancock set to work with a will, galloping about from unit to unit laying out lines of fire, resolving territorial disputes, and bringing a sense of energy and purpose to the defense. Spotting Orland Smith's brigade, part of Adolph von Steinwehr's division, lined up along the crest of Cemetery Hill, Hancock asked its commander if he could hold his position. "I think I can," Smith replied. "Will you hold it?" Hancock demanded. "I will!" Smith declared.

Federal reinforcements began to arrive: at about five o'clock the lead elements of Henry Slocum's XII Corps marched up the back slope of Cemetery Hill along the Baltimore Pike. Slocum was the senior major general in the army, but he was unfamiliar with the ground, and he therefore allowed Hancock to make the initial dispositions of his command. Hancock kept one of Slocum's two divisions behind Cemetery Hill as a reserve and sent the other (Geary's) to guard the army's left by occupying the ground south of Cemetery Hill near the Round Tops. By 5:30, at about the time that Ewell, Rodes, and Early were examining Cemetery Hill and considering an attack, Hancock was reporting to Meade that "we have now taken up a position in the cemetery, and cannot well be taken. I think," he wrote, "we will be all right until night."

Not long afterward, around 7 P.M., Hancock turned the command over to Slocum and, mounting his horse, he began the ride back to Meade's headquarters to report in person. Hancock had spent only about three hours on Cemetery Hill, and he had not participated in any of the desperate fighting for which the day would be long remembered, but his role was nevertheless critical. One Maine soldier recalled the "inspiration of his commanding, controlling presence" and "the fresh courage" that he brought to the defenders of Cemetery Hill.

The first of July ended on a disquieting note for Dick Ewell. Having ordered Johnson to take Culp's Hill as soon as possible, he left to confer with Lee about the next day's plans. When he returned, well past dark, he learned that Johnson had not taken the hill after all. Johnson had sent skirmishers up the slope and found the crest strongly occupied by Federal infantry. Because he had understood that Ewell wanted him to occupy the hill only if it was undefended, he had backed off. Thus both hills remained in the hands of the Yankees.

For the rest of his life and for a century afterward, critics would indict Ewell for failing to follow up on the spectacular victory his forces had achieved north of town. Surely, they posit, Stonewall would have done so. Of course, this assumption is based on the belief that an attack on Cemetery Hill late on the afternoon of July 1 would have been successful, and such a conclusion is questionable. An attack at four might

In describing the movements of both armies in the Battle of Gettysburg, it is perforce necessary to refer to the time of day when certain events occurred. But more often than not, such references are no more than estimates. Occasionally commanders scribbled the time of day on the hurried notes they wrote to their subordinates, which is a great help to historians attempting to piece the events together. But even then there is a large element of uncertainty. At the time of the Civil War, there was no such thing as standard time in the United States. Only with the development of the railroad system in the 1880s did such standardization become necessary. Before that, individual communities set their own local time, often displayed on a clock in the town square. It was not unusual for towns that were only a few miles apart to operate on entirely different time, several minutes or even an hour at variance with one another. For travelers this often caused confusion and uncertainty.

It causes confusion still for scholars attempting to track the movements of armies at Gettysburg. Officers generally carried pocket watches, but the time reflected on the faces of those watches might vary significantly not only when comparing a Union and Confederate officer, but even in comparing officers on the same side but from different commands, say a I Corps and a III Corps officer. As a result, any specific reference to the time that an event took place

A soldier's pocket watch

at Gettysburg must carry with it a cautionary note. In asserting that four brigades of Ewell's corps arrived north of Gettysburg at "about two o'clock," it must be remembered that this might have been as early as 1:30 or as late as 2:30. The same uncertainty applies to the moment when the Federals were driven through town and up onto Cemetery Hill.

This uncertainty about local time is historically significant because it affects the whole debate about Ewell's supposed missed opportunity at Gettysburg. If the opportunity to assail Cemetery Hill occurred as early as three, as Isaac Trimble claimed, then Ewell's guilt is magnified because of the long period of remaining daylight that should have allowed him time to organize and launch an attack. If, on the other hand, the opportunity did not beckon until five, then Ewell's "missed opportunity" is less glaring. General Howard later claimed that he sent Doubleday an order authorizing him to fall back if necessary at "about 4 P.M." and that "at 4:30 P.M. the columns reached Cemetery Hill." This contrasts dramatically with Trimble's assertion that "the fighting had ceased entirely" by three. The time suggested here—four o'clock—is a best-guess estimate based on the preponderance of evidence. The precise moment will almost certainly never be known, and students of the battle will probably debate the question forever.

have been decisive, but despite postwar assertions, the Confederates were in no condition to launch an attack at four. By five it was probably too late. Hancock's arrival at 4:30 stiffened the Federals' morale, and by 5:30 they were ready and waiting for just such an attack as Ewell might have been able to mount. As for Culp's Hill, it was not unoccupied (as Johnson discovered), for Hancock, too, had recognized its importance and had sent Wadsworth's division, including the battle-weary Iron Brigade, to its tree-covered slopes. Trimble's brash claim that he could take the hill with a regiment was foolish bravado. To be sure, a determined attack by the six thousand men of Johnson's division might have wrested Culp's Hill from its defenders, and arguably they should have made the effort. But they didn't, and they would pay dearly for it later.

CHAPTER SIX

The Best-Laid Plans

(5 P.M., July 1–10 A.M., July 2, 1863)

At about the same time that Hancock arrived on Cemetery Hill, James Longstreet rode up onto Seminary Ridge. "Old Pete," as he was sometimes known, had ridden ahead of his I Corps soldiers, who were strung out for several miles behind him along Chambersburg Road. His arrival caused a stir, for Longstreet was hard to miss. At six feet two inches with broad shoulders, a full brown beard, and steel blue eyes, he was a commanding figure. Atop the ridge, he found Lee and Hill in conversation; Lee had just dispatched Walter Taylor to ask Ewell if he could possibly take the hill south of town where the enemy could be seen establishing a new position. Longstreet examined the hill in question through his field glasses. According to his postwar testimony, he did not like what he saw; the position looked to be an especially commanding one. But it occurred to Longstreet that perhaps this was good news. The Federals might well be tempted to cling to their strong position on Cemetery Hill while the Confederates moved around it to take up new positions to the south and east where they would cut the Yankees off from their own capital. Under those circumstances, Longstreet mused, Meade would be forced to assume the tactical offensive, giving the Confederate army a chance to fight from prepared positions as it had at Fredericksburg.

Longstreet expressed these views to Lee in the full expectation that the army commander would agree with him. After all, the two men had talked at length about the kind of campaign that they expected to conduct during the invasion of the North, and Longstreet had convinced himself that they were of one mind about the advantages of the tactical defensive. To his surprise, however, Lee instead declared, "If the enemy is there tomorrow, we must attack him."

Lee's decision to renew the attack on July 2 was critical. It was what turned the fight at Gettysburg from one more in a series of Civil War battles into the historic confrontation that it became. Three factors influenced his decision. The first was that momentum was on his side. The unplanned but spectacularly effective coordination of two of his corps that afternoon had won him the town of Gettysburg and sent the enemy fleeing to the hills south of town. The morale of his army was sky high; that of the enemy was almost certainly flat. It was part of Lee's military instinct to press an advantage when the opportunity offered. Disengaging and maneuvering to the south would jeopardize that momentum and give Meade an opportunity to regain the initiative.

Opposite: In a photo taken in 2000, sunlight filtering through the trees dapples the equestrian statue of James Longstreet on Seminary Ridge at Gettysburg. Not only is Longstreet's statue life-size, but unlike most such monuments, it stands at ground level, almost as if the general and his horse had somehow been turned to bronze in midmovement. The curious legacy of James Longstreet's role at Gettysburg is suggested by the fact that this monument was not erected until 135 years after the battle.

Federal soldiers dig in on Cemetery Hill near the brick archway in an Edwin Forbes sketch. Lunettes for the Federal cannon are being prepared (right) while horses drag the guns and caissons to the crest.

Second, in moving to the south and assuming a defensive position between Gettysburg and Washington, Lee would have to abandon his line of supply through the passes of South Mountain. Without secure supply lines, he would have to maneuver to keep his army fed. But Longstreet's scenario called for the army to assume a blocking position and await an enemy attack. Wait how long? If Lee adopted Longstreet's advice and repositioned the army to the south, there was no certainty that Meade would follow the script and attack immediately. The campaign might drag on for days or weeks, giving Meade time to accumulate overwhelming numbers. At Gettysburg, the two armies were as near equal in size as they had been in any confrontation of the war. Lee could not be sure he would ever have such a chance again.

Finally, and perhaps decisively, Lee still did not know where Stuart was, and he lacked the kind of knowledge about the countryside that Stuart's active presence would have brought him. Without Stuart to screen his move, a maneuver such as the one Longstreet advised would have to take place in an intelligence vacuum. Maneuvering through the Pennsylvania countryside without Stuart had been risky enough when Lee believed the Federal army was safely south of the Potomac; to do so now with the two armies in intimate contact would be hazardous in the extreme. As a result of these factors, once it became clear that Ewell's corps could not storm over Cemetery Hill that afternoon, Lee began to consider what might be accomplished the next morning to complete the victory so advantageously begun.

The argument for continuing the fight the next morning was a strong one, but Longstreet's reaction to Lee's announcement made it clear that Old Pete was more than merely disappointed; he was dumbfounded. "I was at a loss," he wrote later in his memoirs. In evident agitation, he told Lee that "if he is there tomorrow, it will be because he wants you to attack." When Lee did not reply to that sally, Longstreet pressed him. "If that height has become the objective, why not take it at once?" Lee then brought Longstreet up to date: Hill's corps was too badly disorganized from the morning fight to continue the action, and Ewell did not think his corps could take the hill unassisted. Longstreet's own corps was still en route, and the absence of Stuart's cavalry meant that Lee did not know which Federal troops—or even how many—were on the heights. He did not want to commit the army until the rest of his forces arrived. Longstreet did not press the issue, but neither did he abandon his conviction that attacking a well-sited position was both foolish and unnecessary, and he nursed a hope that Lee might yet change his mind. "His [Lee's] manner suggested to me that a little reflection would be better than further discussion," Longstreet wrote later. And so Old Pete bit his tongue and dispatched orders for his command to hasten toward the battlefield, writing his subordinates that "you will be needed for to-morrow's battle." Unless, that is, he could talk Lee out of it in the meantime.

After his conversation with Longstreet, Lee rode over to Ewell's headquarters at about seven o'clock, just as the sun was setting, to consult with his II Corps commander. He met with Ewell and his division commanders in an outdoor arbor north of town to discuss the prospects for the next day. Could Ewell's corps make an attack on the hills south of town in the morning? Lee asked. Before Old Bald Head could even answer, the assertive Jubal Early, who not two hours before had urged Ewell to assail Cemetery Hill or Culp's Hill or both, now expressed the view that the ground around the two hills was too well suited to the defense to make an attack there. It would be better, Early suggested, for the army to swing around the enemy's left and attack from the southwest. Ewell seconded his lieutenant's view. In that case, asked Lee, could Ewell slide his corps westward and move south to take up a position on the Federal left flank? Ewell allowed that he could, but again it was Early who volunteered an opinion: it would be undesirable, he said, to abandon the town. It would be bad for morale and, more importantly, would throw away control of the road network. The plan that emerged from the discussion was that the II Corps would maintain a strong presence where it was, thus holding the Federal army in place, while Longstreet's corps, still en route and unbloodied in the first day's fight, conducted a flank attack from the south. In this scenario, Ewell would play the role that Jackson had played at Second Manassas: pinning the enemy in position while Longstreet rolled up the enemy flank. Lee accepted the proposal, and the meeting broke up just before midnight. Lee rode back to Seminary Ridge, where he met again with Hill and Longstreet, telling them, "Gentlemen, we will attack the enemy in the morning as early as practicable."

At midnight, as July 1 ended, the men of Lee's victorious army were aware that they had won an extraordinary victory. They had captured the town of Gettysburg as well as the good ground north and west of it that Buford and Reynolds had attempted to defend. The Federals had been driven back once again, just as they had at Chancellorsville, Manassas, and a half dozen other battlefields. To be sure, the bluecoats still held some high ground south of town, but few in the rebel army believed that July 2 would be significantly different from July 1. As Early put it, "Not a man of the entire force present lay down that night with any other expectation than that

Jubal Early was a blunt-talking, hard-drinking, assertive, even confrontational division commander in Ewell's corps. In the late afternoon of July 1, he declined an opportunity to assail either Cemetery Hill or Culp's Hill, arguing (not unreasonably) that his command was tired and disorganized after the fighting north of town. That fact did not prevent him from insisting later that Ewell had squandered an opportunity that afternoon to take the heights.

George Gordon Meade (center) poses at a house in Culpeper, Virginia, surrounded by members of his staff in a photograph taken by Timothy O'Sullivan in September 1863. New to army command at Gettysburg, Meade entrusted a great deal of authority to his most trusted corps commanders: first to Reynolds, then to Hancock. But once he arrived atop Cemetery Hill late on July 1, the full burden of command decision making fell on his shoulders. Two days before, he had written to his wife that he was "much oppressed with a sense of responsibility and the magnitude of the great interests entrusted [to] me."

the next day would witness a crushing defeat of Meade's army." Their mood may or may not have affected their commander, but it was clear that Lee was determined to continue the assault the next day. He would send Longstreet's fresh I Corps soldiers on a flanking march to roll up the Union left and complete the victory that lay within his grasp.

Not long after Lee finally lay down for a few hours' sleep, at about one or two in the morning, George Gordon Meade arrived at the gatekeeper's cottage on Cemetery Hill after a fourteen-mile ride from Taneytown. All around him the men of his command slept among the headstones of the cemetery. Meade dismounted wearily amid three of his corps commanders: Slocum, Howard, and Sickles. Meade asked them if the army occupied a good position and they assured him that it did, to which Meade replied, "It is just as well, for it is too late to leave it now." More than likely, if Meade had known from the outset that he would have to fight a defensive battle against Lee's unified army, he would have chosen another site. Indeed, he had already picked out a good position behind Pipe's Creek twelve miles to the southeast. But that morning he had sent Reynolds marching to Buford's support, and that afternoon he had granted Hancock the authority to select the battlefield. He was committed. It would be impossible now to disengage and make a safe withdrawal without the rebel army pouncing on his moving columns. For better or for worse, he would fight Lee's army here at Gettysburg.

Meade spent much of the night inspecting his army's position. First he walked the perimeter of the defenses on Cemetery Hill and, apparently satisfied with what he saw, then mounted and rode southward in the dark trailed by a few members of his staff. It was a moon-drenched night, and despite the hour, he could make out the critical terrain features. South of Cemetery Hill the high ground fell away gradually for more than a mile until it was barely perceptible as a geographical feature, disappearing altogether into level ground before rising up again into the two hills known as the Round Tops. Ever since the battle, this section of ground between Cemetery Hill and the Round Tops has been known as Cemetery Ridge. But christening this gentle fold of Pennsylvania farmland a ridge is a bit of a stretch, for its crest is only slightly

When Meade took command of the army, he inherited Hooker's chief of staff, Major General Daniel Butterfield. At Gettysburg, Butterfield accompanied Meade on his late-night tour of the battlefield and participated in all the discussions within the high command. Afterward he claimed Meade had planned to retreat from Gettysburg after the fighting on July 2. Meade denied it, and the two men engaged in an unproductive quarrel about it for years afterward.

George Sykes was promoted to lead the V Corps when Meade became the army commander. The corps missed the first day's fighting, but its arrival on the morning of July 2 bolstered the Union left and played a major role in preventing a Confederate breakthrough.

higher in elevation than the ground in front of it. Its one indisputable military advantage was that for most of its length it offered a clear field of fire to its front, and though Geary's division of Slocum's XII Corps occupied this part of the line, it was evident to Meade even in the dark that he would need to place more troops along its length to protect his left. And soon. For even as Meade rode back to Cemetery Hill at about 4 A.M., the first streaks of dawn were already coloring the eastern sky.

Years later, some of Meade's critics claimed that he had considered evacuating Gettysburg that first night, but in fact Meade was contemplating an offensive. He talked with Slocum about mounting an attack on Ewell's corps from Culp's Hill once the V Corps arrived. With the growing light, however, an inspection of the ground in front of Culp's Hill revealed that it was too obstructed for an effective attack (the same objection that Early had raised to making an attack there). Meade therefore decided that it would be best to wait and see what Lee intended. But whatever happened, his most pressing concern was to concentrate the army. As the sun came up on July 2 there were only about 33,000 Federal soldiers, including the cavalry, on the high ground south of Gettysburg: this included the tired survivors of the I and XI Corps, plus the XII Corps, and two-thirds of Daniel Sickles's III Corps (four brigades) which had arrived during the night. Meade's anxiety was greatest during the first few hours of daylight, for if Lee launched an all-out assault before the rest of the Union army arrived, the outcome could hardly be doubted.

He was greatly relieved, therefore, when just after sunrise, Hancock's II Corps, 12,000 strong, came marching up the Taneytown Road. It seemed to have arrived just in time, too, for only minutes later, the sound of rifle fire welled up on the lower slopes of Cemetery Hill. Meade ordered the II Corps to Cemetery Hill to meet the expected assault, but by seven it was evident that the firing had been simply the result of overeager pickets, and he countermanded the order, sending the II Corps instead to Cemetery Ridge, which extended his left flank half a mile southward past a little clump of trees to the Joseph Weikert House. Beyond it, Sickles's four brigades relieved Geary's division to extend the Federal left to the base of Little Round Top.

At eight the lead elements of George Sykes's V Corps began to arrive. The men of the V Corps had gone into bivouac only a few miles away late on the previous evening after a heroic march from Hanover and had been roused again at 4 A.M. to finish the march to the battlefield. At nine, when Sickles's last two brigades arrived, they swelled Meade's total strength to more than 60,000. Thus it was that from just past dawn until ten o'clock, a period of nearly five hours, a virtual stream of Federal forces flowed into Meade's lines on Cemetery Hill and the ridgeline south of it. By eleven Meade had most of his army in hand; only John Sedgwick's VI Corps was still

LONGSTREET AND HISTORY

Of all the personalities who played central roles in the Gettysburg campaign—Ewell included—none was subjected to more after-the-fact scrutiny than Lee's "Old War Horse." Once the battle had ended, and especially after the war was over, Longstreet became the centerpiece of a bitter and unbecoming public feud. To his Southern critics he was the villain: the man whose pedestrian deliberateness and childish petulance ruined whatever chance the rebel army had to win a decisive victory at Gettysburg. To his champions he was the victim: a man whose keen insight into modern warfare and understanding of the battlefield was ignored by his single-minded commander. In this second scenario, Longstreet becomes a tragic figure: forced to execute a hopeless offensive despite his deeply held conviction that it was doomed to failure.

Both politics and literature played roles in crafting these opposing views. Longstreet's postwar adherence to the Republican Party (which made him a scallywag, in the parlance of the day) made him a target for advocates of the South's "Lost Cause" in the 1870s. But Longstreet contributed significantly to his fall from grace by offering a self-serving postwar explanation for the South's defeat at Gettysburg that put the blame squarely on Lee. William Swinton's *Campaigns of the Army of the Potomac*, published almost immediately after the war in 1866, cited Longstreet as the source for the author's conclusion that at Gettysburg Lee "lost that equipoise in which his faculties commonly moved." Lee's many friends and admirers took issue with this view, especially after Lee's death in 1870, publishing a score of arti-

Lieutenant General James Longstreet in a postwar photograph

cles in the pages of the *Southern Historical Society Papers*. But Longstreet did not recant; instead he reiterated and even enlarged his criticism of Lee, asserting in his memoirs that at Gettysburg, Lee "was excited and off his balance . . . , and he labored under that oppression until enough blood was shed to appease him." Such a claim about a man revered by many as a near saint, engendered bitterness and anger toward the man Lee had once called "my Old War Horse." By the time Longstreet died in 1904 at the age of 83, his name was nearly as despised in some parts of the South as that of William Tecumseh Sherman.

Then, seventy years later, Longstreet's historical reputation underwent a virtual renaissance due largely to the novelist Michael Shaara, who, relying heavily on Longstreet's account of the Battle of Gettysburg, portrayed him sympathetically in his Pulitzer Prize–winning novel, *The Killer Angels*. The most widely read Civil War novel since *Gone with the Wind*, Shaara's book depicts Longstreet as the unsung and underappreciated military genius of the Civil War, a view that emerges as well in the film *Gettysburg*, which is based on Shaara's novel. *The Killer Angels* triggered a dramatic shift in the popular view of James Longstreet, a shift that reached its culmination with the erection of an equestrian statue of Old Pete on Seminary Ridge in 1998, not far from the statue of Robert E. Lee, though Lee's statue remains by far the most prominent Southern monument on the battlefield. In light of all this, untangling Longstreet's historical persona from the historiographical wars of a dozen decades is both challenging and perilous.

Colonel Armistead Long was Robert E. Lee's military secretary, a position he had held since the fall of 1861. In addition to his administrative duties, Long also occasionally commanded elements of the Confederate artillery, and at Gettysburg Lee dispatched him to select artillery positions to support Longstreet's attack on July 2.

Opposite top: An 1863 photo shows Little Round Top (left foreground), which Captain Johnston's scouting party ascended, sometime between 6 and 7 A.M. Amazingly he saw no Federal troops either on the crest or nearby. He quickly returned to Lee's headquarters to report the astonishing news. Despite his report, however, there were Federals near the Round Tops, and more were soon to arrive.

Opposite bottom: On the morning of July 2, Lee rode into Gettysburg and climbed the stairs of the almshouse, shown in an 1880s photograph, to see what he could of the enemy positions from its upper windows. But on a battlefield as large as Gettysburg, Lee had to rely heavily on the information brought to him by his scouts.

en route. The Federal army commander was very much aware that he had managed this concentration largely because the enemy had left him unmolested through five hours of daylight.

And therein lies a tale.

The principal indictment of Longstreet's generalship at Gettysburg is that he failed to conduct the early-morning attack on July 2 that might have rolled up the weak Federal left flank like a hallway carpet and destroyed Meade's army. Some of Longstreet's critics assert that he had been ordered to attack at "dawn"; others claim only that he was to have done so "at a very early hour of the morning," but all of them argue that he failed to meet the expectations of his commander. Because he did not launch a morning attack, and because Federal reinforcements arrived in significant numbers during those crucial morning hours, Longstreet's accusers conclude that Old Pete's sluggardly ways, exacerbated in this case by deliberate stalling due to his lack of enthusiasm for the orders he was given, cost the South its greatest opportunity of the war. Longstreet's guilt or innocence rests almost entirely on two questions: When did Lee order the attack to begin? And how quickly did Longstreet get his forces into position to execute it? Perhaps no answer to these questions will ever be definitive, but careful attention to the sequence of events can reveal some tentative answers.

Both Lee and Longstreet were up before first light on July 2. Lee was mulling over reports that the Federal V and XII Corps had reached the battlefield when Longstreet arrived at his headquarters and offered the usual salutation. Longstreet claimed later that "Lee was not ready with his plans." Technically this was correct; Lee had not yet determined which units would play what roles in the attack, but he was firmly committed to the idea of attacking the Federals with a flanking movement to the right. On the other hand, Lee continued to wonder what kind of effort Ewell might be able to make on the left to support that attack. To refine his plans, Lee sent a number of staff officers out to investigate conditions on both flanks of the enemy army. Colonel Charles Venable rode over to the left to talk with Ewell, and Colonel Armistead Long went to the right to select artillery positions in support of Longstreet's projected flank attack. Clearly Lee never seriously considered an attack at "dawn," for he would have had to wait to receive the reports of his staff officers before making his final dispositions.

Among the several expeditions sent out to survey the prospective battlefield, the most consequential was the one conducted by Lee's staff engineer, Captain Samuel R. Johnston. Accompanied by Longstreet's engineering officer, Major John Clarke, Johnston rode southward down the west side of Seminary Ridge, then crossed over it and rode eastward to the vicinity of the Peach Orchard on the Emmitsburg Road and beyond it up onto the rocky slopes of Little Round Top. Astonishingly, he saw no enemy forces, even though four brigades of Sickles's III Corps were encamped just below the north face of Little Round Top. The only reasonable explanation is that Johnston ascended the hill's southern face which screened him from Sickles's encampment. Moreover, although the time of day is impossible to determine with precision, it appears that Johnson reached Little Round Top at about 6 A.M., after Hancock's men marched up Taneytown Road but before the arrival of Sickles's last two brigades, which came up Emmitsburg Road at about nine.

Johnston returned to Seminary Ridge between 8 and 9 A.M. and reported to Lee

that the Federal left was unguarded and that Little Round Top was unoccupied. Such news could only have confirmed Lee in his determination to strike there. For his part, Longstreet remained skeptical, his disapproval all too evident in his body language as he strode up and down nearby. By then two of Longstreet's division commanders, Lafayette McLaws and John Bell Hood, had reported their arrival at headquarters, and Lee pointed out to McLaws on a map the position he wanted his division to occupy when it began its attack. "General, I wish you to place your division across this road," he said, indicating a farm lane near the Peach Orchard perpendicular to Emmitsburg Road. Longstreet heard the comment but did not see where Lee had pointed, and coming into the conversation he pointed to Emmitsburg Road and told McLaws, "I wish your division placed so." "No, General," Lee said, "I wish it placed just the opposite." Old Pete made no comment, but McLaws later wrote that Longstreet seemed upset, either because of the pending attack or because he had been publicly contradicted by Lee, or perhaps both.

Having heard from the army's right, Lee decided to ride off to the left to see about Ewell himself. He rode into Gettysburg and, dismounting at the almshouse north of town, climbed the stairs to the cupola. From there he surveyed the twin hills south

While the generals made plans, the soldiers waited: in a drawing by A. C. Redwood, a group of artillerists, one with a pipe, one with a tin cup which may have held ersatz coffee, relax before a fire. Some passed the time improving their positions, piling up rocks and fence rails to make a barricade; others boiled coffee (a pot sits on the fire at right) or attended to their equipment.

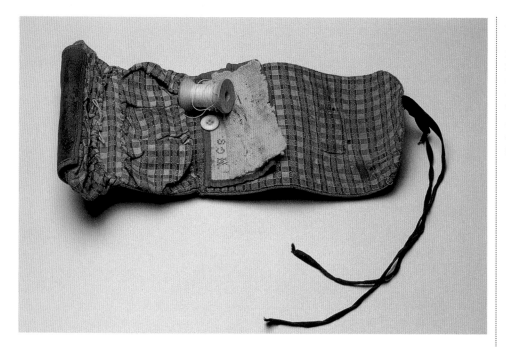

A "housewife"—a kit containing (usually) sewing materials, soap, extra buttons, and other practical items—was a common accoutrement for soldiers. Some also carried a deck of cards or other games. Camp preachers suggested that card games were sinful and often encouraged the men to throw away such tools of the devil. As battle approached, some soldiers would toss away their card decks so as not to risk perdition if killed in battle.

of town in front of Ewell. When Ewell and Venable returned from an inspection of the lines, Lee was there to meet them. He again asked Ewell about the likelihood of the II Corps making a movement around to the right to support Longstreet, and again Ewell argued against it. Lee therefore ordered Ewell to support the attack with "a diversion" on his own front as soon as he heard the sound of the fighting from the south, telling him that the diversion might develop into a genuine attack if "an opportunity [was] offered." Then Lee left to return to Seminary Ridge.

The troops who would conduct the main assault would be mostly Longstreet's. McLaws and Hood were both nearby with their divisions, but Longstreet's 3rd division, that of George Pickett, was still at Chambersburg guarding the army's line of supply, and it would be some time before Pickett could make it to Gettysburg. On the other hand, Richard Anderson's division of A. P. Hill's III Corps had not been involved in the first day's fighting, and it could be attached temporarily to Longstreet for the attack. Longstreet would therefore have three fresh divisions—more than 20,000 men—to undertake the flank attack that Lee had in mind. It was roughly the same number of troops that Lee had assigned to Jackson at Chancellorsville, and as he had with Jackson, Lee did not give Longstreet a timetable for the attack but left the details to his "Old War Horse."

By ten o'clock, or very soon thereafter, all the key decisions had been made and the necessary orders had been issued: Longstreet would attack from the south with three divisions, his front perpendicular to the Emmitsburg Road, and Ewell would pitch into the Federals on Cemetery Hill when he heard the sound of Longstreet's attack. Of course, by then most of Meade's reinforcements had already arrived. Because of that, Longstreet cannot be held accountable for failing to conduct a dawn attack, or even for failing to attack before Meade was significantly reinforced. By the time Lee gave the order to proceed, Meade had most of his army with him.

Of course, there is still the second charge: Did Longstreet execute Lee's order in a swift and efficient manner? And on this charge the evidence is much more incriminating.

CHAPTER SEVEN

A Tale of Two Generals

(10 A.M. – 4 P.M., July 2, 1863)

Effective and timely battlefield communication was—and is—one of the most important elements of military success. In the nineteenth century it was also one of the most difficult. Once commanders were beyond earshot of one another, they had to rely upon an awkward and inefficient system of communicating: either couriers had to carry oral messages that they committed to memory, or they had to deliver handwritten notes scrawled on scraps of paper, and either method took up valuable time. This was why it was so important to have subordinate officers who could intuit the spirit behind their commander's original orders, for as circumstances on the battlefield changed, they needed to be able to adjust their actions to the new circumstances without upsetting the army's overall tactical plan. Absent a full and sympathetic meeting of the minds, the result was often delay, confusion, and disappointment. Such was the case in the six hours between 10 A.M. and 4 P.M. on July 2, when two corps commanders—one from each army—faced circumstances that, in their view, compelled them to make independent decisions that dramatically affected both the character and the outcome of the desperate fight for the Union left flank on the second day at Gettysburg.

The target of the Confederate attack that day was the presumably vulnerable left flank of the Federal army south of Cemetery Hill. Lee's scout, Captain Johnston, had reported that the enemy's left was virtually unguarded ("in the air," as the military phrasing had it), and Lee envisioned a flanking assault not unlike Jackson's at Chancellorsville, where Longstreet would swing around the Yankee army and attack from the south, charging up Emmitsburg Road (as Jackson's men had charged up the Orange Turnpike) to roll up the Yankee line along the crest of Cemetery Ridge from the Round Tops to Cemetery Hill. It was a tantalizing vision, but it was a vision that was based on faulty intelligence. The Federal left was not unguarded, though it was poorly organized—indeed almost disastrously so.

Four brigades of Daniel Sickles's III Corps (about six thousand men) held the

Sickles's prewar career was marked by numerous scandals, the most notorious of them involving his young wife, Theresa (above left), whom Sickles suspected of having an affair with Philip Barton Key. When Sickles saw Key outside his home attempting to signal Theresa by waving a handkerchief, Sickles ran outside and killed him on the spot, as depicted (above right) in a woodcut from the March 12, 1859, issue of *Harper's Weekly*. Sickles's attorney, Edwin Stanton (later Lincoln's secretary of war) succeeded in getting an acquittal for his client on the grounds of temporary insanity. It was the first time an American court accepted such a defense.

Federal left that morning. The only corps commander at Gettysburg who lacked the benefit of a military education, Sickles had a tendency to be dismissive of his West Point–trained peers. But then they were more than a bit skeptical of him as well, not only for his lack of a West Point pedigree but because Sickles's scandalous prewar reputation was that of a womanizer and a manipulator—even a murderer. Trained as a lawyer in the offices of Benjamin Butler, Sickles had entered politics under the wing of Tammany Hall and won election to the New York State Assembly at the age of 28. He had then shocked New York society by nonchalantly escorting a known prostitute onto the floor of the legislature. Five years later, at the age of 33, he set more tongues wagging when he married a 16-year-old girl who almost immediately gave birth to a daughter, and the gossip grew louder when he continued to associate publicly with prostitutes after his marriage. What was good for the gander, however, was apparently unacceptable for the gosling. Sickles was infuriated to learn that his young wife had been secretly meeting Philip Barton Key (the son of Francis Scott Key) during his lengthy absences. Spotting Key outside the Sickles's Lafayette Square home, the enraged husband charged out into the street and shot the unarmed Key to death in broad daylight. In a lurid trial, punctuated by Mrs. Sickles's published confession of infidelity (coerced from her by her husband), Sickles was found not guilty by reason of temporary insanity. Then he provided even more grist for the gossip mill by forgiving his wife for her indiscretions and resuming their married life. Two years later he was a brigadier general in the U.S. Army.

Sickles's metamorphosis into a general was due partly to his political connections and partly to his efforts in raising a brigade of volunteers. To the surprise of many, he prospered in the army, in part because of his friendship with Joe Hooker, who made him a corps commander. When Meade superseded Hooker in command of the army, Sickles (by now a major general) knew he was unlikely to receive preferment from the new army commander. He got a hint of this on June 30, when he received a sharp note from Meade criticizing him for what the commanding general called "the very slow movement of your corps yesterday." But Sickles was not intimidated by Meade. He noted that Meade had issued a flurry of contradictory orders in the first few hectic days of his command: one ordering a concentration along Pipe's Creek and another directing Sickles to march to Gettysburg. Indeed, Sickles received three different sets of orders on July 1, and had finally acted on his own, ignoring a middle-of-the-night order to halt his advance, and pushed on to Gettysburg anyway in the belief that Meade's orders had been overtaken by events, as indeed they had. That experience, however, reinforced Sickles's tendency to rely at least as much on his own judgement as on orders from the commanding general.

Sickles was one of the three corps commanders who had been present on Cemetery Hill when Meade had arrived in the middle of the night after the first day's fighting. Four of Sickles's six brigades arrived about two hours later, and Meade ordered them to relieve John Geary's division on the southernmost portion of Cemetery Ridge. This allowed Geary's men to join their XII Corps comrades on Culp's Hill. Sickles dutifully ordered his men into bivouac, but he did not lay out a defensive line,

Daniel Sickles (seated) poses with his staff in an 1864 photograph. In a blatant effort to secure public sympathy for himself as a wounded veteran after Gettysburg, Sickles deliberately rejected the use of a prosthesis, and most of the post-Gettysburg photographs of Sickles (including this one) include prominently displayed crutches. In this case, the chair was moved into the frame solely for the purpose of displaying the crutches.

The George Weikert House, in a photograph taken in 2000, marked the approximate location of Daniel Sickles's original defensive position (see map, page 127). Sickles believed that the area assigned to him, near the southern end of Cemetery Ridge, denied his troops a clear field of fire and made them vulnerable to an attack from either front or flank.

nor did he send any of his troops to the crest of Little Round Top, the high round hill nearby, which dominated his own left flank and which remained barren of Federal forces throughout the night and into the early morning.

At first light on July 2, Sickles was able to make a careful study of the ground that Meade had assigned to him, and he did not like what he saw. Unlike the higher ground to his right, where the men of Hancock's II Corps lay on their arms, the ground in front of his III Corps soldiers was interrupted by stands of trees that limited both their visibility and their field of fire. Worse, that terrain sloped gradually upward to a piece of commanding high ground three-quarters of a mile in front of him along Emmitsburg Road. Sickles saw that an enterprising enemy could set up batteries there that would make his own position untenable. Why had Meade sent him to this obviously vulnerable position? Sickles knew that Meade had not arrived at Gettysburg until the middle of the night; he very likely concluded that Meade had no real understanding of the topography on this part of the line.

Around 7 A.M. (at about the time that Captain Johnston's scouting party was ascending Little Round Top less than a mile to the south), Sickles received a visit from Meade's son. Barely out of his teens, George Junior had recently been a cadet at West Point but had failed out for excessive demerits. Now he was a volunteer captain on his father's staff. Having Junior there to look over his shoulder did nothing to improve Sickles's mood, and he did not even bother to come out of his tent to talk with him. Nevertheless, young Meade learned from others that the corps commander was unhappy with the position assigned to him. Eager to help, he rode off to refer the issue to his father.

Meade senior had little time for such things. Hastily, he reiterated to his son what he thought he had already communicated to Sickles: the III Corps was to occupy the position formerly held by Geary's division. Such orders were rather vague, and Sickles claimed to remain unenlightened. Geary's men had not occupied a line, he insisted, only a bivouac. Couldn't General Meade send a senior staff officer to look over the ground? Perhaps the army's chief of artillery, Henry Hunt, could come and see what Sickles saw: that this position at the low end of Cemetery Ridge was vulnerable to enemy guns placed along Emmitsburg Road. Dutifully, Captain Meade remounted and rode north again to see his father.

Meanwhile at nine o'clock (as Lee was pointing out on the map where he wanted McLaws's division placed for the attack), the two brigades that Sickles had left behind at Emmitsburg came marching up that road to join their comrades. Now that his corps was at full strength (nine thousand men), Sickles was more convinced than ever that he needed to occupy that high ground in front of him. Just after ten (as Lee was giving Longstreet his final orders) he rode north to talk personally with Meade. Meade was still focused on solidifying the defense of Cemetery Hill, but in response to Sickles's urgent insistence, he agreed to send General Hunt to have a look at the III Corps' position, and he promised to come himself as soon as he could spare the time.

Sickles rode back to his own corps only partially satisfied. Hunt showed up as promised, and the two generals rode out to the Peach Orchard. Hunt agreed that it was good ground and that it commanded the position that Meade had assigned to Sickles's corps, but Hunt also declared that he had no authority to change Sickles's orders. Hunt pointed to the line of thick woods a half mile in front of the Peach Orchard (Pitzer's Woods) and wondered if they concealed any enemy forces. Sickles decided to find out. At eleven o'clock, he ordered Colonel Hiram Berdan to take three hundred men forward on a reconnaissance mission to explore those woods.

Berdan's elite command was unusual. Unlike nearly every other regiment in the army, it did not have a state affiliation. Instead it was composed of men gathered together from several states who shared the ability to shoot accurately over long distances. Entrusted with Sharps rifles (and therefore called sharpshooters), they wore green uniforms instead of the regulation Union blue and were designated as the 1st and 2nd U.S. Sharpshooter regiments. Berdan took a hundred of the 1st U.S. Sharpshooters, plus two hundred men of the 3rd Maine regiment, and moved forward into the tree line across Emmitsburg Road. They had gone no more than a half mile when they encountered Confederate skirmishers. Berdan pressed forward to discover what was beyond them and found himself confronting a triple rank of Confederate infantry moving southward. After a sharp little fight, Berdan withdrew and reported what he had found.

For Sickles this information was decisive. Strong elements of the Confederate army were clearly moving toward the Union left flank—his flank!—and he was determined to do what he could about it before his corps was overrun. Though he still had not received permission from Meade or anyone else, he ordered his two divisions to move forward to the high ground he preferred. The men of David Birney's division took up positions that would soon bear immortal names: Devil's Den, the Wheat Field, and the Peach Orchard. Not long afterward, the men of Sickles's 2nd division under Andrew Humphreys advanced as well, occupying positions along Emmitsburg Road facing west.

Then, at about three o'clock, Meade himself arrived, trailed by a half dozen staff

Hiram Berdan, an engineer by training and a crack shot, first suggested the idea of a special regiment of sharpshooters at the beginning of the war. Occasionally resented by conventional infantry, Berdan's unusual unit was generally employed in skirmishing duty or assigned to guard the army's flanks during maneuvers. At Gettysburg, the sharpshooters saw some of their fiercest action of the war, and they were especially effective in the rugged terrain between the Round Tops and Devil's Den.

officers. The commanding general was appalled to discover that Sickles had taken matters into his own hands and pushed his corps out in front of the rest of the army. Why, Meade asked, had Sickles not placed his corps on Hancock's left as ordered? Sickles replied that he had moved forward to take advantage of the high ground and to deny that ground to the enemy. Meade explained to him that the ground he occupied was commanded by the artillery of both sides; occupying it only made Sickles vulnerable. Sickles volunteered to return to his original position, but Meade knew that it was now too late. "I wish to God you could," he replied, "but the enemy won't let you." For better or for worse, Sickles's corps would now have to fight from its advanced position, and Meade would have to do what he could to support his maverick general.

While Sickles was taking matters into his own hands, his counterpart in the Confederate army was struggling with some crucial decisions of his own. Lee had ordered Longstreet to begin his movement toward the Federal left flank sometime after ten o'clock, but an hour after that, as Wilcox's Alabama soldiers skirmished with Berdan's sharpshooters in the shade of Pitzer's Woods, Longstreet's two divisions under Lafayette McLaws and John Bell Hood, a total of some 15,000 men, remained quietly encamped along the banks of Marsh Creek.

Longstreet was a careful planner. In the Battle of Second Manassas, ten months earlier, he had waited patiently until his forces were deployed just where he wanted them before issuing the order to attack, even though by then Stonewall Jackson's hard-pressed command was hanging on by its fingernails. At Chickamauga, three months after Gettysburg, Longstreet would again delay his attack until he was satisfied that his forces were properly aligned. In both of those cases his delay worked to the Confederates' advantage; Longstreet's attacks—when they came—were decisive. But at Gettysburg, Longstreet's many critics argue, his deliberateness effectively sabotaged Lee's plan. Having received his orders at ten in the morning, he did not get his two divisions into position to execute the attack until four in the afternoon. Why?

Once he received Lee's orders to attack, Longstreet seemed to accept the inevitable and issued orders of his own to Edward Porter Alexander, his talented young artillery officer, to lead the I Corps artillery off in the intended direction of the attack. The idea was to get Alexander's batteries in position near the Peach Orchard (that high ground that so worried Daniel Sickles) so that they could support Longstreet's infantry assault. Alexander wasted no time. Within the hour his guns were on the move heading southward behind the screen of trees on Seminary Ridge. Longstreet's infantry, however, remained in camp. Old Pete wanted to wait for his 3rd division, George Pickett's division of Virginians, which had been last in line as the army advanced to Gettysburg. "The General is a little nervous this morning," Longstreet confided to Hood. "He wishes me to attack; I do not wish to do so without Pickett. I never like to go into battle with one boot off." Soon enough, however, Lee made it clear that there was not enough time to wait for Pickett. Longstreet asked that he at least be allowed to await the arrival of Evander Law's brigade of Hood's corps which was also en route, though much closer. To this, Lee assented, then he rode off to consult one more time with Dick Ewell.

Law's brigade did not arrive until almost noon, and when Lee returned from his consultation with Ewell just past eleven, the I Corps infantry had not yet broken

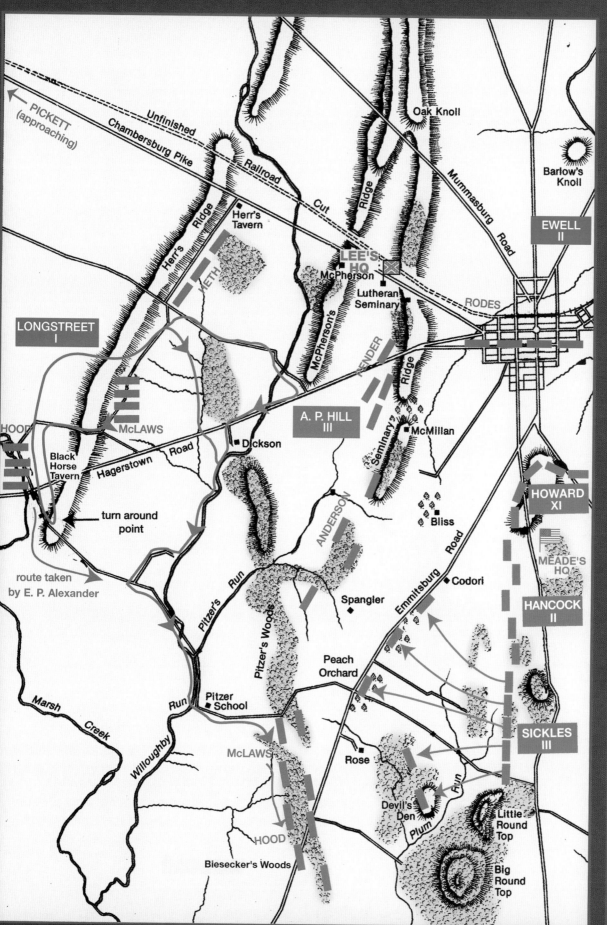

LONGSTREET'S MARCH

July 2, 1863

11 A.M. – 4 P.M.

PICKETT (approaching)

Unfinished Chambersburg Pike

Railroad Cut

Herr's Tavern

Herr's Ridge

HETH

Oak Knoll

Barlow's Knoll

EWELL II

Ridge

LEE'S HQ

McPherson

Lutheran Seminary

Mummasburg Road

RODES

LONGSTREET I

McPherson's Ridge

McLAWS

HOOD

PENDER

A. P. HILL III

Dickson

Seminary Ridge

McMillan

HOWARD XI

Black Horse Tavern

Hagerstown Road

turn around point

route taken by E. P. Alexander

Pitzer's Run

ANDERSON

Bliss

Emmitsburg Road

MEADE'S HQ

HANCOCK II

Spangler

Codori

Marsh Creek

Run

Pitzer School

Peach Orchard

SICKLES III

McLAWS

Rose

Willoughby

Run

Devil's Den

Plum Run

Little Round Top

HOOD

Biesecker's Woods

Big Round Top

Pitzer's Woods

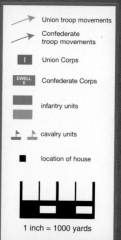

→ Union troop movements

→ Confederate troop movements

▮ I Union Corps

▮ EWELL II Confederate Corps

▬ infantry units

cavalry units

■ location of house

1 inch = 1000 yards

If there was postwar argument and animosity among some of the Confederate generals who fought at Gettysburg, the same is true of some Union generals. The most famous such dispute took place between Meade and Sickles while the war was still raging, and it nearly resulted in Meade's dismissal. Despite Sickles's poor performance at Gettysburg, Meade did not file charges against him for disobedience of orders, mainly because the final outcome of the battle had been so satisfactory and partly, too, because Sickles had lost a leg in the fight and it seemed unnecessary to prosecute him. Nevertheless, Sickles seemed to relish a fight, for he, or one of his acolytes, struck the first blow.

On March 12, 1864, the *New York Herald* carried a lengthy account of the Battle of Gettysburg written by an anonymous author who signed himself "Historicus." It is possible that Sickles was the author, or it may have been written by Major General Daniel Butterfield, the chief of staff Meade had inherited from Hooker. Butterfield was as irascible as Meade, and their personalities clashed. Whoever Historicus was, his account of the battle was astonishingly favorable to Sickles. Moreover, it was probably no coincidence that the article was published just as Meade was testifying before the Joint Committee on the Conduct of the War in Washington. This group of Senators and Congressmen was generally suspicious of West Pointers and equally admiring of volunteer officers like Sickles. The article by Historicus immediately became grist for the mill in Washington and nearly resulted in Meade's removal from command. Instead, President Lincoln stuck by his general, and Meade remained commander of the Army of the Potomac until the end of the war.

Here is part of what Historicus had to say. Note in particular that in this version of events, it is Sickles who first recognized the importance of Little Round Top and sought to defend it in spite of the fact that Sickles never did send troops to occupy the Round Tops:

General Sickles saw at once how necessary it was to occupy the elevated ground in his front toward the Emmitsburg road, and to extend his lines to the commanding eminence known as the Round Top, or Sugar Loaf Hill. Unless this were done, the left and rear of our army would be in the greatest danger. Sickles concluded that no time was to be lost, as he observed the enemy massing large bodies of troops on their right (our left). Receiving no orders, and filled with anxiety, he reported in person to General Meade and urged the advance he deemed so essential. "O," said Meade, "generals are all apt to look for the attack to be made where they are." Whether this was a jest or a sneer Sickles did not stop to consider, but begged Meade to go over the ground with him instantly; but the commander-in-chief declined this on account of other duties. . . .

Two P.M. came, and yet no orders. Why was this? Other orders than those expected by General Sickles were, it appears, in preparation at headquarters. It has since been stated, upon unquestionable authority, that General Meade had decided upon a retreat, and that an order to withdraw from the position held by our army was penned by his chief of staff, General Butterfield, though happily its promulgation never took place. . . .

Meanwhile the enemy's columns were moving rapidly around to our left and rear. These facts were again reported to headquarters, but brought no response. . . .

The critical moment had now arrived. The enemy's movements indicated their purpose to seize the Round Top hill; and this in their possession, General Longstreet would have had easy work in cutting up our left wing. To prevent this disaster, Sickles waited no

George Gordon Meade

longer for orders from General Meade, but directed General Hobart Ward's brigade and Smith's battery . . . to secure that vital position. . . .

General Meade at length arrived on the field. . . . "Are you not too much extended, general?" asked Meade. "Can you hold this front?" "Yes," replied Sickles, "until more troops are brought up; the enemy are attacking in force, and I shall need support." General Meade then let drop some remark showing that his mind was still wavering. . . . Sickles replied, "General, I have received no orders. I have made these dispositions to the best of my judgement. Of course I shall be happy to modify them according to your views." "No," said Meade, "I will send you the

Fifth Corps [Sykes] and you may send for support from the Second Corps [Hancock's]." "I shall need more artillery," added Sickles. "Send to the Artillery Reserve for all you want," replied Meade; "I will direct General Hunt to send you all you ask for." The conference was then abruptly terminated by a heavy shower of shells, probably directed at the group, and General Meade rode off. Sickles received no further orders that day.

SOURCE: *New York Herald*, March 12, 1864. Reprinted in *Official Records of the Union and Confederate Armies in the War of the Rebellion*, series I, vol. 27 (part 1), pp.130–32.

Daniel Butterfield

An 1880s photograph shows the Marsh Creek Bridge on Hagerstown (or Fairfield) Road, with the Black Horse Tavern in the background. Longstreet's corps started out near here but then countermarched when it seemed that their movement might be observed by Federals on the Round Tops. In the end, Longstreet's roundabout march may have delayed his attack by as much as an hour, an hour that some critics suggest may have been critical.

camp. Surprised and not a little unsettled by this discovery, Lee issued peremptory orders for Longstreet to get his men on the move. It was unusual for Lee to deviate from his normal practice of issuing discretionary orders that allowed his subordinates to execute them as they thought best. But time was rushing past, and Lee feared that his great opportunity might be slipping away. Thus prodded, Longstreet ordered his two divisions to begin marching from their campsites along Marsh Creek southward past the Black Horse Tavern and across Hagerstown Road.

Longstreet's lead division was commanded by his fellow Georgian and West Point classmate 41-year-old Lafayette McLaws, whose appearance lived up to his spectacular name: his dark eyes peered out of a bird's nest of curly black hair, both facial and cranial, that surrounded his face like an aura. Only minutes after starting out, McLaws reached the top of a small hill and stopped. The hilltop was barren of trees, and it was evident that the passage of a strong column of infantry over its crest would be visible to Federal observers on Little Round Top. The enemy would be alerted to the movement, and the attack would lose the element of surprise. Longstreet, accompanied by Captain Johnston, rode to the head of the column to determine the cause of the delay. McLaws showed him the problem and suggested that they backtrack and take an alternate route, one that crossed the ridgeline a few hundred yards farther north, where trees would screen their passage. Longstreet was visibly distressed by this news. "Is there no way to avoid it?" he asked. McLaws said there was not. He knew of a more secretive route, he said, but it required a short countermarch. Longstreet agreed.

The easiest way to accomplish the necessary revolution was for all of the men in the column simply to execute an about-face. But that would have put Hood's division in the lead, and Lee had told McLaws that he was to lead the attack. Again Longstreet yielded to his fellow Georgian. Orders were dispatched for the whole column to countermarch. This created some confusion back through the column when Hood's men had to give way and allow McLaws's men to march past them before again falling in behind.

One of the curious and unresolved aspects of this episode concerns the route taken by E. P. Alexander, whose artillery column had already passed this way. When Alexander had noted that the hilltop was visible to the enemy, he had simply directed his guns off the road to the right and around the shoulder of the hill, managing to get his guns past it without conducting an awkward—and time-consuming—countermarch. Why Longstreet did not also seize upon this solution remains a mystery, especially in light of the fact that the tracks from Alexander's guns should have been clearly visible vectoring off from the road and into the nearby fields. Practitioners of psychohistory speculate that Old Pete consciously or unconsciously sought an opportunity to delay an attack he did not want to make, hoping (perhaps) that Lee might yet change his mind. Others argue that Longstreet's decision to countermarch requires no more explanation than a consideration of his innate cautiousness. Lee wanted the movement to be concealed from the enemy, and—good subordinate that he was—Longstreet sought to achieve that goal. Of course, a general eager to confront the enemy might have spent more time exploring the alternatives to a lengthy countermarch and in the process might have discovered Alexander's shortcut. Instead McLaws urged a countermarch, Johnston kept silent, and Longstreet accepted McLaw's suggestion.

Crossing Herr's Ridge north of the Black Horse Tavern, where the route was concealed from the Yankees by thick woods, Longstreet's column then tramped eastward up Hagerstown Road, away from the planned direction of march, until it turned on a farm road that snaked southward again, along the banks of Willoughby Run and past the Pitzer School, before the head of the column finally debouched out of the tree line near Emmitsburg Road, Lee's intended axis of attack. Longstreet had managed to keep his column out of sight of the Federal signal team on Little Round Top, thus preserving the element of surprise, but combined with his late start, he had also used up several valuable hours. Worse, in those several hours, the tactical picture had dramatically changed. When Longstreet asked McLaws how he planned to make his attack, that officer replied that he first wanted to see what forces might be in front of him. Longstreet declared, "There is nothing in your front; you will be entirely on the flank of the enemy." That had been true two hours before, but it was true no longer. When the head of the rebel column broke into the open, it came under fire from Union artillery in the Peach Orchard where Alexander's guns were supposed to be. Sickles's entire corps now occupied positions directly athwart Longstreet's proposed line of advance.

Even now, Longstreet was not yet ready to commit his command to battle. As the South Carolina, Mississippi, and Georgia troops of McLaws's division took up the positions that Lee had pointed out on the map that morning (more than six hours ago now), Longstreet ordered Hood's division to march past them to extend the Confederate flank further east deciding, apparently just then, to let Hood rather than McLaws make the initial attack.

Hood was only 32 years old in July 1863 and in the prime of life. Before the war

Longstreet's fellow Georgian Lafayette (pronounced La-FAY-ette) McLaws was famous within the army for his defense of the stone wall on Marye's Heights at the Battle of Fredericksburg, where his division fought off repeated attacks from seven Federal divisions. At Gettysburg his division was in the lead during the march to the Federal left flank, though when his forces arrived at Emmitsburg Road, Longstreet ordered Hood's division to leapfrog past it and take the lead in the assault.

John Bell Hood (above) commanded Longstreet's right-hand division during the assault on the Federal left on July 2. Hood sought permission from Longstreet to move farther to the right in order to swing around the high ground in front of him. But the march to the jump-off position had taken so long that not enough time remained to reorient the axis of attack.

was over, he would lose both an arm and a leg to battlefield wounds; he would supervise a futile and costly defense of Atlanta against Sherman, and he would lose most of his army in a hopeless offensive into Tennessee. Those experiences would age him prematurely: his dark eyes would sink into his skull, and his face take on an expression of perpetual gloom. But all that was still in the future on July 2, and Hood at Gettysburg, with his flashing dark eyes and red-gold hair, seemed to many the very personification of war. An admiring soldier described him as "a gigantic old Saxon chieftain come to life."

As his Alabama, Texas, and Georgia troops marched past McLaws's men and took up positions east of Emmitsburg Road, Hood's attention was drawn irresistibly to the two high round hills to his right front. These were the Round Tops, left unoccupied by Sickles and even now manned only by a Federal signal team. The white puffs of smoke from enemy artillery pieces west of that high ground showed him where the new Federal line was, even if its details were obscured by the thick woods. Surely those hills, beyond the Union left flank, were the key to this portion of the battlefield. Evander Law, who commanded Hood's lead brigade, thought so too. Both Law and Hood sent out small foot patrols to investigate the location of the enemy line, and in particular to determine how many Federals were on the Round Tops. They returned in less than fifteen minutes with the news that the Round Tops were not occupied in force.

Hood sought permission from Longstreet to change the direction of his attack. Hood's preference was to swing around the Round Tops altogether, passing to the east of the hills, and attack the Federal army in its rear rather than on its flank. He sent an aide to find Longstreet and to urge on him the change in plans. Longstreet turned him down. The reason, apparently, was that there was no time for further marching and readjusting of units. Somewhere back on Seminary Ridge, Lee was waiting for

the sound of Longstreet's attack. Waiting as well was Ewell's whole corps, which was supposed to launch its own attack on Cemetery Hill upon hearing the sound of Longstreet's advance. All those thousands of men . . . waiting. It was nearly four o'clock. There was no more time.

Hood persisted. Years later, he would claim that he asked Longstreet three times for permission to change the direction of the attack. When Evander Law pleaded for permission to assault the Round Tops, Hood called over a staff aide, directed Law to explain his reasoning, then told the aide to find Longstreet and repeat the request. The aide returned in ten minutes with a simple, curt message: "General Longstreet orders that you begin the attack at once." Hood turned to Law: "You hear the order?" Law acknowledged that he had and left to join his command.

It was within a few minutes of four o'clock. Longstreet's forces were finally placed where Lee wanted them: in a broad front more than a mile wide south of the Federal army. In the shade of the trees that flanked Emmitsburg Road, 15,000 men lay prone on their arms awaiting the signal to advance against the 5,000 men of David Birney's division of Sickles's corps. The attackers would have the odds on their side, but this would not be a surprise attack from cover, as Jackson's assault at Chancellorsville had been; the Federal artillery near the Peach Orchard was already finding the range. Apart from skirmishing, there had been no heavy fighting at Gettysburg for a full twenty-four hours. But in the next four hours, the men on both sides would more than make up for it. Some of the fiercest fighting in the history of American arms was about to begin.

This view, in a photograph taken in 2000, is the same that met Hood's eyes on the late afternoon of July 2 as he prepared to attack, stepping out from the edge of Biesecker's Woods and looking north past the Bushman farm to the Round Tops. Big Round Top is on the right, and Little Round Top is visible between the Bushman farmhouse and barn. (Most of the trees directly behind the Bushman farm were not there in 1863.) Hood's orders were to advance northward along the axis of Emmitsburg Road, which would have taken him to the left of the farm. Instead he ordered his men forward to "take those heights."

CHAPTER EIGHT

The Assault Begins
Devil's Den and Little Round Top
(4 P.M. – 6 P.M., July 2, 1863)

For the rest of the war—and indeed for the rest of his life—Daniel Sickles maintained that his bold decision to push his command out to the high ground near Emmitsburg Road saved the Army of the Potomac from destruction. As he saw it, he sacrificed his own corps to protect the army much as a man might throw himself on an explosive to save his comrades. Although his own command was all but annihilated in the fighting that soon welled up on his front, Sickles argued that its presence there, directly across Longstreet's line of advance, blunted the Confederate attack and thereby saved the Union army—and by extension, the Union itself—from disaster. Most scholars disagree. They note that Sickles's move upset the overall architecture of Meade's defensive line, and they point out that in any case Sickles positioned his brigades too far apart to be mutually supportive. This was especially true of the three brigades of David Birney's division holding the left side of Sickles's salient: J. H. Hobart Ward's brigade in Devil's Den; Regis de Trobriand's brigade in the Wheat Field; and Charles Graham's brigade in the Peach Orchard. Unable to provide effective support for one another, they could be overwhelmed and wrecked one at a time by the attacking Confederates. Worse yet, Sickles left the Round Tops completely undefended. Far from saving the army, Sickles's conduct nearly led to its destruction. Three things saved the Union army from disaster that afternoon: Hancock's efforts to rush reinforcements to the threatened spots, the dedication and sacrifice of a few unlikely Union heroes . . . and luck.

Forty-year-old Hobart Ward commanded the brigade that Sickles assigned to hold his new left flank. Ward was not a West Pointer, but he had experience that particularly suited him for the command of a brigade. He had served throughout the 1840s as an enlisted man, including service in the Mexican War, eventually becoming sergeant major of the 7th U.S. infantry. Then, after he left the army, he had served for another decade as a commissary general in New York, thus gaining valuable administrative experience. When the war broke out, he obtained a colonelcy and the command of a regiment, and after Antietam he was elevated to brigadier general. Ward was steady

Opposite: The cannon barrels, shown resting atop stone supports in this 1880s photo, were placed on the crest of Little Round Top after the battle by the Gettysburg Battlefield Memorial Association in honor of the brigade commander Stephen Weed and of Lieutenant Charles Hazlett, whose battery occupied this position on July 2. Both men lost their lives in the bloody fighting for this rock-strewn piece of high ground.

A glowering Hobart Ward affects a truculent pose in a wartime photograph. Not a West Point graduate, Ward was a "soldiers' general," having served as a noncommissioned officer in both the Mexican War and in the peacetime army. Ward's brigade defended the aptly named Devil's Den in the fierce fighting on July 2.

rather than mercurial, unlikely either to stir up trouble or to fail in his duty. At Gettysburg he commanded five regiments: two from New York, and one each from Indiana, Maine, and Pennsylvania. He also had the 4th battery of the New York Light Artillery, consisting of six guns under the command of Captain James Smith.

As directed by Sickles, Ward advanced his 1,600 men to a rocky outcrop of high ground known as Houck's Ridge whose most salient feature was a pile of enormous boulders, some of them more than twenty feet across. Locals called it Devil's Den, and survivors of the fighting there would acknowledge the appropriateness of such a name. Ward deployed his five regiments in a defensive line extending northward from those massive boulders through Rose's Woods toward a wheatfield that was to be occupied by the brigade of Regis de Trobriand on his right. Out in front of this line, Ward placed elements of the 2nd U.S. Sharpshooters as skirmishers. It would be their job to give early notice of an enemy attack, and to slow it down if they could. He put four of Smith's guns atop the boulder-strewn ridge (all that would fit) and put the other two to his left in the valley of a meandering rivulet called Plum Run. From there, they could guard against enemy attempts to get around his left flank.

Ward worried about that flank. From his position in Devil's Den, he could see large numbers of enemy soldiers (Hood's division, though he did not know it yet) crossing Emmitsburg Road and moving toward his left. In response, he ordered Colonel Elijah Walker's 4th Maine regiment to face left, effectively refusing his flank. But the valley of Plum Run, on his immediate left, was not his most serious concern. Almost directly behind him, less than five hundred yards away, loomed the still unoccupied summit of Little Round Top. An enemy on that summit would dominate not only the valley of Plum Run but Devil's Den as well. It is easy to imagine Ward looking back over his shoulder more than once at the crest of Little Round Top as he contemplated his circumstances. Unlike Sickles, however, Ward did not complain about the difficulties of his position. His job was to watch his front and his flank; someone else presumably had the job of guarding Little Round Top.

Such a presumption was unfounded. Sickles's most serious error that afternoon—even worse than his decision to move his command forward in defiance of orders—was that he left both Round Tops unoccupied. Such an oversight is inexplicable. Obsessed as he was about the slightly higher ground in front of him at the Peach Orchard, it is perplexing that he could ignore so completely the impressive height of Little Round Top on his left flank. The seriousness of his oversight became startlingly evident when Union Major General Gouvernor Warren rode up to the crest of Little Round Top at about three o'clock. Warren had been riding southward with

Meade (who was en route to his conversation with Sickles) when the commanding general ordered him to ascend "the little hill off yonder" to see what was going on there. Warren and a few aides rode up onto the crest and found a Federal signal team quietly awaiting orders. But there were no troops. Warren was shocked.

Twenty-five years later, the state of New York placed a life-size statue of Warren on the summit of Little Round Top. Anyone standing near that statue today can well understand the general's alarm, for the site offers a commanding view of the battlefield. Off to the north Warren could see Cemetery Ridge, occupied by Hancock's II Corps, and beyond it the reverse slope of Cemetery Hill; to the northwest he could see Seminary Ridge all the way to the Lutheran Seminary alongside Chambersburg Road, where, even then, Robert E. Lee was waiting for the sound of Longstreet's attack; and beyond Seminary Ridge, he could see the gray smudge of South Mountain on the distant horizon. Directly below him, across Plum Run, was Ward's position in Devil's Den. While Warren surveyed this vista, the commander of the signal team, Captain James S. Hall, pointed out Biesecker's Woods to the southwest, where, according to Hall, a large rebel infantry force had just recently taken up positions. By then, Longstreet's men were under cover, and Warren couldn't see them. It seemed unlikely to him that a large enemy force could have made its way so far to the south, and he was inclined to dismiss Hall's report. Then a Confederate artillery shell

A statue of Major General Gouvernor Warren overlooks the area dubbed the Slaughter Pen from the crest of Little Round Top. Ordered by Meade to investigate the security of Little Round Top, Warren was astonished to find only a Federal signal team on its crest. Galvanized into action when a Confederate artillery shell burst nearby, he issued the orders that brought Strong Vincent's brigade to the hill.

This photograph—showing the western face of Little Round Top looking across Plum Run from the Wheat Field—was taken a few weeks after the battle by a team of photographers led by Mathew Brady, who can be seen leaning against the tree at left. Strong Vincent's brigade occupied positions on the southern slope just over the crest seen here.

exploded nearby, slightly wounding Warren, and Captain Hall irreverently exclaimed, "Now do you see them?" Warren was convinced. He spat out orders that sent his aides galloping off to find a brigade to send to this position at once, before the enemy seized it.

Lieutenant Ranald Mackenzie carried Warren's order to Sickles. That officer noted—accurately but not necessarily to his credit—that his entire command was already committed to its new positions and that he had no reserve. Mackenzie then sought out the commander of the V Corps, General George Sykes, whose troops were just then arriving on the scene, and gave him the same message. Willing to cooperate, Sykes sent a courier of his own to find the commander of his first division, James Barnes. As that courier searched for Barnes, he encountered Colonel Strong Vincent, the 26-year-old Harvard graduate whose brigade had performed so commendably at Upperville in June. The courier asked Vincent if he knew where to find General Barnes. He did not. But true to his nature, Vincent sought to save some time by short-circuiting the chain of command. "What are your orders?" he asked. "Give me your orders." The courier did so, "General Sykes told me to direct General Barnes to send one of his brigades to occupy that hill yonder." Without hesitation,

Vincent replied, "I will take the responsibility," and he quickly issued the orders that would send his four regiments to the slopes of Little Round Top, where they would play a critical—and perhaps decisive—role in the afternoon's fighting.

The Confederate attack—long expected, long delayed—began at 4 P.M. Despite Longstreet's refusal to change the direction of the attack, Hood apparently remained obsessed by the looming mass of the Round Tops on his right front. Hood placed himself in front of Jerome Robertson's Texas brigade, drew his sword, and called out, "Fix bayonets, my brave Texans; forward and *take those heights!*" Whatever Hood's intention, he never got a chance to see it fulfilled. Only minutes into the attack, as his soldiers crossed the open fields between Biesecker's Woods and the Round Tops, a Federal artillery shell exploded near him, and a chunk of shrapnel mangled his left

Alexander Gardner's team took this famous photograph of a dead Confederate soldier in Devil's Den. Though the photo accurately suggests the kind of rocky terrain that characterized Devil's Den, Gardner's assistants moved the body some forty yards and inaccurately labeled the man a sharpshooter in order to create a more poignant image.

Alfred Waud's engraving shows troops of Benning's and Robertson's brigades pushing Hobart Ward's defenders off the crest of Houck's Ridge near Devil's Den. Note the empty cartridge box in the left foreground and the Federal officer at right with his arms raised in an attempt to halt the retreat.

Opposite: The Confederate attack on July 2 began at 4 P.M. Hood was an early casualty, but the men of his division swept over Big Round Top and assailed both Devil's Den and Little Round Top. They captured Devil's Den after a furious fight but failed to gain Little Round Top, which remained the anchor of the Union left.

arm. Bleeding and probably in shock, he left the field and spent the rest of the day in a field hospital near the Pitzer School.

The command of Hood's division fell to Evander Law. In the midst of an attack, Law did not take the time to appoint someone else to take over his own brigade; instead he tried to do both jobs at the same time. In any case, the rush of events compelled him to act immediately, for his front was coming apart—literally. Most of the division was marching eastward toward the high ground of the Round Tops. But Emmitsburg Road, which the Texans on the left had been told to use as a guide in their advance, ran almost due north. As the nine Confederate regiments in the first assault wave moved forward, the front widened until a gap opened in the middle of it: the two left-hand regiments (the 1st Texas and the 3rd Arkansas) pushed their way northward through Rose's Woods toward Ward's command in Devil's Den, while the other seven continued to veer eastward toward the Round Tops. Quickly, Law shifted two regiments from his right to the center in an effort to close the gap.

At about this time—perhaps 4:15 in the afternoon—the attackers left the open farmland, where they had been vulnerable to enemy artillery, and entered thick woods. The men struggled now through difficult terrain; the canopy of leaves overhead filtered the sunlight but also trapped the oppressive heat. Sweat trickled down

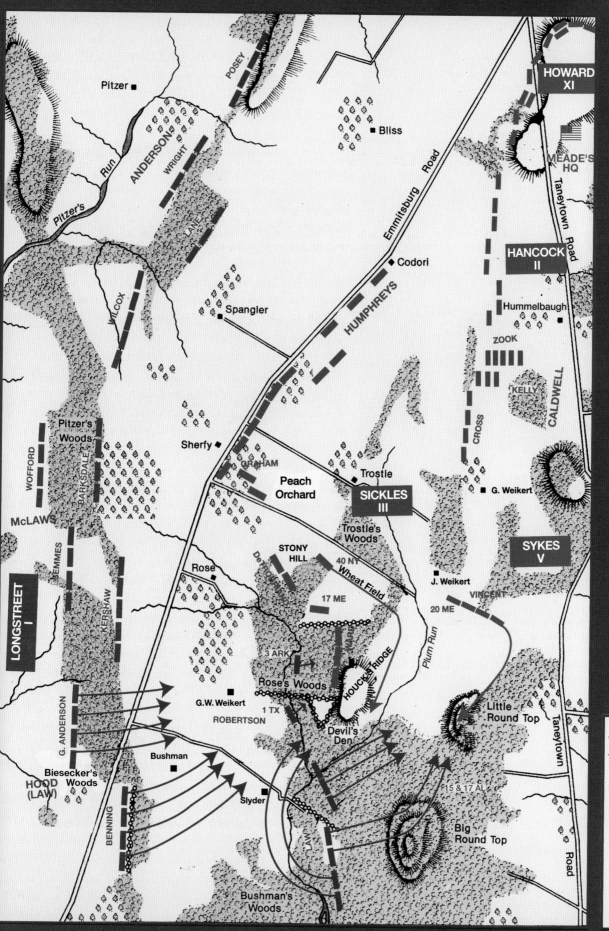

**THE CONFEDERATE
ATTACK:
LITTLE ROUND TOP
& DEVIL'S DEN**

July 2, 1863

4–6 P.M.

Pitzer ■

■ Bliss

ANDERSON

WRIGHT

POSEY

HOWARD
XI

MEADE'S
HQ

Taneytown Road

Ermmitsburg Road

HUMPHREYS

■ Codori

HANCOCK
II

Pitzer's
Run

Pitzer's

WILCOX

LANE

Spangler ■

Hummelbaugh ■

ZOOK

Pitzer's
Woods

WOFFORD

BARKSDALE

Sherfy ■

GRAHAM

Peach
Orchard

■ Trostle

SICKLES
III

■ G. Weikert

KELLY

CALDWELL

CROSS

McLAWS

GEMMES

KERSHAW

Rose ■

STONY
HILL

De
TROBAND

Trostle's
Woods

40 NY

Wheat Field

17 ME

J. Weikert ■

SYKES
V

VINCENT

20 ME

Plum Run

LONGSTREET
I

3 ARK

Rose's Woods

1 TX

HOUCK'S RIDGE

Little
Round Top

G. ANDERSON

G.W. Weikert ■

ROBERTSON

Devil's
Den

Bushman ■

Biesecker's
Woods

HOOD
(LAW)

BENNING

Slyder ■

15 & 17 AL

Big
Round Top

Taneytown Road

Bushman's
Woods

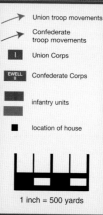

Union troop movements

Confederate
troop movements

| I | Union Corps |

| EWELL
II | Confederate Corps |

infantry units

infantry units

■ location of house

1 inch = 500 yards

their necks, and the men swatted at insects drawn to the moisture. Despite the long delay, many had never had a chance to fill their canteens, and thirst nagged at their consciousness even as they worked their way through the underbrush. Visibility was dramatically limited and units were separated as the soldiers pressed ahead through the leafy tangle of shrub and vine.

The combination of difficult terrain, thick woods, and an uncertain chain of command after Hood's departure from the battlefield meant that much of the subsequent fighting that afternoon devolved into localized contests at the brigade and even regimental levels. The "friction" of war that inevitably modifies the elegant plans of the generals once they are subjected to the confusion of battle was adding its influence to the day's events. In the bitter struggles for Devil's Den and Little Round Top, the men on both sides fought their own battles, mostly at close range, and often isolated from their comrades on other parts of the battlefield.

On the left of the attacking Confederate line, the 1st Texas and 3rd Arkansas regiments pushed through Rose's Woods, driving the Federal skirmishers back onto their own line, and then opened a general assault on Ward's position. Just west of the massive boulders on the nose of Houck's Ridge was a triangular field: a cleared area of about three acres bounded by low rock walls that offered some cover to troops who could shoot down men attempting to cross it. For more than an hour, men from Texas and New York fought each other furiously for control of this unlikely mountain meadow. Ward had ordered his men not to fire until the enemy was within two hundred yards. But given the dense woods, the attackers were often not visible until they were closer than that. Even so, the Federals had the early advantage, for the initial rebel assault

Though his role at Gettysburg is sometimes overshadowed by that of Joshua Lawrence Chamberlain, Strong Vincent may well have been the true hero of the Federal defense of Little Round Top. He took the initiative to send his brigade there, he selected the defensive position, and, in the end, he gave his life in its defense.

consisted of only two regiments. After an initial surge by the Texans, Major James Cromwell of the 124th New York led a Union counterattack across the triangular field. Cromwell was conspicuous on a large gray horse, and his gallantry was so compelling that some Texans were reluctant to shoot him. But a rebel volley from the rock wall at the south end of the field staggered the New Yorkers and cost Cromwell his life. The Union counterattack stalled, and the New Yorkers retreated.

Meanwhile on the eastern face of Houck's Ridge, near the massive boulders, the two Alabama regiments that Law had shifted to fill the gap in his line assailed Houck's Ridge from that direction. Ward's men now fought back to back in defense of Devil's Den. The fighting was at close range and fiercely contested until a second wave of attackers—Henry Benning's brigade of Georgians—tipped the advantage to the attackers. On both sides of Houck's Ridge, the Confederates surged forward.

Even now, however, Ward was unwilling to admit defeat. He organized a counterattack by two of his regiments—the 4th Maine and the 99th Pennsylvania. The men of those units charged southward through the valley of Plum Run between Devil's Den and the Round Tops, then veered to the right and stormed up onto the ridge, reclaiming the high ground. They could not hold it, however, without support,

"THE FIRE OF THE ENEMY WAS VERY HEAVY AND VERY DEADLY"

After every major engagement of the Civil War, it was common for each unit commander, starting with the regimental commanders, to write an official report of the action. Their reports were then used by the brigade and division commanders to write more reports until eventually the army commander compiled his report. Obviously these reports are of inestimable service to historians. In the 1880s and 1890s, the U.S. government collected and published them in a lengthy set of volumes titled *Official Records of the Union and Confederate Armies in the War of the Rebellion*, usually referred to by historians as the *Official Records* or simply the *OR*. In the following excerpt from his official report on the Battle of Gettysburg, Confederate brigadier Henry Benning describes the assault on Devil's Den by his brigade and the 1st Texas regiment.

My line continued to follow the first line [Tige Anderson's], halting once or twice to preserve its interval. At length I saw that the first line would not be able alone to carry the peak [of Devil's Den]. So I advanced without halting again. When my line reached the foot of the peak, I found there a part of the 1st Texas struggling to make the ascent—the rest of the brigade having gone to the right and left—the 4th and 5th Texas to the right and the 3rd Arkansas to the left. The part of the 1st Texas referred to falling in with my brigade, the whole line commenced ascending the rugged steep and (on the right) crossing the gorge [Plum Run]. The ground was difficult—rocks in many places, presenting by their precipitous sides, insurmountable obstacles, whilst the fire of the enemy was very heavy and very deadly. The progress was, therefore, not very rapid, but it was regular and not interrupted. After a while the enemy were driven from their three front guns. The advance continued, and at length they were driven completely from the peak, but they carried with them the three rear guns on its summit . . . so that we captured only the three front guns. These were ten pounder Parrotts. A number of prisoners also were taken, more I suppose than one hundred.

The peak being thus taken and the enemy's first line driven behind his second, I made my dispositions to hold the ground gained, which was all that I could do, as I was then much in advance of every other part of our line of battle, and the second line of the enemy on the mountain itself [Little Round Top] was in a position which seemed to me almost impregnable to any merely frontal attack, even with fresh men. Indeed, to hold the ground we had appeared a difficult task. The shells of the enemy from the adjacent mountain were incessantly bursting along the summit of the peak, and every head that showed itself was the target for a Minnié ball.*

Several attempts by flank movements were made to dislodge us, but by the gallantry of the regiments on the right and left they all failed.

SOURCE: Benning to W. H. Sellers, August 3, 1863, *Official Records of the Union and Confederate Armies in the War of the Rebellion* (Washington: Government Printing Office, 1889) vol. 27 (part 2), pp. 414–15.

Brigadier General Henry Benning

Patrick "Paddy" H. O'Rorke led the 140th New York regiment in a furious charge on Little Round Top that turned back the rebel assault and very likely saved the position for the Federal army, though it cost the young and popular O'Rorke his life.

and Ward sent for reinforcements. The 40th New York arrived from de Trobriand's brigade, and soon afterward, the 6th New Jersey from Humphreys's division. Each in turn charged down the valley of Plum Run, the 40th New York making a particularly dramatic assault. But it was not enough; Ward had to fall back, abandoning three of the four guns of Smith's battery, which the triumphant Confederates seized as trophies of war.

As Ward's men retreated grudgingly from Devil's Den, events were nearing a climax on Little Round Top as well. At four o'clock, just as the Confederate attack was getting under way, Strong Vincent put his men in motion toward the undefended high ground that loomed over Ward's position. Rather than march them straight up the northern slope, however, he decided instead to direct them around its eastern, or unengaged, side. He sketched out the route for Colonel James Rice, whose 44th New York regiment would lead the way, then galloped ahead of his men to survey the terrain. He rode up the southeastern face of Little Round Top and dismounted.

The western slope of the hill directly behind Ward was nearly barren of trees and offered the best field of fire, but since at that time Ward still held Devil's Den, Vincent calculated that Little Round Top was relatively secure from that quadrant, so he looked instead for a position that would allow his men to defend the *southern* slope, from which direction an attack seemed most likely. There he noticed a ledge, or shelf, where the hill broadened out about twenty yards below the crest. Vincent knew that soldiers defending a hill should never place themselves on the actual crest. From there, all too often, the defenders could not depress their rifles to target enemy forces at the foot of the hill. Then, too, on the actual crest they could be silhouetted against the sky and become easy targets. Instead, proper tactical doctrine called for defenders to occupy what was known as the military crest, a line just below the summit. Vincent decided that this ledge—ever after called Vincent's Spur—was just the place, and as his regiments marched up the hill one by one, he placed them on the ledge in a line facing south and ordered their commanders to send out skirmishers.

Vincent's men had barely settled into their new positions when Law's Alabama and Texas soldiers assailed their right, which was held by the 16th Michigan. The attackers passed between and around the boulders at the base of the hill, stopping occasionally to fire, then moving forward to fire again from another position. They kept this up for some minutes before falling back to regroup for a sustained effort. During the respite, Vincent's men obtained some welcome support from Lieutenant Charles Hazlett's four-gun battery of artillery. Hazlett picked out gun sites on the exposed crest of Little Round Top while his men manhandled the guns up its rocky slope. Confederate snipers made life difficult for the Union gunners, but Hazlett's artillerists unlimbered and fired away with a will.

Soon, however, it became evident that artillery support alone would not be enough. The Alabama soldiers at the base of the hill gathered themselves and surged forward. The pressure of numbers was beginning to wear on the men of the 16th Michigan, and in the confusion, someone issued an order to fall back. That produced more confusion. Vincent dashed forward personally to countermand the order and stabilize the line. Rallying his men, he was struck by a bullet and fell mortally wounded. The Confederate flags were coming up the slope, and the rebel yell rose another octave as the attackers sensed that victory was within their grasp.

Desperate to find support for the Union's collapsing hold on Little Round Top, Warren was searching frantically for reinforcements when he espied a column of troops moving on the Wheatfield Road. He rode to the head of the column and found the 140th New York regiment, which was commanded by 27-year-old Colonel Patrick H. O'Rorke. Called Paddy by his friends in honor of his County Caven, Ireland, birthplace, O'Rorke had graduated first in his West Point class only two years ago. Warren rode up to him and gestured toward Little Round Top. The enemy, he said, was advancing unopposed on the other side of the hill. O'Rorke replied that he was under orders to continue eastward on the Wheatfield Road. "Never mind that," Warren told him. "Bring your regiment up here, and I will take the responsibility." At once, O'Rorke turned his column off the road and led his regiment in a mad scramble up the hill. As he reached the crest, the rebels were less than forty yards from the Union right flank; O'Rorke saw at once that any delay would be fatal. He did not bother to deploy his command, but instead drew his sword, called out, "Down this way, boys!" and led them into the smoke and confusion of the battle. In midcharge, O'Rorke turned to shout encouragement to his men, and a rebel bullet smashed into his neck, severing his spine and killing him instantly. But the arrival of the 140th turned the tide. The startled Confederates fell back; scores were taken prisoner. O'Rorke lay dead on the field, and Strong Vincent was dying, but the Union held the high ground.

Colonel William B. Oates commanded the 15th and 47th Alabama regiments that crested Big Round Top and then assailed Strong Vincent's line on Little Round Top, where they struck the 20th Maine. Afterward Oates wrote that "the [enemy] fire was so destructive that my line wavered like a man trying to walk against a strong wind." He denied, however, that his forces were driven from Little Round Top. "I ordered the retreat," he insisted, because "the undertaking [was] too great for my regiment unsupported."

Meanwhile, affairs were reaching a crisis on the left as well. That flank was held by the 20th Maine which was under the command of 34-year-old Colonel Joshua Lawrence Chamberlain, a former Bowdoin College rhetoric professor, whose actions over the next hour would make him an American icon. Aware that his regiment marked the extreme left flank of the Union army, Chamberlain had detached one company (Company B) under Captain Walter G. Morrill to scout in front of the line. Morrill took up a position several hundred yards beyond the regiment's left behind a low stone wall. From there he could give notice of any attempt by the enemy to get around the flank. Before long, Morrill was joined by a dozen or more men from the 2nd U.S. Sharpshooters. They had been out in front of the line trading shots with Law's skirmishers but were falling back in front of the main Confederate assault, which, they reported, was coming this way.

When Law had shifted his two right-hand regiments to fill the gap in his center, it put the 15th and 47th Alabama regiments on what became the new Confederate right flank. Both regiments were under the command of Colonel William B. Oates of the 15th Alabama who was senior to Lieutenant Colonel Michael Bulger of the 47th. Oates was a bluff and vigorous 29-year-old former teacher and lawyer with a full, dark beard and ringlets of dark hair who had obtained his command only a month earlier. Though demanding, he was popular with the men because he shared their discomforts. And discomfort had been a steady diet for the past thirty-six hours. Oates's men had marched twenty-five miles that day to get to Gettysburg (it was Law's brigade that Longstreet had been waiting for that morning). Then, after an all-too-short rest along the banks of Marsh Creek, they had taken part in the lengthy march and countermarch to get to their jump-off positions in Biesecker's Woods. Finally, when the attack began, they had crossed some open farmland and entered a thick wood. Trying to maintain alignment, they had struggled through the under-

Below: The four-gun battery of Lieutenant Charles Hazlett fires from Little Round Top at the advancing Confederate lines in a painting by Edwin Forbes. Hazlett's gunners had to manhandle their guns up to the crest, then worked them with a fury despite their exposed position until the infantry brigade of Stephen H. Weed (inset, left) arrived to support them. By then the crisis had passed, but a sharpshooter's minié ball cut through Weed's spine and left him mortally wounded. Hazlett (inset, right) knelt by his wounded commander, and Weed reached up to grab his lapel in order to whisper something to him. As Hazlett leaned forward to hear, a bullet struck him in the head, killing him instantly. Weed died that night in a field hospital.

Taken on July 6, 1863, Timothy O'Sullivan's photograph shows that the bodies of some of the Confederates who died at the Slaughter Pen remained unburied four days after the fighting. It shows both the ruggedness of the terrain that the Confederate attackers had to overcome and some of the price they paid in the assault.

growth and begun to climb, the ground rising steeply before them, until, huffing and puffing, they reached the summit of Big Round Top.

It was unoccupied. It was also militarily useless, for the heavy forest growth so obscured their vision, despite the elevation, that they could see neither friend nor foe. The sound of the fighting came from their left, where, by now, the battle for Devil's Den was in full fury. Oates's instinct was to give his men a rest and fortify this high ground. But Captain Leigh Terrell, Law's adjutant who spoke with the authority of the brigade commander, ordered him to continue forward. Oates protested that his men were tired and that their canteens were empty, but he got them up and into line again and led them down the northern slope. There in the saddle between the Round Tops, they came face to face with the 20th Maine.

So far, the Maine men had been on the periphery of the fighting for Little Round Top, but when Oates's men appeared on their front, they became the center of the maelstrom. The stone marker that today commemorates the 20th Maine at Gettysburg indicates the approximate spot where Oates's men first attempted to break through. The tired and thirsty Alabama soldiers advanced gamely, but they had no particular advantage of numbers over the defenders, and they had to fall back.

In spite of his success in repelling this attack, Chamberlain worried that the enemy might get around his flank. To prevent this, he reorganized his defense so that his left curled back along the eastern end of Vincent's Spur, thus turning his position into a salient. His line now looked like a backward "J" with four companies constituting the refused flank. Chamberlain entrusted these four companies to his second in command, Major Ellis Spear.

Oates, too, thought Chamberlain's position could be outflanked, and after the repulse of his first attack, he regrouped his command in the saddle between the two hills and moved eastward intending to assail the Union line from its flank and rear. This second assault struck not only Spear's four companies but also extremely difficult terrain. The spur upon which Vincent sited his brigade here turned into a vertical ledge about five feet high. The attackers fought their way up to the ledge, then suffered heavily attempting to clamber over it while Spear's men fired down on them. Once again the attackers had to fall back.

By now the Alabama troops were wearing down. They had marched and fought all afternoon with no water in their canteens, and it was stiflingly hot. Clouds of white smoke from thousands of rounds of black powder wafted among the trees, and the taste of black powder was in their mouths from breathing the air as well as from biting off cartridges to load their muskets. Swallowing had become difficult. Nevertheless, Oates would try one more time. This time he decided to swing well around the hill and attack it obliquely from the rear. And it worked. The Alabama troops reached the ledge and swarmed up onto the high ground behind it. The Confederates were now literally behind the Union line; Chamberlain's defensive line folded back into a hairpin as the men of the 20th Maine, like their comrades on Houck's Ridge, fought literally back to back. They gave way grudgingly, of necessity leaving some of their wounded comrades behind on the hillside. Several of them felt this keenly and requested permission to go forward to recover their wounded.

The fight for the left flank of Vincent's Spur had reached a climax. Soldiers from both sides struggled for the crest; in some cases the fighting was hand to hand. Even worse from Chamberlain's point of view, his men were running out of powder and ball. Timing was everything now, for the momentum was passing to the enemy. In a moment of inspiration, he seized the initiative, calling out in his parade-ground voice,

"BAYONET!"
Joshua Lawrence Chamberlain and the Charge of the 20th Maine on Little Round Top

The desperate counterattack of the 20th Maine regiment on the afternoon of July 2, 1863 has become one of the most famous small-unit assaults in American military history. It is a dramatic story: the regiment's commanding officer, Colonel Joshua Lawrence Chamberlain, a former rhetoric professor at Bowdoin College, was the handsome beau ideal of the citizen soldier; his men were volunteers—friends and even relatives from back home (Chamberlain's brother Tom among them); the regiment held a critical position on the extreme left flank of the extended Federal defensive line at Gettysburg; and they were about to be overwhelmed by an attack that threatened not only their lives but (more importantly) the safety and survival of the Army of the Potomac. Having fought off two determined assaults, the Maine men faced the crisis moment desperately low on ammunition. They could not fall back; they could not hold . . . so they attacked.

Perhaps the most vivid account of this attack came from Chamberlain, who wrote the following description in 1913, a half century afterward:

We were enveloped in fire, and sure to be overwhelmed in fact when the great surge struck us. . . . Already I could see the bold flankers on their right darting out and creeping catlike under the smoke to gain our left, thrown back as it was. It was for us, then, once and for all. Our thin line was broken, and the enemy were in the rear of the whole Round Top defense. . . . Now, too, our fire was slackening; our last rounds of shot had been fired; what I had sent for could not get to us. I saw the faces of my men, one after another, when they had fired their last cartridge, turn anxiously towards mine for a moment; then square to the front again. To the front from them lay death; to the rear what they would die to save. . . . Just then . . . Lieutenant [Holman] Melcher . . . came up and asked if he might take his company and go forward and pick up one or two of his men left wounded on the field. . . . I answered, "Yes, sir, in a moment! I am about to order a charge!"

Not a moment was about to be lost! Five minutes more of such a defensive, and the last roll call would sound for us! Desperate as the chances were, there was nothing for it but to take the offensive. I stepped to the colors. The men turned towards me. One word was enough—"BAYONET!"—It caught like fire and swept along the ranks. They took it up with one shout. . . . It was vain to order "Forward." No mortal would have heard it in the mighty hosanna that was winging the sky. . . . The grating clash of steel in fixing bayonets told its own story; the color rose in front; the whole line quivered for the start; the edge of the left wing rippled, swung, tossed among the rocks, straightened, charged . . . and swooped down upon the serried host.

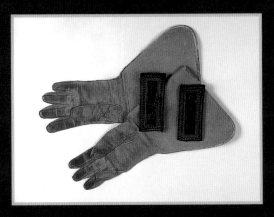

Colonel Joshua Lawrence Chamberlain, above, and his gloves and shoulder straps showing his rank, right.

In his postwar official report on the battle (not written until 1884) and in an address given at the dedication of the 20th Maine monument at Gettysburg (in 1889), Chamberlain implied that the counterattack had been more calculated than spontaneous. He declared on those occasions that he had ordered a "great right wheel," a complicated maneuver that required his left-flank companies to swing down off the hill like a hinged gate to sweep the foe from their front. In *The Killer Angels*, Michael Shaara depicts Chamberlain describing the maneuver to his subordinates. But no contemporary account indicates that he ever gave such an order, and given the circumstances it seems highly unlikely. There was no time for it. Certainly Major Ellis Spear, who commanded the left flank companies and would have had to supervise the maneuver, never heard such an order. This is how Spear recalled the moment:

Major Ellis Spear

Suddenly in the midst of the noise of musketry, I heard a shout on the center of "forward" & saw the line & colors begin to move. I had received no orders, other than to hold my left and guard the flank, and did not understand the meaning of the movement. But there was no time to seek explanation. The center was going ahead, apparently charging the enemy. If any, then all, and we all joined in the shouts and movement, and went in a rush down the slope and over the boulders.

It was the terrain and the circumstances that led Chamberlain's men to execute the great right wheel. The unexpected counterattack, and the even more surprising attack by Captain Morrill's Company B on their rear, compelled the Confederates to flee southward though the saddle of the Round Tops to escape their attackers. As Spear's men pursued, the effect was more or less like that of a swinging gate. To the men in the ranks, however, it was all one spontaneous blur. Here is the testimony of Lieutenant H. S. Melcher, who first suggested to Chamberlain the idea of going out in front of the line to succor the wounded:

. . . each man had fired the 60 rounds of cartridges he had carried into the fight, and the survivors were using from the cartridge-boxes of their fallen comrades, the time had come when it must be decided whether we should fall back and give up this key to the whole field of Gettysburg, or charge and try to throw off this foe. Colonel Chamberlain gave the orders to "fix bayonets," and almost before he could say "charge!" the regiment leaped down the hill and closed in with the foe, who we found behind every rock and tree. Surprised and overwhelmed, most of them threw down their arms and surrendered.

SOURCES: Joshua Lawrence Chamberlain, "Through Blood and Fire at Gettysburg," *Hearst's Magazine* (June 1913); Ellis Spear, *The Civil War Recollections of General Ellis Spear* (Orono, Maine: University of Maine Press, 1997), pp. 34–35; H. S. Melcher, "The 20th Maine at Little Round Top," *Battles and Leaders of the Civil War* (New York: The Century Company, 1887) vol. 3, p. 315.

"BAYONET!" The men of the 20th Maine instantly interpreted this as an order to advance. Without any further orders from their commander, the men of the 20th Maine spontaneously leapt from their positions and charged downhill into the startled Alabama soldiers, who had thought themselves on the brink of victory. At almost the same time, and entirely by coincidence, the men of Morrill's Company B, bolstered by the handful of green-jacketed sharpshooters, came into the fight directly behind the Alabama soldiers. Caught between two fires, the men of the 15th Alabama gave way. Many fled. Others, exhausted from their efforts, threw down their arms.

On both the right and the left, heroic and improbable counterattacks by single regiments had preserved Strong Vincent's line on Little Round Top. Sickles had left the hill unoccupied, Warren had recognized its importance, Vincent had assumed responsibility for defending it, and the men of the 140th New York and the 20th Maine had secured it. Soon afterward, the rest of Stephen H. Weed's brigade, of which the 140th was only one element, arrived to solidify the Union hold on Little Round Top. Weed's men deployed along the eastern face of the hill across the valley of Plum Run from the Confederates in the Devil's Den. Though skirmishing would continue across that valley for the rest of the afternoon, the Union would never relinquish its hold on Little Round Top.

Elsewhere on the field, of course, the fight continued.

The national flag that was carried by the 20th Maine at Antietam, Fredericksburg, and Gettysburg (below left) is housed in the Maine State Museum in Augusta. After Gettysburg, the regiment presented the flag to Adelbert Ames, its first colonel, who commanded a division on Cemetery Hill on July 2. In 1881, the flag was returned to Gettysburg, where it flew once more (below right) over the position defended by the 20th Maine. Flags had an almost religious significance to Civil War soldiers; there are innumerable references in soldiers' writings to the "sacred banners" of their cause. At Gettysburg, as elsewhere, many gave up their lives attempting either to capture or protect a regimental or national flag.

Peter Rothermel's 1867 painting, *Sharpshooters at Round Top*, details the men of Stephen Weed's brigade defending the western slope of Little Round Top from the final Confederate assault by Wofford, Kershaw, Semmes, and G. T. Anderson's brigades. The soldier in the foreground wears a Zouave uniform, inspired by French North African troops and popular during the early years of the war.

CHAPTER NINE

Confederate Breakthrough
The Wheat Field and
the Peach Orchard
(5 P.M. – 7 P.M., July 2, 1863)

A half mile west of Little Round Top, beyond Devil's Den and just past a narrow fringe of trees, was a piece of ground that history would christen simply the Wheat Field. It was not the only wheat field that saw battle action in the Civil War, but as with "the cornfield" at Antietam, the savage and prolonged contest for this patch of open ground would endow it with special distinction. The same was true of the Peach Orchard that lay another half mile beyond the Wheat Field at the very apex of Dan Sickles's salient. There were peach orchards on many a Civil War battlefield, and yet modern students of the war know that when someone mentions "the peach orchard," it is *this* peach orchard they mean. On the afternoon of July 2, these two landmarks witnessed some of the most savage fighting of the war as Longstreet committed the rest of Hood's division (now under Law) and followed it with those of Lafayette McLaws and Richard Anderson as the Confederates attempted to overwhelm the Union left.

Lee's original conception of the attack was for Longstreet to advance his units "en echelon." This meant that instead of his entire command moving forward all at once, his divisions would advance sequentially from right to left, each clearing the way for the next. As a result, though Hood's division stepped off at about four, the men of McLaws's division did not join the fight until nearly five, and Anderson's division pitched in around six. When at five McLaws's men swept forward, battle flags aloft, they charged toward the two Federal brigades that still guarded Sickles's left: those of Regis de Trobriand in the Wheat Field, and Charles K. Graham in the Peach Orchard.

Colonel Philip Regis Denis de Kerendern de Trobriand certainly had the most spectacular name in the Army of the Potomac. The younger son of a French nobleman, de Trobriand had married a wealthy American woman in the 1840s and eventually

Opposite: A now silent Federal cannon points toward Seminary Ridge from the Sherfy Peach Orchard along Emmitsburg Road, which marked the apex of Daniel Sickles's vulnerable salient on July 2.

Despite his aristocratic name and sartorial finery, Regis de Trobriand was a steady and reliable brigade commander. The highest ranking Frenchman in American service since the Marquis de Lafayette, de Trobriand commanded five Union regiments in Rose's Woods and the Wheat Field, and his brigade received the brunt of the initial Confederate onslaught.

moved to the United States, becoming a U.S. citizen on the eve of the war. He raised a regiment (the so-called Lafayette Guards) in New York and became its colonel, then rose to brigade command after Chancellorsville. A stout, round-faced man, he wore his kepi at a jaunty angle and had about him an aristocratic aura of calm confidence that communicated itself to the troops under his command, a habitual demeanor that would be sorely tested this day.

De Trobriand's five regiments occupied positions just west of Devil's Den in an area known as Rose's Woods. The 17th Maine, on de Trobriand's left, took cover behind a low stone wall that marked the southern boundary of the Wheat Field. The rest of the brigade stretched off to the right across a piece of rocky ground that is identified in most battle reports simply as "the stony hill." It was not a strong position: de Trobriand's 1,500 men constituted a salient within a salient, wrapped as they were around the stony hill on a front nearly a half mile wide. In front of them, their visibility was obscured by thick woods through which an enemy could advance under cover. Finally, if they suffered a reverse, they would have to fall back across the open and exposed ground to their rear.

De Trobriand's men could hear the sound of the fight in Devil's Den, less than a quarter mile away, but they could not see any of it because of the density of Rose's Woods. A courier arrived from Ward with a plea for reinforcements, and de Trobriand sent him the 40th New York, which made that valiant charge down the valley of Plum Run noted in the previous chapter. Soon afterward, de Trobriand had all he could handle on his own front as the Confederate brigade of George T. Anderson, part of the second wave from Hood's division, came crashing through Rose's Woods keening the rebel yell. Anderson's nickname was Tige—short for tiger—and with appropriate ferocity his men charged the low stone wall defended by the 17th Maine and successfully planted their flag on it, though the Maine men rallied and drove them back—at least for now. Having sent off the 40th New York, de Trobriand had only four regiments left, and one of those (the 110th Pennsylvania) had only six companies. He needed support, and fast.

Throughout this crisis on the army's left flank, Meade's staff officers frantically directed reinforcements to shore up the collapsing position that Sickles had selected. Once again it was George Sykes's V Corps that they looked to for help. Strong Vincent's brigade had already moved to Little Round Top, where it was engaged in a fight for its life. Now the other two brigades of James Barnes's division—those of Jacob Sweitzer and William Tilton—marched to support de Trobriand. The arrival of Federal reinforcements stalled the momentum of the attacking Georgians, and Tige Anderson decided to wait for support before attempting another push.

⚔ ⚔

While the Federal defenders of the Wheat Field and the stony hill savored a brief respite, Confederate Brigadier General Joseph Brevard Kershaw waited impatiently for permission to go into the fight. His South Carolina brigade was part of McLaws's division, and it was galling for him to wait and watch while Hood's command swept forward. Kershaw was a Confederate true believer who had been part of the Southern bid for independence from its earliest days. As a delegate to the South Carolina state convention in December 1860, he had cast his vote to secede from the union; then he had raised a regiment, becoming its colonel, and participated in the bombardment of Fort Sumter. He had fought with courage and distinction at Bull Run, Fredericksburg,

Confederate Brigadier General Joseph B. Kershaw (pronounced Ker-SHAW) fought in virtually every major battle of the eastern theater from Bull Run to Saylor's Creek. At Gettysburg, his brigade spearheaded the charge into Rose's Woods and the Peach Orchard and suffered 30 percent casualties. Afterward Kershaw wrote that "Every attack was magnificent and successful, but failed in the end for want of cooperation. . . ."

and Chancellorsville. Now he could barely stand it as his men remained on the edge of Biesecker's Woods, watching while the smoke and noise of battle dominated the scene in front of him. At last there came the signal—three guns fired in measured succession—and Kershaw ordered his six regiments of South Carolina troops, some two thousand men, forward. They stepped over a low stone wall, crossed Emmitsburg Road, and advanced toward the battle in disciplined lines. Three of Kershaw's regiments marched due east toward the fight for the stony hill; the other three he sent northward toward the ground that rose up gently toward the Peach Orchard.

Earlier that afternoon, when Sickles ordered his corps forward, his purpose had been to place his artillery on that high ground around the Peach Orchard. He put two of his five batteries there (about a dozen guns) and soon more batteries came up in support from the army's artillery reserve so that by the time Kershaw's men began their advance, more than thirty Federal cannons commanded the ground the South

John C. Caldwell appears here in his prewar guise as the headmaster of a boys' school. Like many others, Caldwell grew a beard during the war, finding, perhaps, that it was easier to give up shaving while in the field. By July 1863, he had grown a luxuriant brown beard. Caldwell commanded the Federal division sent by Hancock to shore up the collapsing Federal front in the Wheat Field. A participant of that fight later recalled that "the yellow grain was still standing. I noticed how the ears of wheat flew in the air all over the field as they were cut off by the enemy's bullets."

Carolinians would have to cross. The Federal gunners loaded and fired as fast as they could, their shells ripping through the ranks of rebel infantry, but despite their losses, Kershaw's men continued to march steadily toward them. Artillery unsupported by infantry was seldom able to hold a position on its own, and a few of the Federal artillerists began to look anxiously over their shoulders as the line of enemy infantry got closer and closer. One battery ran out of ammunition and had to pull back; the crew of another prepared to spike their guns in anticipation of being overrun. Then, inexplicably, the three South Carolina regiments that had been marching steadily toward them suddenly turned right and marched eastward toward the stony hill. This astonishing maneuver was the result of a misunderstanding of orders, and a costly one too, for in turning to obey, the South Carolina troops presented their open left flank to the Federal gunners, who redoubled their fire, sending grape and canister into the enemy's packed ranks. Shattered by this fire, Kershaw's left wing fell back in disorder.

Kershaw's other three regiments were luckier. As they advanced against Tilton's brigade on the stony hill, the firing there swelled to a fury. Smoke from two thousand rifles filled the air, and the sound of whining minié balls added a high-pitched counterpoint to the roar of ceaseless musketry. At the same time, Tige Anderson's Georgians renewed their assault on the stony hill from Rose's Woods. Tilton requested permission to fall back, and fearful that his troops would be caught in a collapsing pocket, Barnes gave his approval at the same time ordering his other brigade—Sweitzer's—to fall back as well. It was a decision with grave consequences, for with their withdrawal the whole Federal position on the stony hill was uncovered. Kershaw's South Carolinians were astonished when the enemy before them dematerialized. Virtually unopposed, they swept up and over the hill.

Thus abandoned, de Trobriand's men were all but cut off and in real danger of being literally surrounded. The men of the 17th Maine, low on ammunition, gave up the stone wall they had defended so valiantly and fell back across the open ground of the Wheat Field, retreating to the protection of Trostle's Woods beyond Wheatfield Road.

All this time, General David Birney had been attempting to hold together his collapsing front. He had sent couriers to find reinforcements, and reinforcements had been promised, but it would take time for them to arrive, and time was exactly what Birney did not have. Anderson's Georgians and Kershaw's South Carolinians were advancing without a check. They had to be stopped, or slowed. To buy time, Birney turned to the 17th Maine. The men of that unit had just escaped from the maelstrom of battle, but they gamely responded and, stepping out of Trostle's Woods, reentered the Wheat Field. Joined by the 5th Michigan, the 17th Maine carried on a stiff and bloody firefight with the Georgia troops of Anderson's brigade for several minutes while Federal reinforcements rushed to the Wheat Field.

To find those reinforcements, Meade turned to the II Corps of Winfield Scott Hancock, telling him to send a division not to Sickles but to General George Sykes since by now Meade had now lost all confidence in Sickles's ability to manage troops. In receipt of this message, Hancock turned laconically to his 1st division commander and told him, "Caldwell, you get your division ready."

John C. Caldwell, formerly the headmaster of a boys' academy in Maine, was a volunteer officer whose curly brown beard and thinning hair made him look older than his 30 years. His command of mostly New York and Pennsylvania troops—3,200 men in four brigades—occupied that portion of the Union line on Cemetery Ridge immediately to Sickles's right. He had been both surprised and curious that afternoon as he watched Sickles's command march out to Emmitsburg Road. When Caldwell expressed his surprise to Hancock, that officer had remarked, "Wait a moment, you will soon see them tumbling back." Now Hancock was sending Caldwell to rescue Sickles from his folly.

It was not a complicated maneuver. Caldwell simply ordered his four brigades to face left and march southward along the low spine of Cemetery Ridge toward the smoke-enshrouded crest of Little Round Top. They paused in the vicinity of the Joseph Weikert House while Caldwell sought orders from Sykes. Those orders, brought to him by a courier, were a bit vague: "Drive the enemy back, and if possible establish the original line on the crest." What crest? Caldwell might have asked. He had not had an opportunity to survey the ground in front of him, and visibility was limited in any case by the clouds of white smoke from the battle that was in full fury all around him. It was evident, however, that there was little time to be lost. Somewhere to his front was a piece of high ground to be reclaimed, and Caldwell was willing to do what he could. Turning right, his lead brigade splashed across the trickle of Plum Run and entered Trostle's Woods from the east. Rather than redeploy his brigades in the formations they had rehearsed on the drill field, Caldwell simply ordered them to file into line as they arrived. It created some confusion: right-hand regiments were on the left; companies within regiments were not in their customary order. But Caldwell's men were veterans, and they soon jostled themselves into line.

The first of Caldwell's brigades to enter the Wheat Field belonged to Colonel Edward Cross. There was virtually no cover in the open field of waist-high wheat, and from the moment Cross's men cleared the tree line, they came under fire. They fired back, and for interminable minutes the two sides simply shot each other down across an open field. Some of Anderson's Georgians used the woods and the low stone wall recently defended by the 17th Maine for cover, but Cross's men simply stood in the open and took it. There was no flinching. When a captain from the 61st New York noticed that one of his lieutenants was instinctively hunching his shoulders amid the storm of minié balls, he whacked him across the back with the flat of his sword and ordered him to "stand up like a man!"

Meanwhile, Caldwell was assembling the rest of his command for a general assault. He deployed Patrick Kelly's Irish Brigade behind Cross's, holding John R. Brooke's brigade in reserve. But his fourth brigade, a mostly German unit commanded by a man with the unlikely name of Samuel Kosciuzko Zook, was not to be found. As it happened, Zook's march to the battlefield had been intercepted by a courier from Sickles, who ordered him to reinforce Birney's division. Zook asked the courier if he spoke with the authority of General Sickles, and the young captain assured him that he did. Zook thereupon turned to the right and headed into Trostle's Woods from the north. It probably made little difference, for the young captain's directions brought Zook up onto the right flank of Kelly's brigade about where Caldwell would have wanted him anyway. Counting Cross's brigade (already engaged), Caldwell now had better than 2,300 men arrayed in a battle line that stretched across the northern edge of the Wheat Field. Caldwell gave the order to advance; it was passed by the brigade commanders to the regimental commanders; the swords rose and fell; and the men of Kelly's and Zook's brigades left the modest protection of Trostle's Woods and entered the Wheat Field.

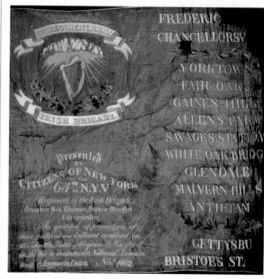

A broadsheet requests Irish volunteers (top) and a flag boasts the famous Irish Brigade (bottom). Though Irish immigrants fought in scores of Federal units (and Confederate units as well), the 2nd brigade, 1st division of Hancock's II Corps became famous as the Irish Brigade. Originally composed of New York regiments (including the Fighting 69th), by July 1863 the brigade had shrunk to the size of a battalion due to its terrible losses at Antietam, Fredericksburg, and elsewhere. At Gettysburg, the Irish Brigade suffered again during its bold charge across the Wheat Field on July 2. By the end of the war, the Irish Brigade bore the distinction of having suffered the third-highest rate of loss of any brigade in the Union army.

In Paul Wood's painting *Absolution Under Fire*, Father William Corby (who later became the president of Notre Dame University) grants absolution to the soldiers of the Irish Brigade as they prepare to make their charge into the Wheat Field. A witness recalled that "the men stood undisturbed by bursting shells, with bowed heads in reverent silence. Then the whole division was marched off at 'double-quick' across fields and through patches of woods in the direction of the conflict."

Federal gunners in the Peach Orchard try to save their guns by hauling them away using a heavy rope called a prolonge, in a sketch by Charles Reed. Captain John Bigelow, commanding one of the batteries, later recalled the experience: "Prolonges were fixed and we withdrew—the left section keeping Kershaw's skirmishers back with canister, and the other two sections bowling solid shot toward Barksdale's men. We moved slowly, the recoil of the guns retiring them, while the prolonges enabled us to keep the alignment."

Opposite: At 5 P.M., Longstreet committed McLaws's division to the attack. As the battle continued in the Wheat Field, the key breakthrough was achieved by Barksdale's brigade, which smashed through the apex of the Union salient at the Peach Orchard. Hancock sent Caldwell's division south to try to stem the tide.

At once they came under terrific fire from three sides. Kershaw's South Carolinians fired on them from the stony hill on their right; Anderson's Georgians fired into them from Rose's Woods on their left; others fired from the cover of the stone wall directly in front of them. Zook himself was among the first to fall; his second in command fell only minutes later. On the other end of the Federal line, Cross was also down, mortally wounded. But in the center of the Federal line, where the men of Patrick Kelly's Irish Brigade followed their green battle flag, the Federal attack made rapid progress. Though this famed unit now boasted barely five hundred men after its heroic bloodletting at Antietam, the Irish Brigade drove forward to the base of the stony hill and fought it out at close range with Kershaw's men. At a word from their commander, they charged the hill and carried it, taking a score of prisoners. Their assault temporarily regained the initiative for Union arms, but the situation was precarious. Both Cross and Zook were down; Cross's men were running out of ammunition; Kelly's men were losing their momentum. Caldwell had to commit his reserves.

The commander of Caldwell's reserve brigade was John Rutter Brooke, who had celebrated his twenty-fifth birthday less than two weeks before. Another volunteer officer, Brooke would later decide that he liked the army, and after the war he stayed in uniform, serving in the Spanish-American War and retiring as a major general in 1902. But in all his long career, he would never see another day like this one. Ordered

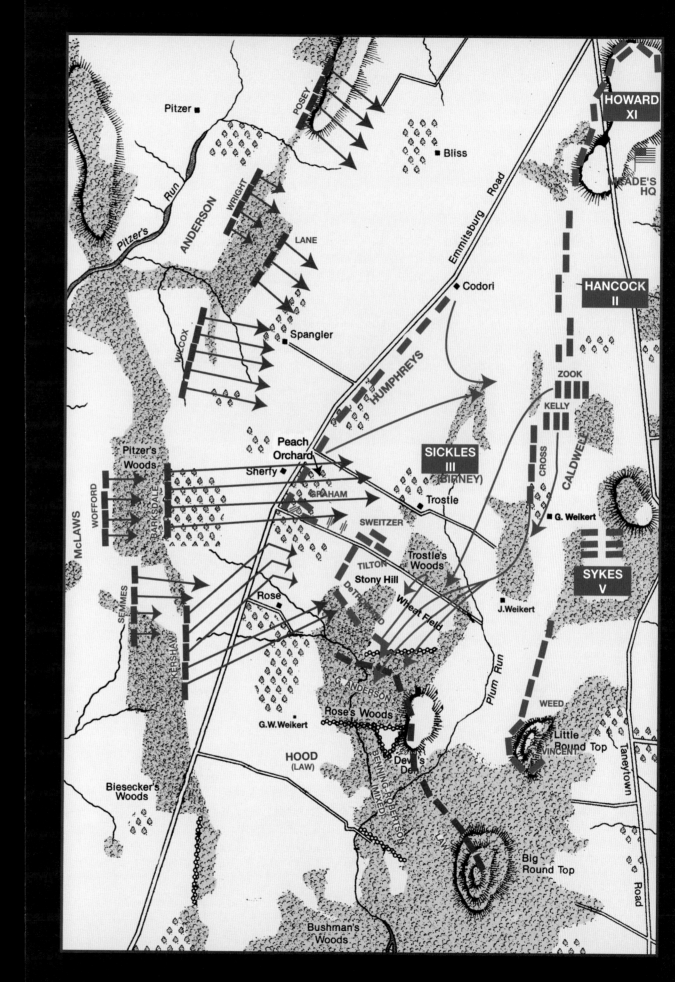

THE CONFEDERATE ATTACK: THE PEACH ORCHARD & THE WHEAT FIELD
July 2, 1863
5–6 P.M.

HOWARD
XI

MEADE'S HQ

Pitzer ■

Bliss ■

Pitzer's Run

Emmitsburg Road

POSEY

ANDERSON

WRIGHT

LANE

WILCOX

Codori ◆

HANCOCK
II

HUMPHREYS

Spangler ■

ZOOK

KELLY

CROSS

CALDWELL

Peach Orchard

Pitzer's Woods

Sherfy ◆

SICKLES
III
(BIRNEY)

McLAWS

WOFFORD

BARKSDALE

GRAHAM

Trostle ■

G. Weikert ■

SWEITZER

Trostle's Woods

TILTON

DeTROBRIAND

Stony Hill

SYKES
V

SEMMES

KERSHAW

Rose ■

Wheat Field

J. Weikert ■

G. W. Weikert ■

Rose's Woods

G. ANDERSON

WEED

Plum Run

HOOD
(LAW)

Devil's Den

BENNING
ROBERTSON
LAW
MIXED

VINCENT

Little Round Top

Biesecker's Woods

Taneytown Road

Big Round Top

Bushman's Woods

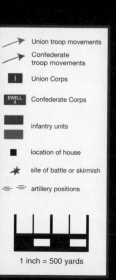

→ Union troop movements
→ Confederate troop movements
▮ Union Corps
▮ Confederate Corps
▬ infantry units
■ location of house
✶ site of battle or skirmish
≡ artillery positions

1 inch = 500 yards

PHOTOGRAPHING THE DEAD

When John Rutter Brooke's Federal brigade counterattacked across the Wheat Field and into Rose's Woods on the far side, it ran headlong into the second wave of Confederate attackers composed of Paul Semmes's Georgia brigade. The fighting was fierce and the casualties appalling—Semmes himself fell mortally wounded. In this series of photographs taken three days later by Alexander Gardner and his assistants, some of the costs of that fighting are vividly evident. In the photograph below of Confederate dead, almost certainly Georgians from Semmes's brigade, as well as men from the 15th South Carolina, lie in a V-shaped arrangement with Rose's Woods in the background. Though the bodies may have been gathered together in this pattern in preparation for burial, the numbers suggest the overwhelming presence of death on this part of the field. And for every soldier killed, at least two more were wounded.

The photo at top right is another Gardner photograph from the same area, again showing Confederate dead on the edge of Rose's Woods. The photo below it, which Gardner titled *A Harvest of Death*, is of Union dead somewhere on Sickles's line, possibly near the Trostle farm. A solitary horseman in the middle distance is probably supervising the collection of bodies for burial. The fact that so many dead remained unclaimed and unburied three days after the fighting ended only hints at the way the field must have looked before the ambulatory wounded hobbled away and the more severely wounded were carried away by their friends. In addition to the screams of the wounded and dying, modern students of the war must also imagine the clouds of acrid white smoke from the black-powder rifles, the heat of a July afternoon, and the sounds of both the rebel yell and the Union hurrah mixed with the sound of a thousand muskets.

William Barksdale (above), a Mississippi lawyer, newspaper editor, and four-term congressman, led his brigade across Emmitsburg Road to smash the apex of the Federal salient in the Peach Orchard. Mounted, and with his silver hair catching the afternoon sunlight, he was a conspicuous figure on the battlefield. He received three wounds—one in each leg and one through a lung. Taken prisoner while trying to rally his men against a Federal counterattack, he died on July 3 in a Federal field hospital. Defiant to the last, he told his captors that they should "beware," for they would have "Longstreet thundering in your rear in the morning."

Andrew A. Humphreys (above) commanded the Federal division along Emmitsburg Road. Forced to give ground when the Union left collapsed in the Peach Orchard, he managed to keep his retreating forces in hand, and though his losses were horrific, his division remained intact. Meade was so impressed by Humphreys's performance in this fight that he elevated him to army chief of staff after the battle.

into the fight, his 850 or so men charged across the middle of the Wheat Field, now trampled flat and spotted with corpses. They passed Cross's brigade on their left and the Irish Brigade on their right and crashed into Tige Anderson's startled Georgians in Rose's Woods. The Georgians gave way, and Brooke's men pursued, chasing them through the woods and across Rose's Run. There they encountered elements of Paul Semmes's brigade, which had followed Kershaw's into the battle. Hardly pausing for breath, Brooke's men assailed these troops, too, and in the ensuing fight, Semmes went down with a mortal wound.

Brooke's headlong counterattack drove a deep wedge into the Confederate front. Except for Devil's Den, still held by the rebels, Caldwell's four brigades had effectively regained all the ground lost in the afternoon fighting: Rose's Woods, the Wheat Field, and the stony hill. But the heady success of Brooke's charge obscured the fact that these positions remained as dependent as ever on the security of the Federal occupation of the Peach Orchard. If the Confederates overran that position, Caldwell's entire division would be cut off. And it was.

About the same time that Brooke launched his impetuous assault across the Wheat Field and into Rose's Woods, the second wave of Confederates from McLaws's division struck the point of the Federal salient at the Peach Orchard. That attack was led by 41-year-old Brigadier General William Barksdale, a former fire-eating congressman from Mississippi. Like Kershaw, Barksdale had chafed at being told to wait while others fought. Pointing to the Federal guns in the Peach Orchard, he told Longstreet that his men could take them "in five minutes" and begged for permission to advance. "Wait a little," the patient Longstreet told him. "We are all going in presently." When the orders finally came, the former congressman gave the obligatory inspirational speech from horseback, then ordered, "Attention, Mississippians! Battalions, Forward!" and his 1,400 men set out at a walk, crossing Emmitsburg Road and marching toward the point of Sickles's original salient, where the Federal line bent back at a ninety-degree angle to follow the line of Emmitsburg Road.

Barksdale's four regiments were packed into a front only 350 yards wide and would have made a prime target for Federal gunners, but most of the Union artillery in the Peach Orchard faced southward to target Kershaw's men, and many of those guns were running low on ammunition. Several crews had already begun to limber up and fall back. Even that was proving difficult since not enough living horses could be found to pull the guns. A few of the artillerists attempted to save their guns by using a maneuver called firing by prolonge: allowing the recoil to propel the gun backward, then hauling on a trailing rope to pull it back further until it was ready to fire again.

At the very point of the salient, Charles Graham's brigade braced itself to receive the onslaught. Graham himself fell early in the fight, and command passed to Colonel Andrew Tippin of the 68th Pennsylvania. That regiment temporarily halted the 21st Mississippi with a well-directed volley, but as other elements of Barksdale's command charged across the road to their right, Tippin saw he was about to be cut off. His men were already looking over their shoulders; the last of the Federal guns limbered up and headed for the rear. Tippin ordered his men to fall back. Though reasonable under the circumstances, that command marked the collapse of the Union position in the Peach Orchard. As the Pennsylvanians retired, the Federal salient in the Peach Orchard burst apart like a ripe melon struck by a hammer blow.

Bad as this was, worse was to come. The collapse of the Union position in the Peach Orchard uncovered the left wing of Andrew Humphreys's division along Emmitsburg Road just as he came under frontal attack from Richard Anderson's division. Anderson's was the unit that Lee had temporarily loaned to Longstreet to fill in for the yet-to-arrive George Pickett. His men began their attack at about six, charging forward in sequential brigade attacks as prescribed in their orders. First came a brigade of Alabama troops on Barksdale's immediate left, then—like fingers drumming on a table—came brigades of Floridians, Georgians, and, finally, another Mississippi brigade. Humphreys had no choice but to order his men to fall back, though most of them did so under strict discipline: walking backward while loading, then at a command stopping to fire a volley before continuing their retrograde movement. By the time they reached the relative safety of Cemetery Ridge, which they had left at three o'clock that afternoon—barely three hours ago—Humphreys had lost some 1,500 men out of his complement of 4,000. Nevertheless, his cool response to the circumstances may have saved the army from disaster.

Disaster still loomed elsewhere. Behind Barksdale's Mississippians came Wofford's brigade of Georgians with Longstreet himself accompanying the advance. As Barksdale's men advanced to the northeast with the men of Anderson's division, Wofford's brigade turned east along the Wheatfield Road, picking up elements of Kershaw's command en route and rolling straight into Caldwell's flank just as Brooke's attack ran out of steam. Indeed, Brooke had already begun to withdraw from his advanced position in Rose's Woods when Wofford's men came crashing onto the scene. Now it became a race to see if Brooke could extricate himself before he was cut off completely. His men had to fight their way back across the Wheat Field just as they had fought their way forward not half an hour before. The rest of Caldwell's division fell back as well. Caldwell later reported that his command withdrew "in good order," but it was a charitable interpretation. Few stood upon the order of their leaving as Wofford's Georgians swept down the Wheatfield Road like a force of nature. The Federals abandoned the stony hill, Rose's Woods, and the Wheat Field. By the time they regrouped along the Taneytown Road behind Little Round Top, Caldwell's division had lost more than 1,200 men from its original strength of 3,200. The onrushing Georgians were finally halted by a counterattack launched by two brigades of Pennsylvania reserves.

On the Federal side of the line, there was considerable anxiety at Meade's headquarters as the Union army commander tried desperately to shuttle reinforcements to his collapsing left flank. Indeed, there was a hint of panic in his order to Slocum for the XII Corps to abandon its position on Culp's Hill and march to the sound of the guns. Slocum asked Meade's permission to leave one brigade behind to hold Culp's Hill, and Meade agreed, but the rest of the XII Corps set out at once. Even then, with some two miles to cover, it might not arrive in time to make a difference.

A Gettysburg battlefield monument commemorates the sacrifice of the 1st Minnesota regiment (see overleaf).

In an oil painting by Rufus Fairchild Zogbaum, Colonel William Colvill (with arm upraised, just to the right of the colors) leads the 1st Minnesota in a hopeless charge against five Confederate regiments in order to buy Hancock the time he needed to establish a defensive line on Cemetery Ridge. Of the 262 men who made the charge, only 47 returned.

Closer to the action, Winfield Scott Hancock, who had already sent Caldwell's division to the Wheat Field, now ordered George Willard's New York brigade to march south as well. Hancock accompanied Willard's men personally, and under the watchful eye of their corps commander, they deployed near the George Weikert House directly in the path of Barksdale's charging Mississippians. Willard did not passively await them. Instead he led his command forward, and within minutes Mississippi and New York collided head on. By this time Barksdale's charge had lost much of its impetus. Thinned by casualties and worn down by fatigue, the Mississippians faced a fresh Union brigade advancing with bayonets fixed. Their advance slowed, then stopped. Barksdale himself was hit three times—one bullet passing through his lungs—and the Mississippians gave way, falling back slowly the way they had come. Taken prisoner, Barksdale died that night in a Union field hospital.

Barksdale's, however, was only one of five Confederate brigades closing in on Cemetery Ridge, and Hancock was running out of troops to put in their path. He had sent Caldwell's division to the Wheat Field and Willard's brigade to meet Barksdale, and few other troops were available to hold the Union center. The survivors of Humphreys's battered division took up positions on the reverse slope of Cemetery Ridge (behind the present-day location of the Pennsylvania monument), but between them and the George Weikert House, there was a yawning gap a quarter mile wide. Behind it was the Taneytown Road and the Federal rear area. If an enemy force gained that road it would split the Federal army in half. After watching Willard's men halt Barksdale's advance, Hancock rode toward that gap and looked about him. Barely two hundred yards in front of him he could see the 1,400 men of Wilcox's Alabama brigade consolidating their line in preparation for a final thrust. Desperately, he looked about for something—anything—to throw in their path. What he found was the 1st Minnesota regiment.

The 1st Minnesota was supporting a battery of the army's reserve artillery. For the past half hour the Minnesotans had watched while refugees from Sickles's broken III Corps streamed past them. Now Hancock rode up with fire in his eyes. "What regiment is this?" he barked. A blue-eyed colonel with bushy side whiskers stepped out to answer him. "First Minnesota," he announced. Colonel William Colvill might have been surprised that Hancock had to ask the question, for the 1st Minnesota was part of Hancock's own II Corps. In fact, Hancock had placed Colvill under arrest only three days before for permitting his men to cross a river single file on a log rather than making them wade through a stream, thus slowing the march. With battle pending, Colvill had been released from arrest, and very likely he was eager to atone. Hancock gave him his chance. He pointed to the regimental flags punctuating Wilcox's line. "Advance, colonel," he ordered, "and take those colors." One regiment against five. It was a forlorn hope, and both men knew it. Nevertheless, Colvill did not hesitate. He ordered his men forward at the double-quick, and the 262 men of the 1st Minnesota jogged forward. As they closed the enemy line, they leveled their bayonets, shouted "hurrah," and charged.

So surprising was this unexpected assault that the Alabama troops recoiled from it. The skirmishers ran back to their support line, where they rallied, then they opened fire. That halted the Minnesotans, and a short-lived firefight ensued. The Alabama troops soon regained the advantage and inflicted heavy casualties on the Minnesota troops, but as Wilcox looked about him, he noted that Barksdale's men on his right had fallen back and that Perry's Florida brigade on his left had stopped at Emmitsburg Road. With both his flanks exposed and no reinforcements at hand, he decided to fall

Brigadier General Ambrose R. Wright led his four Georgia regiments to the very crest of Cemetery Ridge in the late afternoon of July 2, but without support he had to fall back. A furious Wright claimed afterward that had he been supported, he could have held the ridge.

back as well. When he did so, the survivors of the 1st Minnesota slowly made their way back to Cemetery Ridge. Of the 262 men who made the charge, only 47 returned unscathed. Colvill survived, but he had suffered a crippling leg wound. Just as on Little Round Top, where first the 140th New York under Paddy O'Rorke and then the 20th Maine under Joshua Chamberlain had turned the tide, so too here on Cemetery Ridge a heroic act by a single regiment had a disproportionate impact on the outcome of the battle.

The Confederates still had one more arrow in their quiver. Beyond Wilcox's left, Ambrose Wright's Georgia brigade was still advancing. His men crossed Emmitsburg Road near the Codori House and charged up Cemetery Ridge against weak opposition. They ascended the ridgeline and gained its crest. For one breathless moment on that hot, sultry day, as the red glow of sunset spread across the western sky, about a thousand Georgians held the crest

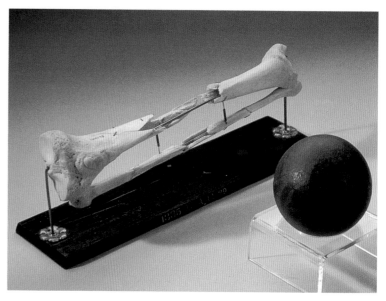

Daniel Sickles's right tibia and fibula illustrate the damage inflicted by a Confederate cannonball similar to the one shown. After the amputation of his lower leg, Sickles directed that it be saved, subsequently donating it to the Army Medical Museum (currently called the Armed Forces Medical Museum) in Washington, D.C., where he occasionally visited it and where it remains today.

of Cemetery Ridge 150 or so yards south of the monument that today marks the traditional high-water mark of the Confederacy. But the moment did not last. Assailed by two of John Gibbon's brigades on their left, and elements of Humphreys's battered command on their right, they engaged in a three-sided firefight for only a few minutes before falling back. Wright later claimed that if he had been supported, he could have pierced through the Federal line and won the day. Wilcox made the same claim. But neither got the support he needed, and both brigades returned slowly back over the bloody fields they had captured to the relative safety of the trees on Seminary Ridge.

By 7 P.M., three hours after it began, the Confederate assault had spent itself. Despite the morning delays, and despite furious Federal resistance, Longstreet's attack had nearly proven decisive. Nearly, but not quite. Though the Confederates held Devil's Den, the Wheat Field, the stony hill, and the Peach Orchard, two Federal brigades still clung to Little Round Top, and, thanks largely to Hancock, they still held a continuous line from the Round Tops to Cemetery Hill. Of course, they had suffered horribly. Unlike most Civil War battles, where the attackers generally suffered significantly greater losses than the defenders, the afternoon's fighting had claimed some nine thousand Federals while the Confederates had lost "only" six thousand.

One of those Federal casualties was Daniel Sickles. All day, Sickles had warned anyone who would listen to him of the dire consequences that would ensue if rebel gunners got possession of the high ground around the Peach Orchard. And, sure enough, after Barksdale's Mississippians seized the Peach Orchard, Confederate gunners set up batteries there and opened fire on the Federal rear area. A chance shot from one of those guns struck Daniel Sickles in the leg, smashing his right tibia. Sickles ordered a soldier to improvise a tourniquet out of a saddle strap, and he was carried off to a nearby field hospital stoically smoking a cigar. At the hospital, surgeons amputated his right leg, and Sickles ordered the doctors to set it aside so that he could keep it as a souvenir. Enemy guns in the Peach Orchard had found him after all.

CHAPTER TEN

The Struggle for the High Ground

Cemetery Hill and Culp's Hill

(6 P.M. – Midnight, July 2, 1863)

While Union and Confederate soldiers fought each other to exhaustion on the Union left, two miles to the north Ewell's corps prepared to pitch into the Union right. There, as on the left, two high hills dominated the terrain. The first was Cemetery Hill, a broad, gentle rise of ground immediately south of Gettysburg, where Howard had established his headquarters on the morning of July 1. Its name derived not from the carnage that was about to take place there but from the presence of a community burial ground—Evergreen Cemetery, the entrance to which was marked by a distinctive brick archway alongside Baltimore Pike. The Union I and XI Corps had fallen back to this high ground after the fighting on July 1, and it was now the anchor of the whole Union position. South of it, Cemetery Ridge stretched for a little over a mile down to the Round Tops; east of it, the ground dipped into a shallow swale then rose up again to the crest of an even higher hill only eight hundred yards away, a hill that loomed 180 feet above Rock Creek, which meandered past its eastern approaches. This was Culp's Hill, and it was as dominating at this end of the battle line as Big Round Top was at the other end, though like that of Big Round Top, its military utility was limited by the fact that it was so thickly covered with trees as to be all but useless for the placement of artillery.

In their discussions of the previous night, Ewell and Early had convinced Robert E. Lee that the ground in front of these two hills was unsuitable to an attack, but at the same time they had also argued that it would be bad for morale to give up possession of the town in order to strike elsewhere. Perhaps so. But Lee could not afford to let Ewell's entire corps—one-third of his army—remain idle while the great battle of the campaign was fought. Accordingly, Lee ordered Ewell to await the sound of Longstreet's attack on the left, and when he determined that the attention of the Federals had been drawn southward, he was to strike at those two hills in front of him. At the very least it would create a diversion; at best it might lead to a decisive double-envelopment of the Yankee position. For Ewell, this was something of a second

Opposite: Federal guns from Battery B of the 4th U.S. Artillery aim harmlessly over Gettysburg in a 1977 photograph of Cemetery Hill. The equestrian statue of Winfield Scott Hancock in the background presides over the pastoral setting, which on July 2 and 3, 1863, saw some of the fiercest fighting of the Civil War.

chance. He might yet be able to satisfy his critics by seizing the two hills that some said he ought to have taken the night before.

🔫 🔫

Ewell had his men up early on July 2. His understanding of Lee's plan was that Longstreet was to attack in the morning, and he did not want to be late for it. He left orders for the men to be roused at first light and ready to attack at dawn. But dawn passed without any indication of activity on Longstreet's front, and Ewell became

impatient. Around eight Charles Venable arrived from Lee's headquarters. Ewell accompanied Venable on a tour of the front lines, and when they returned, Lee was waiting for them. Lee again broached the idea that Ewell might move away from this ground to support Longstreet's attack, but Ewell remained skeptical of such a maneuver, and Lee did not force the issue. His orders remained unchanged: Ewell would support Longstreet by launching a diversionary assault once he heard the sound of Longstreet's guns. By now, however, it was clear that Longstreet's attack would not take place until the afternoon. Ewell ordered his men to stand down, and they settled in to wait.

In an Edwin Forbes painting, troops of Samuel Carroll's brigade rush forward past the tombstones of Evergreen Cemetery to help the men of Adelbert Ames's division (formerly Barlow's) fight off the assault of Isaac Avery's North Carolina brigade and Harry Hays's Louisiana brigade, both of Early's division. The hinge of the Federal defensive line, Cemetery Hill was the target of furious Confederate attacks late on July 2, after Longstreet's attack to the south had already run its course.

Waiting was not easy under the circumstances. It was hot and sultry, and shade was scarce. Intermittent skirmishing continued all morning and into the afternoon, and the men on both sides had to keep their heads down to avoid the singing minié balls. Federal artillery was another annoyance. The Yankees had turned Cemetery Hill into a virtual artillery park. More than fifty Federal guns bristled from its crest, and more than half of them faced north and east toward Ewell's command. Since artillery could outrange muskets, the Confederates behind the line of skirmishers could do little besides hug the ground when explosive shells fell among them as they waited. The Confederate artillery replied perfunctorily. Not only did the Federals have more guns; they had better positions. The only piece of ground that seemed to offer an advantage to Southern gunners was Benner's Hill, a modest rise about a half mile north of Culp's Hill and a mile northeast of Cemetery Hill. The Confederates put a six-gun battery there, but except for a ranging shot or two, they did not open fire since they were preserving their ammunition to support the afternoon attack. If all of that were not enough to discourage the waiting Confederate soldiers, they could hear the distant, hollow thump of axes on Culp's Hill, evidence that the Yankees were building breastworks.

To conduct his attack, Ewell had three divisions. Two of them—those of Early and Rodes—had been in the thick of the fighting the day before and were not at top strength, though their morale remained high. In Ewell's plan, three of Early's four brigades were to charge straight up the north slope of Cemetery Hill, while Rodes's five brigades assaulted the hill from the northwest. Meanwhile the fresh division of Edward "Allegheny" Johnson was to seize Culp's Hill. The entire enterprise seemed a daunting task, even for troops brimming with confidence. As it turned out, however, fate would ensure that the odds were not so daunting after all. For just as Lee had hoped, Longstreet's assault on the Union left would dramatically—indeed, almost fatally—distract the Union high command.

At six feet five inches, Federal Major General John Geary was a dominating figure on the battlefield with a personality to match. Before the war he had been the first mayor of San Francisco and then governor of "Bleeding" Kansas; after the war he would serve two terms as governor of Pennsylvania. At Gettysburg, his division occupied the crest of Culp's Hill, one of the highest points on the battlefield.

On the Federal side of the line, Cemetery Hill and Culp's Hill were occupied by the XI and the XII Corps, respectively. The men of Howard's XI Corps were still smarting from the whipping they had taken the day before. Directly in front of Early's men, on the north side of Cemetery Hill opposite the town, was Howard's 1st division, composed of the same soldiers Early's men had driven headlong through town twenty-four hours earlier. Because Francis Barlow had fallen wounded and been captured on the knoll that still bears his name, that division was now commanded by 27-year-old Adelbert Ames. Ames had come a long way in a short time. He had graduated from West Point only two years earlier, in May of 1861, one month ahead of Paddy O'Rorke. Two months before the Battle of Gettysburg, Ames had been a colonel commanding the 20th Maine, but he had turned the regiment over to Chamberlain when Ames was promoted to brigade command. Now with Barlow's fall, Ames commanded the division. Ames had two small brigades on Cemetery Hill. Both brigades had been badly bloodied in the first day's fighting, and though he could boast a total of nine regiments, the number of soldiers in those regiments did not exceed 1,200. Against them, Early and Rodes could send more than 7,500 men.

To Ames's right, the Union had better odds on Culp's Hill. There, the Federals had what was left of Wadsworth's division from the I Corps, including the remnants

of the Iron Brigade. More importantly, Slocum's entire XII Corps was there. With nine thousand men, the XII was the smallest of the Union corps at Gettysburg, but it significantly outnumbered Johnson's Confederate division of about six thousand, which Ewell planned to send against it, and the Union men held the heights—both of them. In effect, Culp's Hill had two crests: a higher one closer to Cemetery Hill, and a lower one farther south near the extreme right flank of the Union line. Slocum spread his two divisions out over both crests, placing the division of John W. Geary on the higher summit, and Alpheus Williams's division under Thomas Ruger's on the lower rise.★

The six-foot-five-inch Geary had led a colorful life. During the Mexican War he had risen to command a regiment. He then left the army and made his way to California, where he had organized a postal system and become the first mayor of San Francisco (which still has a street named for him). In the late 1850s, he served briefly in a politically sensitive job as territorial governor of "Bleeding" Kansas. Now he found himself atop the high ground at Gettysburg in command of three brigades. It was a strong position, and it was about to become stronger. Geary was not a particular advocate of breastworks—like many officers of long service, he was convinced that fighting from behind fieldworks made men reluctant to accept battle in the open.

Edwin Forbes based this painting on sketches he had produced of the breastworks erected by the Federal defenders of Culp's Hill. Formal breastworks like these were rare at Gettysburg, which was mainly a stand-up fight, but the works proved their worth in the fighting on Culp's Hill and were instrumental in halting the Confederate attacks on both July 2 and 3.

★There was some confusion on the Union right about the command structure of the XII Corps. Slocum was under the impression that he commanded the Union right wing, and as a "wing commander" he had delegated control of the XII Corps to Alpheus Williams, who then entrusted his own division to Thomas Ruger. But no one at Meade's headquarters, least of all Meade, thought of Slocum as a wing commander. The practical result was that Williams acted as a conduit for Slocum's orders to the corps. Throughout this narrative, however, Williams's division will be designated as Ruger's since it was Ruger who exercised effective control of the division while Williams exercised tactical control of the corps.

But his brigade commanders, especially George S. Greene, argued that fieldworks could prove useful here, and Geary did not forbid it. Axes were found and distributed, and the men set to work felling trees. They stripped off the branches and piled up the logs to make a wall, piling dirt and rocks against it to make it more impervious to shot. In a few places they even erected "head logs": thick logs that were placed four to six inches above the wall, leaving a narrow gap below for the defenders to shoot through without exposing themselves. By late afternoon, about the time that Longstreet's attack finally got under way more than a mile to the south, the XII Corps' position on Culp's Hill might have been described as unassailable.

Soon after four o'clock the defenders of Culp's Hill heard the sounds of battle wafting up from the south, and they strained their ears hoping to gain some clue about the progress of the fighting. Then orders arrived from Meade. To Slocum's surprise, if not his astonishment, Meade ordered him to abandon Culp's Hill and take his

In another Edwin Forbes painting, skirmishers of the 14th and 15th Louisiana fire uphill at the New York soldiers of George S. Greene's brigade atop Culp's Hill at twilight on July 2, while the rest of Johnson's division prepares to attack at lower right. Badly outnumbered, Greene's men benefited from both the difficult terrain and their log breastworks in the fierce fighting that followed.

entire corps south to shore up the collapsing Union left. Slocum was shocked. He sent a staff officer to headquarters to ask if he could leave a division behind on Culp's Hill. Meade agreed that Slocum could leave a brigade there, but he emphasized that the real danger was on the left and that Slocum should send his corps there at once. Ruger's men left first, pulling out of their positions on the lower crest of Culp's Hill and marching south toward the sound of the guns. Once they had cleared the road, Geary's men followed. The brigade that Slocum left behind to defend the breastworks was that of George S. Greene, which consisted of four New York regiments with a total of 1,500 men. Even as Greene's men watched the last of their XII Corps comrades march off to the south, Johnson's 6,000 Confederates were preparing their assault.

Mathew Brady took this photograph of the Federal breastworks on Culp's Hill two weeks after the battle (two of Brady's assistants pose on the Federal side of the line). This portion of the line was defended by two New York regiments (the 78th and 102nd), which successfully fought off repeated attacks by the five Louisiana regiments of Nicholl's brigade. The fighting was so fierce that leaves and twigs clipped off by flying minié balls rained down on the troops below. One visitor to this portion of the battlefield a few weeks later counted seventy bullet holes in a single tree no more than a foot in diameter.

Major Joseph W. Latimer, known as the boy major, was only 19 years old when he commanded the artillery battalion of "Allegheny" Johnson's division at Gettysburg. He was popular throughout the division; even the infantry took pride in his accomplishments and often cheered him when he rode by. On July 2, Johnson ordered Latimer's sixteen guns on Benner's Hill to support the infantry attack by opening fire on the thirty-three Federal guns on Cemetery Hill. In the unequal duel that followed, Latimer was mortally wounded.

It began with an explosion of artillery. Johnson wanted Confederate gunners on Benner's Hill to support his attack, and he ordered Major Joseph Latimer (only 19 years old and known as the boy major) to take sixteen guns to that hill and open fire. Latimer did so, but his guns immediately attracted a storm of counterbattery fire that all but overwhelmed them. Though Latimer's guns fired off more than a thousand rounds, they were pounded by twice as many guns from Cemetery Hill. Latimer had to withdraw all but four of his guns from the exposed hilltop. While Latimer was supervising the fire of those four guns, a Union shell exploded nearby and mortally wounded him; Latimer would never see his twentieth birthday. Moreover, it was evident that whatever the Confederates might hope to accomplish on this end of the line would have to be done with infantry.

Johnson sent his infantry forward in a three-brigade front. His two right-hand brigades splashed across Rock Creek and started gamely up Culp's Hill. It was already late in the afternoon, and the attackers were ascending the shady side of the hill in a thick wood. Visibility was poor and rapidly getting worse. Federal skirmishers in the woods slowed the attackers, but they pushed on and soon came within musket range of the Federal breastworks. The sound of the fighting rose to a crescendo as both sides loaded and fired as quickly as possible. A virtual storm of bullets tore through the gloaming of the forest, thudding into tree trunks and breastworks, snipping off small branches, and occasionally finding a human mark. The next morning, one soldier in the 149th New York counted no fewer than eighty-one bullet holes in the regiment's flag. As dusk turned into full dark, the firing continued, but Greene's thin line held.

Johnson's 3rd brigade, that of Marylander George H. Steuart on the left, started late. It was delayed not only because it had a greater distance to travel but also because a thousand yards downstream at McAllister's Mill, a dam across Rock Creek turned that stream into a small lake where Steuart's men had to cross. Finally, however, they worked their way across the swollen creek holding their rifles over their heads, then they scrambled up Culp's Hill through the thick woods all the way to the lower crest, where they found . . . nothing. Ruger's division was gone! The Federal lines were empty! Steuart's men passed over the crest and turned right. They were now on Greene's open flank and nearly behind the 137th New York regiment. In the dark, the New Yorkers heard rather than saw Steuart's men coming, and they pulled back northward, falling in behind a traverse that Greene had ordered to be built in anticipation of just such an emergency. Greene's four regiments were now arrayed in a tight semicircle around the upper crest of Culp's Hill. Outnumbered and assailed on front and flank, they were in a perilous spot. If help did not arrive soon, they might easily be overwhelmed despite their breastworks.

Meanwhile in front of Cemetery Hill, Early's men began their advance against the linchpin of the Union position. Just at dusk, two of Early's brigades sent skirmishers out in front, the men dodging from point to point as they moved up to the base of the hill, and behind them came two ranks of infantry. Harry Hays's Louisiana Tigers targeted that part of the Union line closest to town, the handsome brick gatehouse marking its approximate center. A brigade of North Carolinians advanced on Hays's left. It was nominally Hoke's brigade but was commanded now by Colonel Isaac Avery since Hoke's wound at Chancellorsville had compelled him to stay behind when the army went north. It was well past twilight and heading toward full dark-

The men of Harry Hays's Louisiana brigade (called the Tigers) begin their assault on Cemetery Hill in an 1863 lithograph. Originally the nickname Tigers belonged to one company of toughs in C. R. Wheat's battalion of Louisiana troops, but it soon spread to the entire brigade. Hays's Tigers charged to the crest of Cemetery Hill late on July 2 and for a brief moment occupied the hinge of the Federal position.

Overleaf: In Peter Rothermel's 1868 painting *Repulse of the Louisiana Tigers*, the Tigers storm up Cemetery Hill (at left background) at twilight on July 2 while the artillerists of the 5th Maine battery (foreground) open devastating fire on their flank. A gunner in the battery later recalled the moment: "The whole battery at close range was pouring a most destructive, demoralizing, enfilading fire of double canister into a confused mass of the enemy struggling in the uncertain shadows of the crest of East Cemetery Hill." Meanwhile, the men of Carroll's brigade (left) rush to counterattack.

AN ARTIST'S VIEW OF THE ATTACK ON CEMETERY HILL

Alfred Waud was the most prolific sketch artist of the Civil War era. A special correspondent for *Harper's Weekly*, a popular illustrated newspaper, Waud accompanied the Army of the Potomac on all its campaigns from Antietam to Appomattox. The 34-year-old was present during the fighting at Gettysburg, and he drew the images shown here. Three days after the battle, he was still sketching the terrain when he was photographed (top left) by Timothy O'Sullivan.

The drawing at bottom left depicts the guns of Captain Greenleaf T. Stevens's 5th Maine battery as it fired into the flank of Hays's Louisiana Tigers during the Confederate attack on Cemetery Hill late on July 2. The view here is essentially the same as that portrayed in Rother-

mel's painting (pp. 184–185). Waud's own handwritten notes at the bottom read: "Ground over which Louisiana Tigers charged. Entrenched guns Stevens battery."

The sketch at top right shows the Tigers atop Cemetery Hill as they struggled hand to hand with the Federal gunners of Rickett's battery. Two Federal officers are firing point blank with their sidearms. Federal infantrymen rush up from the right to help stanch the breakthrough and hold the crest. Many of Waud's drawings (including this one) were subsequently turned into engravings

such as the one at bottom right, which appeared in *Harper's Weekly* in August 1863.

The assault Waud depicted was conducted by only two Confederate brigades. It might have been decisive if it had been supported, but Early could not bring himself to commit Gordon's brigade, and Rodes's division never got properly started. Like so many other apparent Confederate opportunities at Gettysburg, this one went aglimmering for lack of effective coordination.

Just prior to the charge of the Louisiana Tigers, Colonel Charles Wainwright told Captain R. Bruce Ricketts, commanding a New York battery on the crest of Cemetery Hill, that his battery was the key to the whole Federal position. "In case you are charged here," Wainwright told him, "you will not limber up under any circumstances, but fight your battery as long as you can." The gunners fought hand to hand with the Confederate infantry long enough for reinforcements to arrive.

ness, giving the attackers a ghostly quality as they advanced over the landscape toward the cemetery. The Federal gunners on Cemetery Hill fired round after round, the bright muzzle blasts of the big guns punctuating the darkness. As the Confederates came closer, the gunners switched to canister, then double canister—a fierce antipersonnel weapon that turned a cannon into a giant shotgun.

In spite of that, the Louisiana Tigers charged across the Brickyard Road and into the thin rank of Ames's men. The XI Corps' defenders had seen altogether too much of this. Individually, and then in groups, they began to fall back despite Ames's pleas to stand their ground. The Confederates surged forward, charging up the hill toward the hated Federal batteries on the crest. One group of about seventy-five men headed directly for the four-gun battery of Captain Michael Wiedrich. Ordinarily, gunners would try to haul their guns out of the way before enemy infantry got close enough to seize their precious weapons. But this time the gunners knew that there was no place to fall back to. They stuck to their guns, defending them with whatever was at hand: swords, pistols, even ramrods. To no avail. Gleefully and triumphantly, the Confederates claimed Wiedrich's guns as trophies of war. Guns and flags were the tangible symbols of victory in the Civil War, and when Hays's men found themselves in possession of these guns they must have believed that they had won the day—or rather the night, for by now it was fully dark.

On their left, Avery's North Carolinians also broke through the line of Federal infantry. Like the Louisiana Tigers, they charged up the slope directly toward the guns of Captain R. Bruce Ricketts's battery, where they engaged in furious hand-to-hand fighting with the Yankee artillerists and their supports. By then their brigade commander was no longer with them. While leading his men in the initial charge, a bullet had struck Avery in the throat, and he had fallen to the ground. Left behind by the advancing line, alone in the gathering darkness, he scribbled out a final message to his friend Major Sam Tate: "Major, tell my Father I died with my Face to the enemy. I. E. Avery." He was still holding the note when his body was discovered.

Atop Cemetery Hill, Hays's Louisianans and Avery's North Carolinians had gained a precarious hold on the crest, but they could not stay there without support. Luckily, support was at hand. Early had a third brigade—that of John B. Gordon, whose men had helped break Howard's front the afternoon before—and there was still all of Robert Rodes's five-brigade division. Early called up Gordon's brigade

"THE MUSKETRY SHOWED WHERE TO GO"

When those members of the 6th Wisconsin regiment who had survived the battle at the railroad cut on McPherson's Ridge were ordered to occupy the heights of Culp's Hill on the evening of July 1, they may have thought they were being sent to a relatively secure part of the line. Late the next night, however, Dawes received an urgent call for help from Greene's hard-pressed New York brigade, and for the second time in two days the 6th Wisconsin found itself called upon to save the day. The following is from Dawes's memoirs:

The crash of Union muskets breaks out on our right and we know that the attack is on the twelfth corps. Soon a staff officer came along, calling: "Where is Colonel Dawes?" I answered: "Here." He said: "Take your regiment, sir, and report to Colonel Greene." I said: "Where is he?" "He is over in the woods where they are attacking." I commanded: "Attention, battalion, right face, forward by file right—march!" and we started for Colonel Greene. Who he was I did not know, but the musketry showed where to go. The first mounted officer I saw proved to be General [sic] C. S. Greene, of the twelfth army corps. Taking from his pocket a card, he wrote in the darkness his name and command, which he handed to me. He then directed me to form my regiment, and go into the breastworks; to go as quickly as possible, and to hold the works after I got there. I did not then understand, nor did he, that the rebels already had possession of these works. Facing the regiment to the front, I ordered: "Forward—run; march!" We received no fire until we neared the breastworks, when the enemy who had possession of them, lying on the lower side, and who were completely surprised at our sudden arrival, rose up and fired a volley at us, and immediately retreated down the hill. This remarkable encounter did not last a minute. We lost two men, killed—both burned with the powder of the guns fired at them. The darkness and the suddenness of our arrival caused the enemy to fire widely. We recaptured the breastworks on our front, and the fourteenth Brooklyn, which came in on our right, also got possession of the works. We remained here until midnight, when we were relieved by troops of the twelfth corps, who had left these works to support General Sickles' corps against Longstreet's attack and now returned. We then marched back to our own breastworks on [upper] Culp's Hill.

SOURCE: Rufus R. Dawes, *Service with the Sixth Wisconsin Volunteers* (Marietta, Ohio: Alderman & Sons, 1890), pp. 181–82.

The 29th Pennsylvania Regiment on Culp's Hill, a drawing by William L. Sheppard

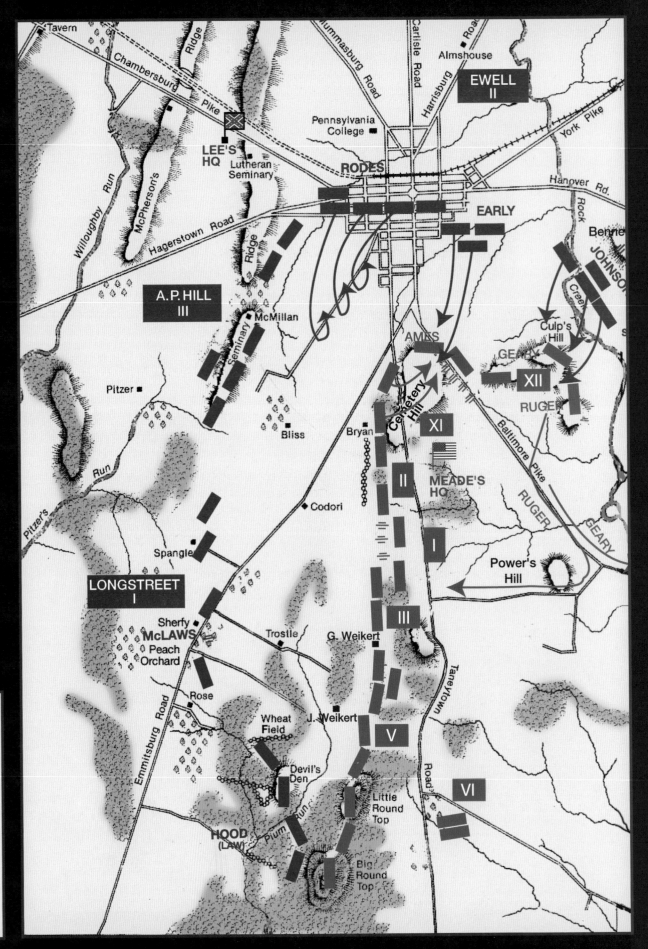

THE CONFEDERATE ATTACK: CEMETERY HILL & CULP'S HILL

July 2, 1863

6 P.M.–Midnight

Legend:

→ Union troop movements

→ Confederate troop movements

| I | Union Corps
| EWELL II | Confederate Corps

infantry units

■ location of house

★ site of battle or skirmish

artillery positions

1 inch = 900 yards

Map labels:

Tavern, Chambersburg Pike, McPherson's Ridge, Willoughby Run, LEE'S HQ, Lutheran Seminary, Hagerstown Road, Seminary Ridge, A.P. HILL III, McMillan, Pitzer, Pitzer's Run, Bliss, Bryan, Codori, Spangle, LONGSTREET I, Sherfy, McLAWS, Peach Orchard, Rose, Emmitsburg Road, Wheat Field, Devil's Den, HOOD (LAW), Plum Run, Trostle, G. Weikert, J. Weikert, Little Round Top, Big Round Top, Pennsylvania College, Mummasburg Road, Carlisle Road, Harrisburg Road, York Pike, EWELL II, Almshouse, RODES, EARLY, Hanover Rd., Benne..., JOHNSON, Rock Creek, Culp's Hill, GEARY, XII, RUGER, AMES, Cemetery Hill, XI, MEADE'S HQ, II, I, Baltimore Pike, RUGER, GEARY, Power's Hill, Taneytown Road, III, V, VI

when he sent Hays and Avery forward, intending to send it into the fight hard on their heels, but because Early had seen no sign of an advance by Rodes, he held Gordon back in case he needed a reserve. It was not the moment for prudence. Even without Rodes, Gordon's veteran brigade might have been just enough to sustain the Confederate momentum on Cemetery Hill. But waiting for Rodes, Early held back, and the moment was lost.

Reinforcements arrived on Cemetery Hill, but they were Federal reinforcements. First came two New York regiments led by the Polish immigrant Colonel Wladimir Kryzanowski of Howard's corps. By now it had grown so dark that as the New Yorkers approached, Hays could not tell if they were friend or foe. Thinking—certainly hoping—that these were Rodes's men, he ordered his troops to hold their fire. A line of muzzle flashes at close range revealed the allegiance of the new arrivals, and belatedly, Hays's men fired back. But behind the New Yorkers came more Yankees—Coster's brigade, also from Howard's corps. Hays determined that he must fall back, and his men abandoned the guns they had briefly claimed and retreated down the hill.

The story was much the same on the other side of Cemetery Hill. Here it was Samuel Carroll's brigade, sent from the II Corps by the ever active Hancock, that arrived in time to drive back the North Carolinians. Like Hays's men, they withdrew to the bottom of the hill and then back into Gordon's line of reserves. The attack on Cemetery Hill had failed, and Early was furious. Where was Rodes? he wanted to know. It was a good question.

Gettysburg was not Robert Rodes's finest hour. A tall, spare, sharp-faced man, Rodes was a graduate of the Virginia Military Institute (class of 1848). On July 1 his men had paid dearly when he had ordered two of his brigades to go forward on Oak Knoll across unfamiliar ground against an enemy whose strength and position he did not know. On July 2 his great error was not anticipating the length of time it would take to get his command out of town and deployed into line west of Cemetery Hill. By the time his five brigades were lined up in proper position, it was fully dark, and his brigade commanders informed him that Early's men had already fallen back. After advancing a few hundred yards to the base of the hill, his front-line brigadiers held a hurried conference and decided that the opportunity had passed. Rodes concurred, and he pulled his entire division back to a supporting position.

Just as the crisis passed on Cemetery Hill, it was reaching its apex on Culp's Hill. Steuart's men were somewhat surprised to find the lower crest of Culp's Hill unoccupied. But the late-night darkness made it difficult, if not impossible, to take full advantage of the opportunity. Though he had an open path to the Federal rear, Steuart concentrated on attacking Greene's refused right flank, unaware that if he had continued forward another four hundred yards he would have emerged onto Baltimore Pike, Meade's line of supply—and retreat. Instead, for the next several hours, confusion was king on Culp's Hill. As Steuart's men wheeled to the right, they bunched together. In the darkness, it was difficult to tell blue from gray, and the 1st North Carolina fired a volley into the 1st Maryland (Confederate) before its identity was discovered.

To increase the level of confusion, Federal reinforcements from Howard and Hancock were also heading toward Culp's Hill. Greene had sent for help as soon as he came under attack, and despite delays caused by confusion in the darkness, support was arriving. Howard sent several regiments from von Amsberg's brigade. From the

Opposite: At dusk, just as Longstreet's attack was grinding to a halt, Ewell's corps north of town began its assault on Cemetery Hill and Culp's Hill. Two of Early's brigades gained a temporary foothold on Cemetery Hill, but they were unsupported and had to fall back. The story was much the same on Culp's Hill, where "Maryland" Steuart's brigade occupied some abandoned Union lines but could not exploit their success, due to nightfall.

Iron Brigade, Dawes brought the 6th Wisconsin, heroes of the fight in the railroad cut the day before. For the second time in two days Dawes's regiment executed a charge that reclaimed a valuable position from the enemy.

As all these forces converged on the lower slope of Culp's Hill, it created a situation that might have been considered a comedy of errors if the stakes had not been so great. The worst error was made by John Geary, the erstwhile mayor of San Francisco and former governor of Kansas territory. Just before dusk, he had received orders to follow Ruger's division southward in response to Meade's call for help. Ruger's men eventually reached the area behind the George Weikert House and played a small role in repulsing the last remnants of Longstreet's attack, though two of Ruger's three brigades never got into the fight at all, suggesting that they need not have been sent. But if Ruger's division was largely wasted, Geary's division was squandered entirely. Ordered to follow Ruger, Geary became disoriented in the growing darkness and missed the turnoff onto the Granite Schoolhouse Road. Instead he continued down Baltimore Pike, across Rock Creek Bridge, and virtually out of the fight. Eventually, someone (several claimed the credit) noticed the error and got the division turned around. Geary's two brigades then marched back up Baltimore Pike toward Culp's Hill where Confederates and Federals were groping uncertainly through the darkness trying to distinguish friend from foe.

Spangler's Spring, shown here in a nineteenth-century drawing, sat in a low swale of ground on the shoulder of Culp's Hill that was occupied by both sides at various times during the fighting and used as a source of water by both sides in the muggy July heat. Several stories emerged after the battle about accidental meetings between Union and Confederate soldiers who chose not to acknowledge one another's presence.

Geary's men were in for a surprise as they tried to reoccupy the positions they had abandoned an hour or two earlier. Wary brigade and regimental commanders sent out scouts to discover what, if anything, was in front of them. One man from the 2nd Massachusetts, sent forward to investigate, found men encamped in his old bivouac and innocently asked them, "Boys, what regiment do you belong to?" "Twenty-third," came the answer. A slight pause. "Twenty-third what?" asked the Massachusetts man. The question gave him away. "Why, they are Yanks!" a Virginian called out, and men scrambled about for their arms while the scout dashed back into the woods.

Not all such confusions of identity were hostile. Around Spangler's Spring, below the southern shoulder of Culp's Hill, men from both sides sought to fill their canteens. More than once, a man glanced sideways to note that the man next to him wore a suspicious uniform. But no challenges were issued, and after filling their canteens the men backed off the way they had come without speaking.

By midnight all the firing had ceased. On Culp's Hill, Greene's New Yorkers still held the upper crest, thanks partly to their stout breastworks and partly to the arrival of reinforcements

from the I and XI Corps. On the lower crest, the situation was more complicated. Confederate forces occupied some of the trenches that the Federals had abandoned earlier, but because of the late-night return of the XII Corps, their hold on that ground was more precarious than they knew.

It had been a long day, and the casualties had been horrific. At least 15,000 men had fallen in the three hours between 4 P.M. and 7 P.M.; 1,500 more fell in the late-afternoon and evening battles for Cemetery Hill and Culp's Hill. Nowhere else in the war was there such a concentration of death as in the late afternoon and evening of July 2, 1863. Though the one-day Battle of Antietam, fought the previous September, had been bloodier, that battle had begun at dawn and lasted all day. At Gettysburg, the serious fighting on July 2 had not started until four o'clock in the afternoon. More-over, when combined with the 16,300 men who had fallen on July 1, the 32,800 casualties at Gettysburg made it by far the bloodiest battle in American history to date, surpassing even Antietam. And, despite that, the outcome was still very much in doubt. As the men on both sides drifted off to sleep with the pleas and moans of the wounded in their ears, almost every one of them knew that the battle was far from over.

A 1993 photo of the area around Spangler's Spring shows the uneven terrain and thick woods that dramatically reduced visibility, especially at night, and that made any attack difficult. This ground was occupied by the Confederates late on July 2, but two Union regiments tried to recover it the next morning.

CHAPTER ELEVEN

The Calm Before the Storm

(9 P.M., July 2–1 P.M., July 3, 1863)

In the uneasy peace that settled—finally—on the hills and valleys south of Gettysburg after midnight, each of the army commanders reflected on the day's events and made plans for the dawn. Neither had any doubt that the fighting—and the bloodshed—would resume at first light. For much of the day, Meade and Lee had been compelled to concede many of the critical command decisions to subordinate commanders. The expanse of the battlefield, the difficult and unfamiliar terrain, and the ubiquitous "fog of war" had turned both army commanders into less-than-omnipotent beings. Now in the full darkness of a summer's night, each man sought to assess the consequences of the day's fighting and make plans for the morning. It would be another short and busy night.

On the Federal side of the field, Meade had been a tornado of activity all afternoon: riding furiously about the battlefield trailed by a few staff officers and issuing orders that sent various units here and there as he patched up weak spots in his line. His sense of urgency had been evident in his body language, and occasionally his actions had betrayed a hint of panic, especially when he had ordered Slocum to abandon Culp's Hill and march his entire corps to the Union left. Only once, however, was he swept up by the moment. Watching the approach of Wright's brigade from Cemetery Ridge late in the afternoon, he looked about impatiently for the reinforcements he had summoned, and when he finally spotted them, he lifted the cap from his head and waved it about him shouting, "Come on, gentlemen!" as he accompanied them forward. It was a tableau reminiscent of Reynolds waving the Iron Brigade into action on McPherson's Woods thirty-six hours earlier, but this time no marksman's bullet shattered the tableau, and Meade survived the day unscathed.

That night at about nine, with the fighting still in progress on the lower crest of Culp's Hill, Meade met with his generals at his headquarters in the Leister House just behind Cemetery Ridge. They crowded into a tiny bedroom, dimly illuminated by a single lantern. It was hot and stuffy in the small room, but the Union generals were

Opposite: *Night Bivouac of the Seventh Regiment New York at Arlington Heights, Virginia,* **by Sanford Robinson Gifford, depicts a portion of the Army of the Potomac at camp. After the bloodiest afternoon in American military history, the two armies at Gettysburg bedded down on July 2 within a mile or two of each other, aware that the slaughter would surely begin again with the coming of dawn. One Federal soldier recalled that "the stillness was only broken by the moans of the wounded yet uncared for in our front."**

Meade and his corps commanders crammed themselves into a bedroom in the Leister House, just behind Cemetery Ridge, late on July 2 for a strategy conference that lasted almost until midnight. After nearly three hours of discussion, the only firm decision that emerged was that the army would stay and fight it out at Gettysburg for at least another day.

too tired and emotionally drained to worry much about creature comforts. Some sat on the edge of the bed; others leaned against the wall; Gouvernor Warren, who had played such an important role on Little Round Top that afternoon, curled up in a corner and went to sleep. Besides Meade and his two senior staff officers (Warren and Daniel Butterfield, the chief of staff he had inherited from Hooker), all seven of the corps commanders were there, with Birney in place of the wounded Sickles and John Newton in command of the I Corps in place of Doubleday.★ Two others, John Gibbon, from Hancock's II Corps, and Alpheus Williams, from Slocum's XII Corps, were there, too. The mood was cautiously optimistic. After all, despite a number of close calls, the rebels had failed to drive them from their position, and despite the virtual destruction of Sickles's corps (now Birney's), the army was as strongly positioned at the end of the day as it had been when the battle opened, perhaps more so.

The discussion was general and unfocused until Butterfield imposed order on the conversation by posing three questions: First, should the army remain where it was, or should it select a different position to defend? Second, if it stayed, should the army

★Meade had little confidence in Doubleday as commander of the I Corps and replaced him with Newton on the night of July 1. Doubleday felt aggrieved by this, and wrote a postwar account of the battle justifying his performance on the first day of fighting.

The Leister House (left, in a photo taken in 2000) where Meade met with his generals on the night of July 2, still stands on the grounds of the Gettysburg National Military Park.

remain on the defensive or seize the initiative and attack? And, finally, if it stayed, how much longer should it remain? This last question derived from a rather awkward circumstance: the army was nearly out of food! Expecting a fight, Meade had ordered the army's supply wagons to remain behind, and now there was only enough food on hand for one more day—two if the men were able to take advantage of local produce and rationed themselves. Despite this, and despite some concern that the army's position was too extended, the response of the officers to Butterfield's first question was unanimous: the army should maintain its current position. In addition, they declared that it should remain on the defensive and await the enemy's next move. As for how long it might stay, . . . well, the next day might provide the answer to that. The meeting lasted three hours and broke up around midnight, just as the last shots on Culp's Hill were sputtering out.

Like so many other aspects of the battle, this meeting became the subject of much postwar discussion. Meade's enemies, particularly Sickles and Butterfield (who was still loyal to the displaced Hooker), claimed that Meade called the council of war because he was too timid to make a decision on his own, and because he had hoped that the generals would vote to retreat. Such charges were groundless. Several hours *before* the generals voted—unanimously—to stay and fight it out on the ground they held, Meade had already dispatched a telegram to Halleck in Washington telling him, "I shall remain in my present position tomorrow, but am not prepared to say, until better advised of the condition of the army, whether my operations will be of an offensive or defensive character." In other words, if he wanted any advice at all from his corps commanders it was not about whether the army should remain or fall back but whether it should attack or defend. Very likely Meade was willing to let the generals vote because it made each of them a participant in the decision and served to cement them in a common bond.

Dan Butterfield (above), Meade's chief of staff, became the focus of controversy after the battle, when he implied that Meade had planned to retreat from Gettysburg and had to be talked out of it by his subordinates. Meade and Butterfield continued the argument into the postwar years.

A sketch by Edwin Forbes shows a gun crew in action firing into a mass of infantrymen in the near tree line. A wounded or dead gunner lies nearby while the soldier next to him holds the ramrod used to load new charges into the muzzle. The gun captain sights along the barrel, while another soldier pulls the lanyard. At close range, a 12-pound Napoleon gun was a terrible weapon against infantry.

If Meade had been a whirlwind of activity on the afternoon of July 2, Lee had remained characteristically detached. It was Lee's habit to ensure that his subordinates understood their orders and then allow them to execute those orders without close oversight. Like some kind of divine clockmaker, he set the various components of his army in motion, then stood back to allow his mechanism to function. That afternoon, after seeing Longstreet (finally) on his way, Lee had taken up a position near the center of the Confederate battle line on Seminary Ridge and watched the fight unfold before him. Hood's initial advance had been beyond his line of sight, but he had watched through his field glasses as McLaws's division went into action, and he had admired the way Barksdale's Mississippians had burst through Federal defenses in the Peach Orchard. He had watched Anderson's men join the fight at dusk, and he had seen Wright's brigade ascend Cemetery Ridge and reach its crest only to fall back for lack of support. Throughout the afternoon, he had admired the courage and steadfastness of the men in the ranks, but at the end of the day he was disappointed by the lack of what he would later call a "proper concert of action." The worst example of this was the fact that Ewell's attack on Culp's Hill and Cemetery Hill had not begun until after Longstreet's attack had fizzled out. Lee still had faith in his soldiers; he still believed that they could successfully assault any Yankee position. What was needed was concentration and coordination.

While he was thinking about how he might achieve the necessary coordination the next day, Lee learned of the arrival—at last—of the missing elements of his army. First, George Pickett showed up to report the approach of his division of Virginians.

It was too late to throw his three brigades into the fight that day, and Pickett was forced to watch in frustration as the battle waxed and waned before him. Without a doubt, however, these fresh forces would play an important role in the next day's fighting. Then, late in the afternoon, a tired and bedraggled-looking Jeb Stuart rode up, dismounted, and reported to the commanding general.

For Stuart the road to Gettysburg had been an arduous one. When the battle had begun on July 1, his three brigades of cavalry had been some thirty miles to the east riding northward toward Carlisle, still searching for the van of Ewell's corps. What had begun as a raid to reassert the superiority of the Confederate cavalry had become an ordeal. Horses and men alike were exhausted. None of Stuart's troopers had managed more than a few hours sleep since the ride had begun nearly a week before, and stupid with exhaustion, they plodded on like zombies, a few of them occasionally toppling unconscious from the saddle. When the column reached Carlisle, Stuart discovered that there were indeed troops there, but they wore Union blue. Two brigades of Pennsylvania militia had reoccupied the town after Ewell's withdrawal. Stuart might have bypassed it, but his men needed food almost as much as they needed sleep. He therefore sent in a demand for the militia to surrender, which the Yankees refused, and Stuart ordered his horse artillery to unlimber and shell the town. While he was at it, he burned the U.S. Army cavalry barracks, the temporary capture of which Ewell had celebrated with a modest ceremony three days earlier.

Then, late that afternoon, one of Stuart's scouts returned with news that he had found the army. It was at Gettysburg, thirty miles to the south, and it was engaged in a fight with the enemy! In the predawn hours of July 2, Stuart abandoned Carlisle and started his exhausted troopers southward. After one more brief skirmish with Union cavalry, he rode ahead of his column to find Lee on Seminary Ridge.

Lee's greeting was less than enthusiastic: "Well, General Stuart, you are here at last," he said. Just that, nothing more; no word of greeting or welcome. For Stuart, the implied rebuke was chilling. The two men had always had a convivial, even an affectionate, relationship. Like other young officers in the Confederate high command, Stuart looked upon Lee (who was almost twice his age) as a kind of father figure. And apparently the father was disappointed in him. Stuart tried to regain Lee's favor by reporting that he had brought with him 125 enemy wagons, fully loaded—a housecat dropping a mouse at its master's feet. But the news did not seem to please the army commander; indeed, by now it hardly mattered. Stuart's face fell. Noticing it, Lee relented. He asked Stuart to bring up his command and let the men and the horses rest; there would be work for them on the morrow.

With Stuart's appearance, Lee's army was at last united. What was he to do with it? His instinct, as always, was to attack. Longstreet's men had gained a purchase on the Union left that afternoon; Ewell's men had secured a portion of Culp's Hill that evening. If either, or both, of these flank attacks could be pushed forward—especially if it could be done simultaneously—the whole Union position would become untenable. The enemy would fall back in disorder, and Stuart's cavalry would be in a position to cut them up as they retreated. A decisive victory could still be had. Unlike Meade, Lee did not survey the opinions of his senior generals. Confident that his troops could overcome the army before them if their assault was properly coordinated, he dispatched orders to Ewell and Longstreet to renew their attacks on the enemy flanks at first light. Then he lay down for a few hours' sleep.

Major General George Pickett achieved immortal glory at Gettysburg. His division was the last Confederate unit to arrive at Gettysburg, and the ebullient Pickett was anxious lest he miss the fight altogether. He needn't have worried, for his name and his command will forever be associated with Gettysburg.

PHOTOGRAPHERS AND THE BATTLE OF GETTYSBURG

Photography was a new art during the Civil War. One might also say that it was a new science as well, for mid-nineteenth-century photography required a wagonload of equipment and a great deal of technical expertise. Moreover, because the photographic plates (film) had to be exposed for several seconds in order to record an impression, only still shots were possible. Surviving Civil War photographs, therefore, are dominated by formal portraits and landscapes.

Culp's Hill was one of several scenes that drew the interest of photographers after the Battle of Gettysburg (Little Round Top and Devil's Den were others). All three images shown here were taken in 1867 by three different photographers, each attempting to portray the nature of the terrain where heavy fighting took place late on July 2 and 3.

The most famous photographer of the Civil War era was Mathew Brady.

Before the war he had studios in both Washington and New York and made a good living taking formal portraits and preparing what were known as *cartes de visite*— small personal calling cards that were used socially in the nineteenth-century. When the war broke out in 1861, Brady left his studio to follow the armies and photograph the scenes of battle. He traveled with a number of assistants (some of them famous photographers in their own right), and took thousands of images of the war. He arrived in Gettysburg on July 15, twelve days after the battle, and took thirty-five photographs; many of them subsequently became famous. The scene above shows Culp's Hill after the battle, with one of Brady's assistants posing as a felled soldier. Note the bullet damage to the trees.

The photo at left, also of Culp's Hill, was taken by Charles John Tyson, a local photographer who had opened a photo gallery in Gettysburg with his brother Isaac just before the war. When the opposing armies arrived there in the summer of 1863, Tyson was kept busy taking studio photographs of Union soldiers, but he fled the town with the arrival of the Confederates on July 1. He returned after the fighting had ended to discover that his photographic equipment was uninjured. After the battle, he took photographs of the areas where the fighting had been the heaviest and offered them for sale. His photo shows the difficulty of the terrain on Culp's Hill, with rocks underfoot and trees so thick that visibility, especially at night, was severely limited.

The photo below was taken by an amateur photographer, Samuel Fisher Corlies, an attorney from Philadelphia who visited Gettysburg in the late fall of 1863, after the trees had dropped their leaves, giving the hill a forlorn look some four months after the fighting. It is possible that Corlies made the trip in order to be present for the dedication of the new cemetery in November, where Lincoln gave his famous address.

SOURCES: William A. Frassanito, *Gettysburg: A Journey in Time* (New York: Charles Scribner's Sons, 1975) and *Early Photography at Gettysburg* (Gettysburg: Thomas Publications, 1995). Students of the Battle of Gettysburg are much indebted to William Frassanito, whose careful assessment of contemporary photography at Gettysburg has revealed much new information about what happened there.

In receipt of Lee's orders, Ewell judged that his best chance for success was on the heavily forested slopes of Culp's Hill, where elements of "Allegheny" Johnson's division still held the abandoned Union positions on the lower crest. During the night, therefore, Ewell strengthened Johnson's position on Culp's Hill, adding the famous Stonewall Brigade (which had spent the day fending off Federal cavalry on the extreme left flank), as well as two of Robert Rodes's brigades, effectively doubling the size of Johnson's command. Thus reinforced, Johnson was to execute a general advance at first light to finish the job he had started. It was the second time in two days that Ewell planned an attack to coordinate with a similar assault on the other end of the Confederate battle line.

On the Confederate right, however, Longstreet continued to nurse ideas of his own about how the battle should be fought. While Ewell reinforced Johnson for a dawn assault on Culp's Hill, Longstreet was sending out scouts to investigate the possibility (once again) of slipping around the Union left altogether. Surely, he reasoned, the results of the attack on July 2 would convince Lee to accept the wisdom of such a move. Longstreet's scouts returned in the predawn darkness to report that a route around the Federal left was still open, and on his own Longstreet issued orders to move his command in that direction. Once again, Lee's subordinates were working at cross purposes.

The 52-year-old Alpheus S. Williams, whom the soldiers called Old Pap, assumed de facto command of the XII Corps since Slocum was acting as a "wing commander." It was Williams who orchestrated the Federal effort to recapture the lower crest of Culp's Hill from the Confederates on the morning of July 3.

The Confederates were not the only ones making plans that night. When Slocum and Williams left Meade's headquarters just past midnight, they returned to their command to learn that the lower crest of Culp's Hill was in the hands of the enemy. Williams asked Slocum for permission to retake it, and Slocum readily granted it. "Drive them out at daylight!" he advised.

Williams, whom the soldiers called Old Pap, was 52 years old in the summer of 1863. He had performed well in the war so far, though his lack of a West Point education prevented him from advancing beyond division command. At Gettysburg, however, Williams was a de facto corps commander because of Slocum's conceit that he had been designated as a "wing commander," though what constituted that "wing" besides his own XII Corps he could not have said. He therefore delegated to Williams, his senior division commander, the responsibility of commanding the corps and putting together a plan to "drive out" the rebels at daylight. With the return of Ruger's division, plus Geary's two prodigal brigades, Williams now had as many troops on hand as Johnson did—even with Johnson's reinforcements. More importantly, he also had artillery, which the Confederates did *not* have. The terrain on Culp's Hill was so forbidding that Johnson's men could not move any field guns into position to support the infantry attack. Williams therefore planned to concentrate his artillery along Baltimore Pike and on Powers Hill to shell the rebels from their position.

Williams created a clear line of fire for his big guns by rearranging his infantry. Greene's brigade still held the redoubt on the top of Culp's Hill, and from his right flank, Williams placed Geary's other two brigades in a line that bent westward, away from the high ground, back to Baltimore Pike. (Improbably, these two brigades were commanded by men named Candy and

Kane!) Then along the pike itself, Williams arrayed some two dozen guns, which could fire at the lower crest of Culp's Hill without fear of hitting friendly forces and from beyond the effective range of rebel musketry. Ruger's men took up positions to the right of these guns south of Culp's Hill. Williams's plan was to open up with the artillery at first light. Of course "first light" was also when Johnson's men were supposed to begin their own assault on Culp's Hill in conformance with Ewell's orders, and when Longstreet, Lee's Old War Horse, was to renew his attack on the Federal left some two miles to the south.

The eastern sky turned from pitch black to dove gray sometime after 4 A.M. on July 3. All across the rolling countryside around Gettysburg, men blinked themselves awake, stretched, and took stock of the morning—it was going to be another hot day. Lee was up early despite having slept little. In the half-light before dawn, he called for his horse, Traveller, and rode southward along Seminary Ridge to talk to Longstreet. He had not spoken personally to Old Pete since the afternoon before, and he wanted to ensure that this time there was close coordination between his corps commanders and no misunderstanding about orders.

Longstreet, too, had slept little. Uncharacteristically, he had not reported personally to Lee after the fighting ended on July 2, instead sending a courier with an oral report. He had been disappointed by the outcome of the fighting, and he continued to believe that a movement around the Union left flank was the army's best course of action. When Lee arrived, Longstreet was ready with his plans. "I have had my scouts out all night," he told Lee, "and I find that you still have an excellent opportunity to move around to the right of Meade's army, and maneuver him into attacking us." Lee heard him out, but he remained unconvinced. Such a maneuver would surrender all that had been gained the day before; it would depress morale; it would let the Yankees off the hook and allow them to regain the initiative. Instead of that, Lee told his Old War Horse, the army would renew its assault on both of the Union flanks.

Not possible, Longstreet replied. The divisions of Hood and McLaws were simply incapable of a renewed offensive, and they were no longer in position to execute it in any case. Even with Pickett's fresh division on hand, it would not be enough. Lee could hardly challenge a corps commander about the condition of his own forces. If Hood and McLaws could not execute the attack, other forces would have to do. Heth's division had not been heavily engaged the day before, and other units could be borrowed from Hill's corps. Of course, those forces could not be moved from where they were to the right flank in time for a dawn attack. The assault would have to be delayed, and the target of the attack shifted from the flank to the center.

Longstreet resisted this idea as well. How many men did Lee plan to send against the enemy center? They discussed it: Besides Pickett and Heth, at least two of Dorsey Pender's brigades could participate, perhaps others—ten, maybe twelve brigades, a total of some 15,000 men. Longstreet shook his head. Years later he claimed that he said to Lee, "General, I have been a soldier all my life. I have been with soldiers engaged in fights by couples, by squads, companies, regiments, and armies, and

At Gettysburg, the burden of command rested heavily on Robert E. Lee, who posed for this photograph in 1865. Ordinarily a hands-off commander, he had attempted for two days to coordinate the movements of his corps by delegating the conduct of the attacks to his commanders. But despite local successes, those attacks had failed to drive the Federal army from its position, due at least in part to the lack of coordination between Longstreet's I Corps and Ewell's II Corps.

Brigadier General George Hume "Maryland" Steuart rallies his forces for a charge across Pardee Field on Culp's Hill on the morning of July 3 in this 1886 lithograph by A. C. Redwood. When he heard the order to attack, Major William H. Goldsborough, who commanded the 1st Maryland battalion in Steuart's small brigade, declared that "it was nothing less than murder to send men into that slaughter pen." Events proved him right.

should know, as well as anyone, what soldiers can do. It is my opinion that no 15,000 men ever arrayed for battle can take that position." If those were not his exact words, they certainly captured his sentiment, for it was obvious that Longstreet opposed the idea of renewing the attack. But Lee, too, had been a soldier all his life, and in a longer and more distinguished career. He saw no other realistic alternative, and he was in command. Nevertheless, given the new plan, it was evident that the dawn assault would have to be delayed until midmorning. Lee dispatched a courier to find Ewell and tell him to postpone his attack until ten. But it was too late. Already the sound of a heavy cannonade could be heard coming from the direction of Culp's Hill.

The guns were not Ewell's. Old Pap had amassed some twenty-six guns for his preliminary cannonade, and they were supported by ten more from James A. Rigby's battery of the army's artillery reserve. Rigby's battery was a Maryland unit, so that Maryland artillerists (Union) were shelling Maryland infantrymen (Confederate). The thirty-six Union guns opened briefly around 3:30, then stopped to await better visibility at first light. That came at around 4:30, and with it the Union guns began to pound the lower crest of Culp's Hill. At almost the same moment, the Confederate infantry began its attack, and many of the attacking Confederates assumed the shelling was a response to their assault.

The target of the Confederate infantry attack was the log breastwork at the crest of Culp's Hill that was manned by Greene's New York brigade. The Yankee defenders fired from behind their fieldworks, picking off the attackers as they advanced in the growing light. The attack stalled, but the attackers did not fall back. Instead they stayed put and engaged in a full-scale firefight, the sound of which soon matched that of the artillery. Both sides kept up such a rate of fire that their rifles became fouled with the residue of black powder, and the soldiers feared running out of ammunition. Members of the 149th New York ripped pieces of cloth from their shirts and jammed them down the muzzles of their muskets with their ramrods in order to clear the powder residue; volunteers from both sides ran back through the woods to haul wooden boxes of cartridges to the front lines. Two enterprising Confederates ran back to the supply wagons, dumped boxes of cartridges into a blanket, then slung the blanket on a pole, and hauled it to the front. Officers cautioned the men to conserve their ammunition and not to fire unless they saw a specific target, but the firing did not abate—there were too many targets.

The Confederates made two distinct attacks in the early morning, and both of them were beaten back. Johnson nevertheless ordered a third attack to be spearheaded by Steuart's brigade. George Hume "Maryland" Steuart was one of several thousand from the Old Line state who had chosen to side with the Confederacy. An 1848 graduate of West Point, he had commanded the 1st Maryland (Confederate) regiment before his promotion to brigade command. As he prepared to renew the assault on Culp's Hill, he was unaware that among the troops facing him was the 1st Maryland (Union) regiment.

Steuart protested his orders. His command had been reduced to no more than nine hundred men in the heavy fighting of the night before, perhaps half the amount it had been when the fighting began; some of the regiments in his brigade numbered no more than a few dozen. To execute the attack he was now ordered to make, his men would have to cross a piece of cleared ground that was defended in part by the 147th Pennsylvania regiment under the command of Lieutenant Colonel Airo Pardee. (Ever since, that piece of open ground has been known as Pardee's Field.) Steuart's protests fell on deaf ears, and he dutifully aligned his shrunken command and started it forward. It was supported by the North Carolina brigade of Junius Daniel and by the Stonewall Brigade—Jackson's old command, but led now by Brigadier General James A. Walker. It was Steuart's men, however, who had the honor—and who bore the consequences—of leading the attack. Exposed in the open field, targeted by well-placed defenders, Steuart's men fell by the score. They pushed forward hopelessly and gave up their lives profligately. The few who survived long enough to get near the Union lines found themselves under such a storm of fire that they hugged the ground and raised white handkerchiefs in gesture of surrender. Seventy-eight were taken prisoner. One, to avoid such a fate, put his loaded musket under his chin and pushed the trigger with his ramrod. The attack collapsed and Johnson had to call it off. After the fight, Steuart wept openly, muttering, "My poor boys! My poor boys!"

Only then did Steuart learn that a courier had arrived at Ewell's headquarters sometime after dawn to inform the II Corps commander that for the second day in

Overleaf: Federal troops in the foreground fire from cover on the men of Steuart's small brigade charging across Pardee Field in *Repulse of General Johnson's Division by General Geary's White Star Division,* an 1868 painting by Peter Rothermel. Ahead of the charging Confederates is a small dog who charged forward with the men, barking in the excitement of the moment. The soldiers on both sides tried to spare him, but there were so many bullets flying across that field that he fell along with the rest, riddled with minié balls. A Federal soldier who tried to comfort the dying dog after the Confederates fell back, reported that the animal licked his hand before it expired. The Federal brigade commander, Thomas L. Kane, ordered that the dog be buried with honors as he was the only being on the field that had behaved like a Christian.

Ordered to regain the lines on the far side of Spangler's Meadow, seen at right in an 1860s photograph, two Union regiments duplicated the heroism of Steuart's Confederates—and with similar results. When Lieutenant Charles R. Mudge of the 2nd Massachusetts heard the order to attack, he responded, "Well, it is murder, but it is the order. Up, men; over the works." In that attack the 2nd Massachusetts suffered 50 percent casualties, including Mudge, who was killed.

Mending the Flag, a sketch by Edwin Forbes shown below, depicts Sergeant William C. Lilly splicing the flagstaff of the 149th New York regiment, part of Greene's command, during the heavy fighting on Culp's Hill on the morning of July 3. A witness later claimed to have counted no fewer than eighty bullet holes in the regimental flag, and bullets cut through the staff twice.

a row, Longstreet's morning attack had been delayed, and that Ewell, too, was to postpone his attack. The news had come too late; by the time the courier arrived, Johnson's attack was already under way. It had all been for nothing.

All this time, Lee was piecing together the force that would make the assault that he now planned to send against the Union center. With hindsight, it is possible to look back in puzzlement, if not in horror, in consideration of Lee's decision to launch a frontal assault at Cemetery Ridge. Visitors to the battlefield today can stand near the Lee statue on Seminary Ridge and look across the open fields to the little clump of trees and wonder how Lee could have made such a desperate decision, even as they wonder also about the mettle of the men who would receive and obey those orders with unblinking stoicism. But looking at the matter from the perspective of July 3, 1863, the notion seems somewhat less desperate than it does in hindsight. Walter Taylor, Lee's loyal aide-de-camp, noted the headquarters' view of things when he remembered how "disjointed" the attacks had

A monument to the 72nd Pennsylvania regiment (Baxter's Fire Zouaves) dominates the skyline on Cemetery Ridge just north of the little clump of trees (visible at left) that Lee used as a landmark to guide his attacking infantry.

been on July 2. Several times that day Confederate forces had pierced through the enemy line: on Little Round Top, on Cemetery Ridge, on Cemetery Hill, and on Culp's Hill. If only help had been at hand to support Wright or Early. If only. . . .

One of the problems, Lee knew, was that he had necessarily been forced to confer the execution of his plans on his subordinates: on Hill, who was physically not at his best; on Ewell, who was inexperienced in corps command; and on Longstreet, who had made it clear from the beginning that his heart was not in it. Then, too, the very size of the battlefield meant that it was difficult to coordinate attacks at opposite ends of the line. But perhaps a single thrust on a particular point, a thrust that was supported and reinforced, perhaps that would apply the kind of irresistible pressure necessary to pierce through the enemy line. Lee knew that the Federals had been compelled to reinforce the heights on both their left and their right. He knew as well that those reinforcements had come mainly at the expense of the center. Perhaps there, near that small copse of trees on Cemetery Ridge, would be the place to strike.

Lee met with both Hill and Longstreet to make sure they understood what he had in mind. He pointed to the distinctive clump of trees he had noticed earlier and explained to them that the advance of their infantry would be covered by a massed artillery bombardment. Some 160 field guns would be arrayed in an arc from the high

"I FELT A BURNING, STINGING SENSATION IN MY THIGH"

One of the seventy-eight Confederate prisoners captured during the assault on Culp's Hill on the morning of July 3 was Private David R. Howard of the 1st Maryland battalion in Steuart's brigade. Wounded and captured, Howard survived imprisonment and was eventually exchanged. After the war, he recalled the events of July 3 when Steuart's brigade was shattered in its assault across Pardee's Field and when he was taken prisoner:

We pressed on near their breastworks, when, turning my head to the right, I saw a sight which was fearful to behold. It appeared to me as if the whole of my company was being swept away. . . . Not wishing to surrender, I turned to go back, not expecting to reach my command alive, but determined to fight as long as I could. Catching my gun by the muzzle, I attempted to get a cartridge out of my box to reload, but before I could do so I felt a burning, stinging sensation in my thigh, and as if all the blood in my body was rushing to one spot. Finding I was falling on my face, I gave myself a sudden twist which brought me to a sitting position, facing the Federals, with my

broken leg doubled up over the other. Taking it up tenderly, I put it in its natural position; then tied my handkerchief above the wound, took the bayonet off my gun and made a tourniquet with it; then took my knapsack off and put it under my head for a pillow. Having made myself comfortable, I turned my attention to finding out who were lying around me and how they were wounded.

I don't know how long I laid there . . . it could not have been more than an hour after the charge, when several of the Federals came out from their works, and beckoned for our men to come into their lines. Believing it was my duty to get out of danger if I could, I pulled myself towards them by placing my hands behind me as far as I could reach, and then pulling my body up to them. After going in this manner for a few yards, two Federals ran out and caught me under the arms, raising me just high enough from the ground to let my feet drag, and in this manner ran back with me into their lines. . . .

SOURCE: David R. Howard, "Left on the Field," *The Baltimore Telegram*, #26, 1879.

One of the most poignant of the many state monuments at Gettysburg is this one honoring the soldiers from Maryland who fought on both sides at Gettysburg. A Union soldier from Maryland helps a wounded Confederate from the field.

A Federal gun on Cemetery Ridge overlooks the open fields between the two armies. The low stone wall in front of the cannon marks the position that was occupied by the Federal infantry of Alexander Hays's brigade. Confederate troops occupied the tree line on Seminary Ridge in the distance, almost exactly a mile away. The small clearing by the distant tree line just to the right of the cannon's muzzle marks the location of the modern-day Lee statue and the approximate position from which Lee identified the target for his massed infantry assault on July 3.

ground near the Peach Orchard to Seminary Ridge. After the Confederate guns silenced the Union guns in the center, the infantry would advance, break through the line, and split the Federal army in half. Thus broken, the enemy would have to give up its position and fall back. To spearhead the infantry assault, Pickett's fresh division of 5,400 Virginians would deploy on the right. To their left, would be Heth's division, now under the command of James J. Pettigrew since Heth had been wounded. Behind Pettigrew, Lee would assemble another "division," composed of two of Dorsey Pender's brigades, entrusting them to Isaac Trimble, the Marylander who had come North with the army hoping that something would turn up. To Pickett's right, two brigades from Anderson's division would cover that flank. Altogether there would be eleven brigades, perhaps 12,500 men, to commit to the assault. Longstreet would exercise tactical control.

He didn't want it. Consciously or unconsciously, Longstreet attempted to delegate the responsibility onto Edward Porter Alexander, the lieutenant colonel who commanded the seventy-six guns of the I Corps artillery. "If the artillery does not have the effect to drive off the enemy," Longstreet wrote him, "I prefer you should not advise Pickett to make the charge." Deciding whether the army should or should not attack was hardly a decision for a lieutenant colonel to make. Aware of that, Alexander wrote back: "If, as I infer from your note, there is any alternative to this attack, it should be carefully considered before opening our fire for it will take all the artillery ammunition we have left to test this one thoroughly." Longstreet's reply offered little clarification and again seemed to leave the matter in Alexander's hands. The intention, he wrote, was to attack with the infantry only if the artillery either drove off the Yankees or so weakened them as to make success "certain." But how was Alexander to know if success was certain? Alexander answered Longstreet's curious message this way: "When our fire is best, I will advise General Pickett to advance." There the matter rested.

It was one o'clock in the afternoon. The fighting had long since died down on Culp's Hill, and the sun was at its peak. A nearby weather station recorded the temperature at eighty-nine degrees. Amid the silence of the battlefield, 2 guns near the Peach Orchard banged out a signal, and in just the time that it took to draw a breath, all 160 guns of the Confederate army fired a thunderous salvo that could be heard in Harrisburg, forty miles away. Lee was about to play his last card.

Edward Porter Alexander (above), only 28 years old at Gettysburg, commanded the artillery of the I Corps on July 3, in which capacity he was charged with the conduct of the preliminary artillery bombardment that preceded the grand assault by Lee's infantry.

CHAPTER TWELVE

The Grand Assault

(1 P.M.– 4 P.M., July 3, 1863)

The infantry assault that is popularly known as Pickett's Charge is enshrouded by a multilayered mythology that has a powerful history of its own. The very phrase conjures up notions of courage and heroism, of sacrifice and tragedy. Eventually, it became a metaphor for the war itself: a tableau to exhibit the gallantry of the South and the steadfastness of the North. It became a symbol for the wastefulness of war: all those young men cut down in a hopeless charge conducted on behalf of a doomed cause. Once the war was over, many Southerners looked back to the Battle of Gettysburg—and to Pickett's Charge in particular—as the moment the Confederacy died. Such a conclusion is valid more as metaphor than as history. The war did not end at Gettysburg; indeed, it had nearly two more years to run, during which the loss of life would exceed that of the first two years. Nevertheless, for Southerners in the postwar years, Pickett's Charge became a kind of psychic milestone. They recalled that after Gettysburg the war changed: troops fought more frequently from field entrenchments; more and more it became evident that bravery, leadership, and tactical daring could not overcome logistic realities or superior firepower. While the Army of Northern Virginia continued to fight valiantly, the buoyancy and jauntiness so evident during its march into Pennsylvania was replaced by a kind of defiant fatalism. Thus, in hindsight, Pickett's Charge seemed to subsequent generations to represent not only the moment when the Battle of Gettysburg was won and lost but the moment when the South itself—or at least the South as it conceived of itself—ceased to exist.

Eventually, it became difficult to separate history from metaphor. Pickett's Charge became part of the national culture, invoked by generations of Southerners to honor and validate all that was noble about what came to be known as the Lost Cause. In his 1948 novel *Intruder in the Dust,* the South's great literary spokesman, William Faulkner, suggested something of the role that this historic event played in molding the popular culture of the twentieth-century South:

> For every Southern boy fourteen years old, not once but whenever he wants
> it, there is the instant when it's still not yet two o'clock on that July afternoon
> in 1863, the brigades are in position behind the rail fence, the guns are laid and
> ready in the woods, and the furled flags are already loosened to break out and

Opposite: In *The Bloody Angle,* an undated painting by N. C. Wyeth, desperate hand-to-hand fighting takes place on July 3, when Armistead led his troops into the Federal lines in the assault that was later called the "high tide of the Confederacy." Armistead was killed during the attack and thirty-three regimental colors fell into Federal hands.

Pickett himself with his long oiled ringlets and his hat in one hand probably and his sword in the other looking up the hill waiting for Longstreet to give the word and it's all in the balance, it hasn't happened yet, it hasn't even begun yet, it not only hasn't begun yet but there is still time for it not to begin . . . yet it's going to begin, we all know that.

It began with the artillery bombardment, the purpose of which was to neutralize the Federal artillery on Cemetery Ridge so that the rebel infantry could cross the open ground between the armies without having to endure the fire of the Union big guns. The initial salvo of that barrage was spectacular as the Southern batteries fired in rapid sequence, like a giant fuse burning down, from the Peach Orchard all the way to the Lutheran Seminary. It may well have been the loudest man-made sound on the North American continent until the detonation of the first atomic bomb at Alamogordo, New Mexico. But despite that, the bombardment failed to achieve its objective, and, for that, much of the responsibility belongs to the Confederate high command.

Porter Alexander commanded the batteries assigned to Longstreet's corps (a total of some seventy-six guns), but the overall commander of the Confederate "long arm" was Brigadier General William Nelson Pendleton. Pendleton had graduated from West Point only a year after Lee, then he had left the army to become an Episcopalian priest. He entered Confederate service after Fort Sumter and rose to command the army's artillery branch despite several notorious disappointments in the field. His age and his spotty record of performance led the troops to pin on him the nickname Old Mother Pendleton. Ordinarily Lee would have quietly transferred him elsewhere (Lee's usual solution to inefficiency in high rank), but he forbore in this case largely because of Pendleton's friendship with Jefferson Davis. At Gettysburg, Lee's awareness of Pendleton's shortcomings was one reason he assigned such a prominent role to the competent Porter Alexander despite that officer's relatively junior rank. Nevertheless, Pendleton retained overall command of the army's artillery, and it fell to him to coordinate the fire of Alexander's I Corps guns with those assigned to the army's other two corps. Because Lee's forces were arrayed in a giant arc west and north of the Union position, Pendleton should have been able to coordinate the fire of the army's field guns to place the Federals on Cemetery Hill and Cemetery Ridge in a destructive cross fire. But due largely to Pendleton's lack of supervision, this was never done. Worse, some eighty-two Confederate guns never participated in the bombardment at all. The vacuum of leadership and coordination in the artillery branch might have been filled by Longstreet if he had chosen to take a more active role, but Old Pete's heart was not in it, and the opportunity was lost.

The Confederate artillery barrage was hampered not only by poor coordination but also by the limitations inherent in the science of long-range artillery fire as it was practiced during the Civil War. The artillery pieces of both sides used black powder, which generated great clouds of white smoke when fired, thereby dramatically obscuring the vision of the gunners after the first few salvos. In addition, the guns recoiled violently after each shot. Even if the first round was on target, the gunners could not be sure how to resight their guns for subsequent rounds amid the smoke and confusion of a massed barrage. Ten minutes into the cannonade, Southern gunners could do little better than guess where their shots might be falling.

Lee's plan for July 3 was to concentrate and coordinate his attack against a single vulnerable point in the Federal line. To allow his infantry to cross the milewide cleared ground between the armies, he ordered his artillery to suppress the Union field guns on Cemetery Ridge. Lee managed to mass more than 160 guns on the objective, but in contrast to the careful attention he paid to the coordination of the infantry, he did not personally oversee the arrangements for the artillery barrage, leaving that to his artillery chief, Brigadier General William Nelson Pendleton. Pendleton did not effectively coordinate the artillery of the several corps either. As a result, the bombardment not only was less efficient than Lee had hoped but it also used up a lot of ammunition that might have been used more effectively in other ways. Long after the battle was over, the I Corps artillery chief, Colonel Edward Porter Alexander, discussed in his memoirs the reasons that this represented a lost opportunity for the Southern long arm:

The great criticism which I have to make on the artillery operations of the day is upon the inaction of the artillery of Ewell's corps. Our position on the exterior line . . . placed us under many & serious disadvantages. But it gave us one single advantage. It enabled us to enfilade any of the enemy's positions, near the centre of their line, with our artillery fire. Now, a battery estab-

**Brigadier General
William Nelson Pendleton**

Colonel Edward Porter Alexander

lished where it can enfilade others need not trouble itself about aim. It has only to fire in the right direction & the shot finds something to hurt wherever it falls. No troops, infantry or artillery, can long submit to an enfilade fire. But, both the artillery & infantry lines which we were to attack could have been enfiladed from somewhere in our lines near Gettysburg. There is where the use of a chief of artillery for the army comes in. He visits & views the entire field & should recognize & know how to utilize his opportunities. The chief of each corps only sees his own ground. I never had an idea of the possibility of this being done at the time, for I had but the vaguest notion of where Ewell's corps was. And Ewell's chief doubtless had as vague ideas of my situation & necessities. But Gen. Lee's chief [Pendleton] should have known, & given every possible energy to improve the rare & great chance to the uttermost. Only one of Ewell's five fine battalions . . . participated in our bombardment at all. It only fired a few dozen shots, for, apparently, it could not see what it was doing. But every shot was smashing up something, &, had it been increased & kept up, it is hard to say what results might have resulted.

SOURCE: Edward Porter Alexander, *Fighting for the Confederacy: The Personal Recollections of General Edward Porter Alexander*, edited by Gary Gallagher (Chapel Hill: University of North Carolina Press, 1989), p. 251.

This photo taken after the battle shows some of the effects of the Confederate artillery bombardment on the Federal rear area. The house at left is the Leister House, which Meade used as his headquarters. The view is northward up Taneytown Road toward the southern (reverse) slope of Cemetery Hill. Because many Confederate shells passed over Cemetery Ridge, Meade and his staff found themselves under a virtual rain of shells, and they evacuated this building to find a safer vantage point. Note the damage to the rock wall along Taneytown Road and the dead horses in the road itself.

One of the most vivid firsthand accounts of the Federal defense of the the angle during the Confederate grand assault was composed by Lieutenant Frank A. Haskell, who was a staff officer to Brigadier General John Gibbon in Hancock's corps. Haskell was ideally placed to observe both the Confederate bombardment and the subsequent infantry assault. After the war, he penned this account of the beginning of the massive Confederate artillery barrage that began at about one o'clock on July 3:

We dozed in the heat and lolled upon the ground with half-open eyes. Our horses were hitched to the trees, munching some oats. A great lull rests upon all the field. Time was heavy; and for want of something better to do, I yawned and looked at my watch. It was five minutes before one o'clock. I returned my watch to its pocket and thought possibly that I might go to sleep and stretched myself upon the ground accordingly. "Ex uno disce omnes." My attitude and purpose were those of the general [Gibbon] and the rest of the staff.

What sound was that? There was no mistaking it! The distinct sharp sound of one of the enemy's guns, square over to the front,

Lieutenant Frank A. Haskell

caused us to open our eyes and turn them in that direction, when we saw directly above the crest the smoke of the bursting shell and heard its noise. In an instant, before a word was spoken, as if that was the signal gun for general work, loud, startling, booming, the report of gun after gun, in rapid succession, smote our ears, and their shells plunged down and exploded all around us. We sprang to our feet. In briefest time the whole Rebel line to the west was pouring out its thunder and iron upon our devoted crest. The wildest confusion for a few moments obtained among us. The shells came bursting all about. The servants ran terror-stricken for dear life and disappeared. The horses, hitched to the trees or held back by the slack hands of orderlies, neighed out in fright and broke away and plunged riderless through the fields . . .

The men of the infantry have seized their arms; and behind their works, behind every rock, in every ditch, wherever there is any shelter, they hug the ground, silent, quiet, unterrified, little harmed.

SOURCE: Frank A. Haskell, *The Battle of Gettysburg*, printed in *Gettysburg*, edited by Glenn LaFantasie (New York: Bantam Books, 1992), pp. 201–03.

Most of them fell long, passing over Cemetery Ridge and tearing up the rear area. Several score fell around Meade's headquarters where the horses of the headquarters' staff became early casualties. Meade and his entourage had to abandon the Leister House and migrate away from the line of fire, ending up on Powers Hill near Baltimore Pike. Other Confederate shells landed near the Federal guns, killing and wounding Union artillerists, exploding a few caissons, and damaging some of the guns. But overall, instead of a coordinated and carefully orchestrated pinpoint bombardment of the Federal lines, the Confederate gunners squandered much valuable and irreplaceable ammunition on an indiscriminate barrage that, despite its sound and fury, failed to achieve its objective.

On the Union side of the line, the sudden eruption of more than 160 guns stunned the Federal infantry along Cemetery Ridge. No one in either army had ever seen or heard such a massive artillery barrage, and even if its effectiveness was minimized by weak coordination, the very scale of it was psychologically paralyzing. The men of Hancock's II Corps, who occupied this section of the line, flung themselves to the ground and clung to it, scrambling to find cover as hundreds of shells flew overhead or exploded nearby. Union artillerists ran to their guns to respond.

Pendleton's counterpart in the Union army was Major General Henry Hunt, a career officer who had instructed Porter Alexander at West Point and who had become chief of artillery just prior to the Battle of Antietam. Hunt was a vocal advocate of centralized control of the army's big guns. He had frequently quarreled with Meade's predecessors about this issue, insisting that overall coordination was more efficient than parceling out batteries to the control of individual corps or division commanders. Though Meade never officially endowed Hunt with supervisory authority over all the army's artillery, Hunt acted as if he had. On July 3, Hunt's biggest concern was ammunition. On his own authority he had ordered the batteries to carry twenty extra rounds to the battlefield, but the gunners had shot away much of that the day before. Now Hunt issued orders for his men to respond to the rebel artillery slowly and deliberately and to save their ammunition for the expected infantry assault.

Such orders were hard to obey while being targeted by hundreds of howling shells screaming overhead or exploding nearby. Hancock, whose II Corps soldiers bore the brunt of the bombardment, worried about his troops' morale and ordered Captain John G. Hazard, who commanded the twenty-eight guns along Hancock's immediate front, to fire back as fast as his men could load. Hazard protested the order, citing Hunt's previous instructions, but Hancock insisted and Hazard perforce complied. Just south of Hancock's position, however, Hunt had placed Colonel Freeman McGilvery with forty-nine guns from the army's artillery reserve, and McGilvery obediently husbanded his ammunition, withholding his fire despite the rain of shells until Hancock ordered him, too, to start firing. Even then, however, he fired deliberately, and because most of his guns were not visible from Seminary Ridge they effectively constituted a "masked battery" that would be able to enfilade the Confederate infantry when it eventually attacked.

An hour passed. As far as Porter Alexander could tell, there was no evidence that his guns were silencing the Federal batteries, but he could see quite clearly that his own supply of ammunition was rapidly dwindling. One of Pendleton's several errors that afternoon had been his decision to move the army's ammunition reserves well to the rear. That protected them from a chance shot fired by Federal gunners, but it also required Southern gun crews to make lengthy round trips to obtain more ammunition as their supplies ran low. Even as Alexander studied what he could see of the enemy position on Cemetery Ridge, some of his own gun crews were standing idle having expended all their rounds. Alexander knew that he needed to save some of his ammunition to support the infantry attack.

Henry Hunt was having similar thoughts. He doubted that his counterbattery fire was doing much good, and decided that he should cease firing altogether. There was even a chance that such a move might delude the rebels into assuming that the Union guns had been silenced. They might launch their infantry attack prematurely. Hunt tried to find Meade to suggest this idea, but Meade was not at his headquarters, and Hunt decided to act on his own. Ironically, Meade was coming to the same conclusion independently. As Hunt rode to the front to order his gunners to cease firing, a courier reached him from Meade authorizing just such an order, though Hancock kept his own II Corps' guns firing until they literally ran out of ammunition.

Forty-four-year-old Henry Jackson Hunt commanded the Union artillery at Gettysburg. Hunt was a professional soldier who had co-authored the army manual for light-artillery tactics in the 1850s. At Gettysburg, Hancock urged him to respond to the thunderous Confederate bombardment, but Hunt knew that such long-range counterbattery fire was unlikely to be decisive, and he wisely husbanded his ammunition for the expected infantry assault.

Watching from across no-man's-land, Alexander had already decided that it was now or never. He sent Pickett a note stating that if he was ever going to go, he should do so now while there was still enough artillery ammunition left to support him. Then, through gaps in the billowing smoke, he saw that some of the Federal batteries were limbering up and moving away. Other batteries had stopped firing. Quickly he scribbled out a second note to Pickett: "For God's sake, come quick." Referring to the disappearance of some of the guns on Hancock's front, he added, "The eighteen guns have gone. Come quick or my ammunition will not let me support you properly."

In receipt of Alexander's first note, Pickett rode to where Longstreet stood watching the fall of shot on the far ridge line. Old Pete read the note but made no comment. To prompt him, Pickett asked, "General, shall I advance?" Longstreet

In this postwar painting by H. A. Ogden, a mounted George Pickett beseeches James Longstreet for permission to begin the attack. Ogden has made Longstreet's reluctance evident in this portrayal as the I Corps commander seems to be unable to look Pickett in the face. After the war, Longstreet wrote that when Pickett asked if he should advance, "I could only indicate it by an affirmative bow."

Charles Reed's sketch of the Confederate infantry lining up for the grand assault on the Federal center shows several important landmarks, including the Round Tops, at right, the Codori House, at left center, and the "little clump of trees" that the infantry was to use as a guide, which is indicated by a small arrow to the left of the Codori House.

found that he could not speak the words. After an awkward silence, Pickett seized the moment. He saluted and declared, "I shall lead my division forward, sir." Soon afterward, Pickett received Alexander's second note, and he hurried off to set the attack in motion.

As he did so, Longstreet rode over to talk with Alexander. That officer was fidgety with impatience. He told Longstreet that he was so low on ammunition he feared he would not be able to sustain the attack. This information jolted Longstreet out of his torpor. "Go and halt Pickett right where he is," Longstreet ordered, "and replenish your ammunition." That was not possible, Alexander told him. The reserve trains were nearly empty, and they were not within supporting distance anyway. It had to be now or not at all. With that, Longstreet relapsed once again into lassitude. "I don't want to make this attack," he told Alexander. "I believe it will fail—I do not see how it can succeed—I would not make it even now, but that Gen. Lee has ordered and expects it."

It was a pregnant moment. Alexander wrote later that he believed Longstreet was on the verge of recalling the attack, that a single pessimistic word from him about the likely outcome would have led Old Pete to call the whole thing off. But Alexander remained silent, and Longstreet engaged in a lonely internal struggle as his tactical instinct warred with his sense of duty. Duty won. Out of the tree line behind him, Pickett's men moved into the open and deployed, and the issue became moot. All along Seminary Ridge, butternut-clad veterans of the Army of Northern Virginia moved forward into the open fields behind the artillery. Garnett's and Kemper's brigades of Pickett's division formed up on the right; to their left, the four brigades of Heth's division, now commanded by Pettigrew, came into line. From end to end, these six brigades formed a front nearly a mile wide though there was a quarter-mile gap between the two divisions. Three more brigades deployed behind these six in a second line, and two more brigades occupied their right flank. All along the line, the color bearers shook the folds out of the flags. It was just past three o'clock.

Few men did more to earn a monument at Gettysburg than Winfield Scott Hancock (left) who played a critical role on each of the three days of the battle. On July 1 he shored up the defense of Cemetery Hill; on July 2 he sent the reinforcements that bolstered Sickles's collapsing line; and on July 3 it was Hancock's II Corps that defended the center of the Union line on Cemetery Ridge.

Only a week before the Battle at Gettysburg, Alexander Webb (below) considered resigning from the army. Despite an outstanding combat record, others less qualified had been promoted over him. A former mathematics instructor at West Point, he noted bitterly that even some of his former students now outranked him. But his promotion to brigadier general came through at last on June 28, and five days later he stood at the epicenter of the war commanding a brigade at the angle directly in front of the clump of trees.

On the Federal side of the field, the cessation of the artillery fire was a relief. As the smoke settled slowly over the open fields between the armies, men who had clutched the ground with clawed fingers raised their heads and peered across no-man's-land, their ears still ringing from the sustained fire of more than three hundred field guns. What they saw gave them little cheer. As they shielded their eyes from the bright sun that had dropped well past its zenith, they could see the rebel infantry deploying for an assault, the flags of a score of regiments dotting the front line. More men formed a second line behind them.

Winfield Scott Hancock watched the panorama fully aware of what was coming. Hancock had already played a crucial role in the battle. He had selected the ground on the first day, and he had been largely responsible for patching up the Federal left on the second day. Now, apparently, it was his corps that was to be the target of the Confederate grand assault. As he gazed across the field, he estimated the attacking force to consist of at least 15,000 men, and he knew that his own force did not exceed 6,000. Even as he made these calculations, he could not help but admire the scene before him. "Their lines were formed with precision and steadiness," he wrote later in his official report, "that exhorted the admiration of the witnesses of that memorable scene."

Hancock had come to Gettysburg with a corps that numbered in excess of 12,000, but he had sent one of his three divisions—John Caldwell's—to fight in the Wheat Field the day before, and that night he had sent most of John Carroll's brigade to succor Cemetery Hill. Now he had but five brigades to man his front: three under John Gibbon and two under Alexander Hays. In Gibbon's small division, the Pennsylvania brigade of Alexander Webb held that portion of the line just in front of the little clump of trees that Lee had pointed out to Longstreet that morning. Webb had succeeded to command of the brigade only a week before—most of his own men did not know him by sight. Now his three regiments of Pennsylvanians stood literally at ground zero in a thin line that ran from in front of the clump of trees northward to where the low stone wall marking their front took a ninety-degree turn to the east, a site that has ever since been known as "the Angle."

Webb's men had some artillery support. As Porter Alexander had observed just before writing Pickett to "come quick," some of the Union gun crews here had limbered up and left: Brown's battery was wrecked, and Arnold's had fired all its ammunition. But three of Lieutenant Alonzo H. Cushing's six guns just north of the clump of trees were still working, and six more under Captain Andrew Cowan came up at the gallop after the artillery fire had ceased and set up south of the trees. Webb knew the artillery would be critical, and he assigned fifty of his infantrymen to assist the gunners. Cowan opened with shell and shrapnel, but as the ranged shortened, he ordered his men to load with canister.

Just north of Webb's position, from the Angle up to the Bryan Farm near Ziegler's Grove, were the two brigades of Alexander Hays's division, some 2,500 men, who would bear the brunt of Pettigrew's attack. Hays was a large, bluff, square-faced man whose visage bore the usual beard and mustache of the era. A classmate of Hancock's at West Point, he had left the army after the Mexican War to pursue business interests, but had reentered after Fort Sumter, assuming command of a regiment. Wounded at Second Manassas, Hays had been promoted to brigadier general and assigned a post in the Washington defenses during his recovery. Like Webb, he had been elevated to the command he held at Gettysburg only days before the battle, but his behavior on July 3 suggested that he was the right man at the right place. Instead of allowing his men merely to hug the ground and cover their ears during the bombardment, he rode up and down the line assigning various individuals the job of rounding up discarded muskets. He ordered them to clean and load the muskets and lay them aside to be ready for the infantry assault. When the bombardment lifted, he gathered up those men who had taken refuge in Ziegler's Grove and placed them into line. Then, instead of allowing his men to gape at the milewide front of bayonets advancing

Alexander Hays commanded the Federal division posted just north of the Angle near the center of the Union line. The men of that command had once been stigmatized for their part in the surrender of Harpers Ferry during the Antietam campaign, but at Gettysburg they behaved as heroes, defending the low stone wall with ferocity and capturing three battle flags. During the Confederate bombardment, Hays maintained a stoic calm, riding up and down the line to reassure his men.

toward them, he supervised them in the manual of arms, which served both to quiet their nerves and to occupy their minds.

Hays benefitted from one other circumstance that was not of his doing. When Carroll's brigade had marched to Cemetery Hill the previous evening, its commander had left the 8th Ohio regiment behind. That unit occupied a position on Hays's right some two hundred yards in front of the main Union line, and Carroll had told its commanding officer, Colonel Franklin Sawyer, to hold the position "at all hazards." The 8th Ohio had come to Gettysburg with a complement of more than 300, but losses the day before had left it with barely half that many. All that night, all through the next morning, and throughout the afternoon bombardment, Sawyer's 160 or so men held their advanced position and were all but forgotten. But as time would prove, they, too, were in the right place at the right time.

This scene, part of the giant cyclorama canvas by Paul Philippoteaux (see also pp. 228–31), depicts Federal gunners on Cemetery Ridge firing on the advancing Confederate infantry, savaging their ranks with explosive shell and (at closer range) shrapnel and canister.

Smoke from a thousand muskets enshrouds Cemetery Ridge in the distance as Confederate forces prepare to cross the killing ground in this Edwin Forbes painting. The troops in the foreground are probably part of Isaac Trimble's division. The McMillan House is at left, and the clump of trees is just visible on the ridgeline through the smoke at right.

To those watching, the advance of the rebel infantry seemed inexorable. Hays thought "their march was as steady as if impelled by machinery." To another Union officer it seemed like "an overwhelming, resistless tide of an ocean of armed men sweeping upon us!"

Despite such impressions, Lee's plan was already beginning to unravel. He had based it on the assumption that his artillery could neutralize the Federal gunners and allow his infantry to cross the open ground more or less unscathed. But although some Union guns had been disabled and others had been hauled away, nineteen Union guns on Cemetery Hill, Rittenhouse's battery on Little Round Top, and McGilvery's forty-nine guns south of the clump of trees remained in position and undamaged. They were silent as the rebel infantry began its advance, but at 1,200 yards they opened fire with a fury. For the advancing foot soldiers this was a catastrophe. Because the Confederate officers did not want to exhaust their men en route, they held them to a steady, disciplined walk. But at a regulation walk (roughly 100 yards per minute), it took the attackers a seeming eternity to cross that deadly ground, and for every second of it, they were under constant and accurate fire from the Union big guns. Union gunners from Cemetery Hill fired into Pettigrew's left flank, while McGilvery's guns and those on the Round Tops fired into Pickett's right. With nearly every shot, men fell dead or wounded, the effectiveness of the Union "long arm" evident in the hundreds of bodies, some writhing in pain, some ominously still, that spotted the ground behind the advancing line. But the men in gray and butternut closed up, filling the holes, and the advance did not slow or falter. Hunt himself grudgingly acknowledged that "the enemy advanced magnificently, unshaken by the shot and shell which tore through his ranks."

Despite the almost superhuman courage of the men who bore that fire and pressed forward with barely a backward glance at their fallen comrades, the advancing formation began to change shape from a line into a crescent as the flanks lagged behind the center. On the left flank, the brigades of Joe Davis and J. M. Brockenbrough in Pettigrew's division got a late start and fell behind almost at once. The men of Brockenbrough's small Virginia brigade (commanded this day by Colonel Robert Mayo) came under particularly heavy artillery fire from Cemetery Hill, and just as they began to falter they encountered Sawyer's 8th Ohio regiment, left out in front of the main line by Carroll the night before. Sawyer's men stood their ground and poured a disciplined volley into the Virginians' weakened ranks, a volley that stopped them cold. Mayo's men turned and headed for the rear. Their absence made Joe Davis's Mississippi brigade the new Confederate left. Davis's men had been roughly handled in the railroad cut on the first day of the fight, and the unit had lost nearly all its experienced field-grade officers. Now, as they pushed ahead, their left was exposed by the collapse of Mayo's brigade, and as they passed across the front of the 8th Ohio, Sawyer's men wheeled left and fired a volley into their exposed flank. The Mississippians continued forward, but much of their impetus was gone.

On the Confederate right, the brigades of Wilcox and Perry (under David Lang) did not advance at all. They were under orders to support Alexander's artillery and therefore didn't move forward until much later. The effect of this, combined with Pettigrew's losses on the left, was that the Confederate grand assault was reduced by at least one-fourth before the serious fighting even began.

Worse, the attackers had to do without any substantial artillery support. Lee had intended for the Confederate field guns to go forward with the infantry, and Porter Alexander was eager to comply. He had kept back a dozen short-range guns just for

Opposite: The grand Confederate assault known as Pickett's Charge was preceded by a gigantic artillery bombardment that began at 1 P.M. At 3 P.M. the infantry assault began with some 12,500 men aiming for the landmark little clump of trees near the center of the Union line.

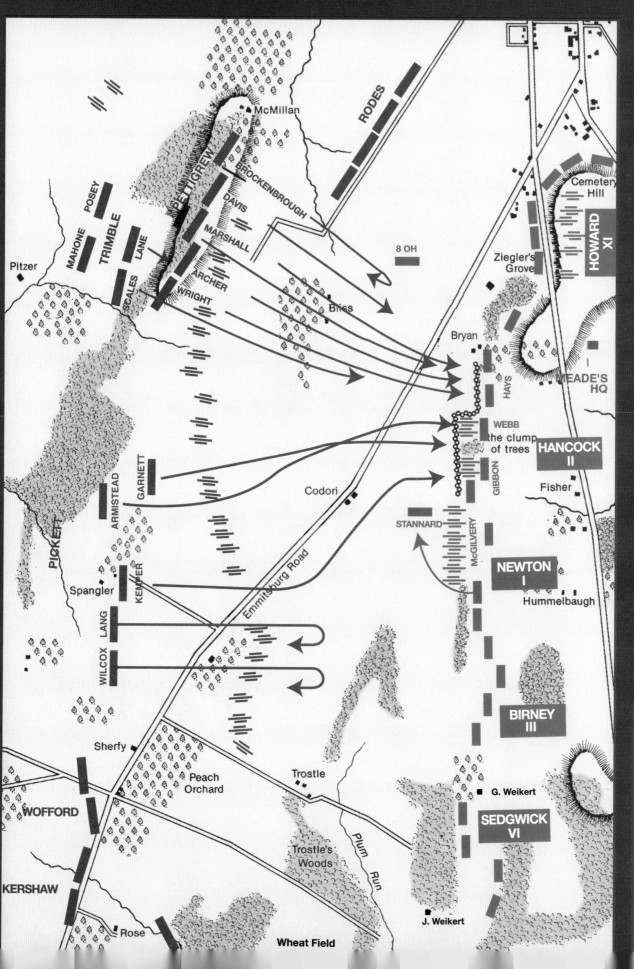

McMillan

RODES

PETTIGREW

BROCKENBROUGH

DAVIS

MARSHALL

MAHONE

POSEY

TRIMBLE

LANE

SCALES

ARCHER

WRIGHT

Pitzer

8 OH

Bliss

Ziegler's Grove

Cemetery Hill

HOWARD XI

Bryan

HAYS

MEADE'S HQ

WEBB

the clump of trees

HANCOCK II

GARNETT

Codori

GIBBON

Fisher

ARMISTEAD

STANNARD

McGILVERY

PICKETT

KEMPER

NEWTON I

Spangler

Hummelbaugh

LANG

WILCOX

Emmitsburg Road

Sherfy

BIRNEY III

Trostle

Peach Orchard

G. Weikert

SEDGWICK VI

WOFFORD

Trostle's Woods

Plum Run

KERSHAW

J. Weikert

Rose

Wheat Field

Union troop movements

Confederate troop movements

Union Corps

Confederate Corps

infantry units

location of house

site of battle or skirmish

artillery positions

1 inch = 440 yards

The scene at left and on the following spread are details of Paul Philippoteaux's copy of the famous cyclorama depicting the climactic moment of the Battle of Gettysburg from a vantage point just behind the Federal lines. In 1882, Philippoteaux completed a gigantic painting, 400 feet long and 50 feet high. A copy, done in 1884, was first exhibited in Boston but then came to Gettysburg in 1913 for the fiftieth anniversary. It remains there today at Gettysburg National Military Park. This second version is approximately 370 feet long and 26 feet high. In the late nineteenth century, cycloramas were a popular way to bring history to the public. The idea was to paint an image of a battlefield as if the viewer were in the midst of the action.

Winfield Scott Hancock (mounted on the black horse crossing the road) directs reinforcements toward the critical point in the Federal line just to the right of the clump of trees. Alexander Webb (on the white horse) encourages his brigade, leading the 72nd Pennsylvania to counterattack the Confederate breakthrough.

this purpose and hoped to send as many as eighty guns forward with the infantry. But when he called for them, the twelve guns he had kept in reserve were gone, shuttled by Pendleton to some other mission, and when Alexander ordered every gun crew with fifteen or more rounds of ammunition to go forward with the infantry, the total came to only eighteen pieces. Though those eighteen guns did go forward, McGilvery's artillery made short work of them. Whatever was to be accomplished in the attack would have to be achieved by the infantry.

In spite of all this, the Confederate infantry marched inexorably toward the distant Federal line, their cadence steady and unhurried. Hundreds of dead and

wounded carpeted the ground behind them. Here and there skulkers found reasons to fall out of line: some stopped to assist a fallen comrade; others simply fell to the ground and kept their heads down; a few, seized by panic, made for the rear. But most marched onward, their muskets at right-shoulder shift, their discipline a marvel to all who witnessed it. The men of Pickett's division veered sharply to the left to close the gap between them and Pettigrew's division. Halfway across, in the modest protection of a slight dip in the ground, they stopped briefly to dress ranks, then they headed directly for that landmark clump of trees, where Webb's Pennsylvanians lay waiting.

Near Emmitsburg Road, the Confederate skirmishers encountered a Union skir-

Repulse of Longstreet's Assault at the Battle of Gettysburg, **a rather fanciful painting by James Walker, depicts a sea of soldiers stretching from the Round Tops, at left, to Ziegler's Grove, at right. In the center foreground, a group of men tend to the mortally wounded Lewis Armistead, who hands his gold watch to a Federal soldier to give to his old friend Hancock.**

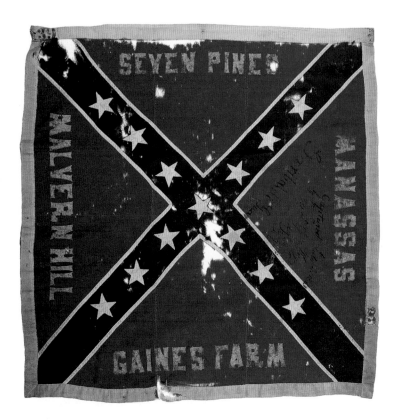

Confederate attackers carried these battle flags of the 11th Mississippi (above left) and the 28th North Carolina (above right) up the slope of Cemetery Ridge, where they were seized by the Federal defenders of Alexander Hays's division just north of the Angle. Flags had an almost religious meaning for the soldiers of both sides, and their loss was commonly held to be a matter of shame. On the day of Pickett's Charge, the attackers lost a total of thirty-three regimental flags.

mish line and exchanged shots with it until the main body came up and the Federal skirmishers quickly ran back to their main line to await the onslaught. At the road itself, the Confederates stopped to tear down the post-and-rail fence that was blocking their way. Their parade-ground alignment dissolved as units crowded into one another and men bunched together to push through the gaps in the fence. By now their numbers were much reduced. Of the 12,500 that originally mustered for the assault, perhaps only about half that number actually made it across Emmitsburg Road to ascend Cemetery Ridge. Still, compressed into that narrow front, they remained a potent force. Perhaps here, at last, was the assault in depth that had been missing earlier. To the watching Federals, the scene was dreadful to behold. One Yankee recalled that "the enemy was moving toward us like an avalanche."

On the left, Pettigrew's men, with Trimble's two brigades in close support, pressed forward against Hays's division. Pettigrew's horse was shot from under him, but he scrambled to his feet and went forward on foot. Most of the Union infantry held their fire until the attackers were within a hundred yards, then they stood and fired a volley at close range that all but swept the field. One Union regiment, the 12th New Jersey, was armed with old .69-caliber smoothbore muskets and had loaded them with buckshot, which made them appallingly effective at close range. On the initiative of two junior officers—both of them captains—most of two New York regiments swung out of line north of Ziegler's Grove into the open fields on Pettigrew's flank, from which position they fired into the mass of Confederates who were battling the rest of Hays's men behind the low stone wall that marked their front. The Confederates tried to struggle forward; a few got to within mere feet of that wall, but despite a number of postwar claims, none got over it. The fighting was hand to hand in a few places, especially when the defenders attempted to wrest regimental flags from the Confederate color-bearers.

Trimble's two brigades came up in support behind Pettigrew, but they were ravaged by the flanking fire of the three Union regiments to their left, and only a few of them got closer than two hundred yards. After a fierce and brutal struggle at the wall, Pettigrew's men simply lacked the numbers or the momentum to continue the assault. They attempted to withdraw or waved scraps of white paper in gesture of surrender. Trimble, himself wounded in the leg, decided that it would be "a useless sacrifice of life" to continue the fight any longer and did not protest when his men began to fall back. "No," he told an aide who was attempting to rally the men. "Let them go."

At virtually the same time that Pettigrew's men assailed Hays's division, the men of Pickett's three brigades slammed into the Federals near the clump of trees. Pickett stopped at the Codori House alongside Emmitsburg Road and watched as his men threw down the post-and-rail fence along the road and scrambled up the gentle slope of Cemetery Ridge toward Webb's Pennsylvanians. They broke into a stumbling run, the rebel yell at last bursting from their throats. Behind the low stone wall, Alonzo Cushing fired off his last round of canister. "I'll give them one more round, Webb," he called out as he pulled the lanyard. Then he fell dead beside his guns with a bullet through his head.

As they charged toward the wall, a few of Pickett's men noted "a long dark mass, dressed in blue" to their right. It was the Vermont brigade of Brigadier General George

In this drawing, George J. Stannard's brigade of Vermont troops swings out of line from Cemetery Ridge south of the clump of trees to deliver an enfilading fire into the right flank of Pickett's division just as the charge was losing its momentum. This unexpected fire, along with the counterattack by regiments of John Gibbon's division on the ridge itself, compelled the Confederates to withdraw as best they could back across the open fields to Seminary Ridge.

A detail from a lithograph of Thure de Thulstrup's painting *Hancock at Gettysburg* depicts General Hancock leading the defense of Cemetery Ridge during Pickett's Charge.

at wave rushing up a sloping beach, the size
of Pickett's Charge diminished as it neared the
rees. By the time it lapped up against the low
marking the Union position, it simply lacked
s to break through. The spot where Brigadier
ewis Armistead fell while charging the guns of
battery has traditionally been considered the
mark of Confederate fortunes at Gettysburg.
, however, a dispute arose among Confederate
bout what constituted the true high-water mark
ault. To North Carolinians in particular, it was
ugh that the assault came to be known as Pick-
ge even though Pickett's division of Virginians
only about a third of the attacking troops. The
he only breakthrough was achieved by a hand-
under Armistead's command seemed to rein-
rimacy of Virginia's role in the charge.
Carolinians acknowledged that the hundred or
o followed Armistead over the low stone wall
ed, the only Confederates to break through the
, but they noted that this portion of the line
yards in advance of the line defended by
gade on their right. It is altogether likely, they
that some of Pettigrew's men ascended farther
pe of Cemetery Ridge, thus achieving a true
mark beyond the point where Armistead fell,
y never breached the wall itself.
North Carolinians even claimed to have crossed
all. Lieutenant Colonel William Morris of the

37th North Carolina in Lane's brigade (part of Tri
command) later insisted that "we drove the enem
front of us from his position in the [Emmitsburg]
then *from behind the stone fence* and held this po
least half an hour." Such claims are unreliable, ho
since virtually every contemporary source from t
Union side insists that no Confederate soldier on
part of the field got closer than a dozen yards to
stone wall.

True as that may be, a dozen yards from the st
would still place those troops farther up the slope
Armistead got. It is in fact likely that some of the
Pettigrew's division, specifically those in Fry's bri
Alabama and Tennessee troops, or in J. K. Marsha
North Carolina brigade (formerly Pettigrew's), asc
further up the slope of Cemetery Ridge than did A
tead's Virginians. Today a small pink-granite monu
just north of the Angle marks the spot where som
ars believe soldiers from the 26th North Carolina
the true high-water mark of Pickett's Charge.

In terms of calculating the decisive moment o
charge, however, it is important to consider that
tead's fall marked the collapse of Confederate mo
tum. Given that, it remains appropriate to consid
older stone marker inside the Angle at Cushing's
the high-water mark. There is, however, one final
circumstance of this debate. Though he led a brig
Virginians at Gettysburg, Armistead was born in
Bern, North Carolina.

lina Monument

Stannard that, like the New Yorkers on Pettigrew's front, wheeled forward out of line to take the attackers in a cross fire. In effect, the Confederates had entered a three-sided box where enemy bullets came not only from their front but also from both flanks. Officers became particular targets. James Kemper, the full-bearded 40-year-old who had been speaker of the Virginia House of Delegates, fell wounded; Richard Garnett, who had commanded the Stonewall Brigade in the Valley, was shot dead, his riderless black horse galloping back toward Seminary Ridge, eyes white and nostrils flaring. Of all the generals in the assaulting force, only Lewis Armistead survived long enough to reach the low stone wall in front of Webb's Pennsylvanians.

Armistead had spent two years at West Point, but he had never graduated (the story in the army was that he had been dismissed for fighting after he broke a dinner plate over Jubal Early's head). Nevertheless, he had served in the prewar army and had twice been brevetted for gallantry during the Mexican War. In the years that followed, he had become a particular friend of Winfield Scott Hancock's, and in the midst of the secession crisis, the two men had pledged to one another that whatever else might happen, at least they would never be personal enemies. Now Armistead was the only surviving brigadier in Pickett's division, and it was he who led the final Confederate assault against Hancock's corps. If he felt the irony of this circumstance, it did not affect his resolve. At the stone wall, the Confederates stopped, some knelt, and opened fire on the defenders. Armistead did not want to lose what little momentum remained. Removing his hat and placing it on his sword point as a guide to his command, he called out, "Come on boys! Give them the cold steel. Who will follow me?"

Too few. Perhaps a hundred men, maybe twice that, accompanied Armistead over the wall. Nevertheless, for one brief moment, a moment often called the high-water mark of the Confederacy, they burst through the Federal line forcing elements of the 71st Pennsylvania to give way before the fury of their assault. In front of Armistead were the now silent guns of Cushing's battery. He raced toward them, eager to claim them as a prize, when he suddenly lurched forward, dropping his hat and sword, and clutching at his stomach. He staggered forward two or three more steps, reaching out with his hand as if trying with his last desperate effort to touch the Union cannon before he fell to the ground. Today a small stone scroll, weathered by the years, marks the spot where he fell, a spot long considered the apogee of what history has ever since labeled Pickett's Charge.

The few Confederates who had accompanied Armistead over the wall were leaderless now, surrounded and outnumbered. Webb rallied the men of the 71st Pennsylvania and brought them back into the fight alongside the 69th which had refused its

right flank and held its position. At about the same time, Norman Hall's entire brigade of five regiments—the rest of Gibbon's command—came charging into the melee from the south. It was too much. A few Confederates tried to escape; others threw down their arms and raised their hands. All across the Federal front, the Confederates fell back or surrendered. Cheers began to rise from the throats of the defenders. Hays grabbed a captured rebel flag and rode up and down the line with it, provoking more cheers from the parched throats of the Union soldiers.

According to tradition, Armistead's last words were for Hancock. William Mitchell of Hancock's staff later claimed that Armistead asked him to "tell General Hancock . . . I am sorry." By then, Armistead would have learned that Hancock, too, had fallen in the fight, struck in the groin by a minié ball even as he watched Armistead's attack from atop the ridge. Lowered gently from his horse, Hancock saw the blood pumping from his wound as several officers tended to him. "Don't let me bleed to death," he muttered through his teeth, and the officers fashioned a tourniquet out of his handkerchief. Hancock would survive; Armistead died two days later in a Federal hospital.

There was one more tragic postscript. Only now, with the outcome no longer in any doubt, did the brigades of Wilcox and Lang make a tardy and futile charge across that bloody ground. Their assault achieved nothing except to add to the butcher's bill. "My men acted with their usual gallantry," a bitter Wilcox wrote later, "though they accomplished but little."

The illustration above depicts Lee riding out to greet his soldiers returning from the fight after the repulse of the grand assault. He accepted full responsibility for the reverse and urged them to take shelter in the tree line to prepare for a possible counterattack. "All good men must rally," he told them. "We want all good and true men just now." But his veneer of confidence concealed a disappointment. The next day he told Longstreet: "It's all my fault. I thought my men were invincible."

Observing the repulse of his command from the vicinity of the Codori House, a disconsolate George Pickett turned his horse back toward Seminary Ridge. The fields were full of retreating Confederate soldiers walking along singly or in groups, the healthy aiding the wounded, a few using their muskets for crutches. Lee rode out to meet them, offering words of encouragement. "All will come right in the end," he assured them. When he saw Pickett, he ordered him to place his division behind the ridge and prepare to receive a counterattack should one be forthcoming. Pickett's reply was terse, but all too accurate: "General Lee, I have no division now."

Opposite: Painter H. A. Ogden captured the moment when Meade sees the retreat of the Confederate infantry back across the open fields in front of Cemetery Ridge. "Have they turned?" he asked upon riding to the front. "They are just turning," an aide replied. Another officer, taking in the panorama of victory, suggested to Meade that he was in great danger of becoming the next president of the United States.

CHAPTER THIRTEEN

The Cavalry

(1 P.M. – 6 P.M., July 3, 1863)

Even as the men of Pickett's and Pettigrew's divisions assailed the stone wall in front of Hancock's corps, another engagement—this one involving cavalry—took place three miles to the east, behind the Federal center, where Jeb Stuart struck at the enemy rear. Ever since the fight on McPherson's Ridge that had initiated the battle two days before, the cavalry forces on both sides had been largely inert. But with Stuart's arrival late on the afternoon of July 2, Lee planned to include his horse soldiers in his overall design for the next day by sending them around the army's left flank to threaten the Federal rear even as Longstreet's infantry broke through the center. Not only would this divert the attention of the Union high command, but (assuming the infantry charge was successful) Stuart's men could then harass the Federal army as it retreated. Thus it was that while Pickett, Pettigrew, and Trimble arrayed their forces for the grand assault, four brigades of Confederate cavalry trotted eastward out of Gettysburg heading for the Federal rear.

For Jeb Stuart, July 3 offered a chance for atonement. It is not difficult to imagine that after his chastisement by Lee, Stuart was filled with a determination to make up for his lapses in the campaign so far. Returning to his command that evening, Stuart's first order was for his troopers to remain in the saddle all night, thus to be ready for any opportunity that might arise. Gently, his subordinate officers suggested to him that while Stuart might be insensible of the physical limits of mere mortals, his troopers were not. They needed food and rest; they needed sleep. Reluctantly acknowledging this reality, Stuart changed his orders and allowed his men to slip from horseback, unsaddle their weary horses, and stretch out on the ground, most of them dropping off instantly to sleep. With first light, however, Stuart was eager to be on the move again.

The precise role that Lee envisioned for his cavalry has never been determined; he barely mentioned the cavalry in his subsequent reports to Richmond. Very likely, his orders to Stuart were sufficiently discretionary as to leave open a variety of possibilities. Stuart later claimed that his role was merely to guard the army's left flank and look for an opportunity to strike a blow. Presumably, if the infantry attack succeeded, he was to fall on the retreating Federals and cut them up as they fled, thus

Opposite: This 1865 painting titled *The Fight for the Standard* suggests the kind of close-quarters fury that characterized the cavalry action east of Gettysburg on July 3. Even as Armistead led his small cadre of survivors over the low stone wall on Cemetery Ridge, Confederate and Union cavalry engaged in an equally furious action, if somewhat smaller in scale, a few miles to the east.

turning a victory into a rout. But it is almost certain that Stuart had more than this in mind. Very likely, he envisioned some kind of massed cavalry attack against Meade's rear that would erase the stigma of his tardy arrival.

At midmorning on July 3, therefore, as the fighting on Culp's Hill was dying down and several hours still before the artillery barrage that preceded the infantry assault on Cemetery Ridge, Stuart led four brigades of cavalry out the York Road heading east. Three of those brigades had accompanied him on his famous ride around the Federal army: those of Wade Hampton, John Chambliss, and Fitzhugh Lee, the commanding general's nephew. In addition, Stuart also had with him the brigade of Albert Gallatin Jenkins that had screened Ewell's advance into Pennsylvania, though that brigade was now under the command of its senior colonel, since Jenkins, too, was among the wounded. In those four brigades, Stuart had a total of perhaps five thousand men. It was a substantial force, and it made a great show riding in a column of fours out the York Road, but it was less imposing than the numbers suggested. First of all, the men and the horses were tired. A night's rest had done wonders for the veterans of the lengthy and circuitous ride to Gettysburg, but the horses remained worn down, if not worn out. Ammunition was another problem. The men of Jenkins's brigade had only about ten rounds per man for their Enfield muskets, not enough for a serious fight. Nevertheless, Stuart still hoped to achieve something decisive.

Five thousand cavalry stirred up a substantial cloud of dust, and Stuart's move could hardly be kept a secret. Alert Federal pickets on Cemetery Hill noted the activity and forwarded the information to XI Corps headquarters. From there the news was passed to the Federal cavalry commander on the scene, David McMurtrie Gregg,

Stuart's lieutenant Wade Hampton (below left) assumed command of one of Stuart's cavalry brigades in the reorganization after Chancellorsville. Six feet tall and a natural horseman, the aristocratic Hampton soon emerged as one of Stuart's favorite subordinates. In the cavalry battle east of Gettysburg, he was wounded three times—two of them saber slashes to the head. Fitzhugh Lee (below right) was Robert E. Lee's nephew and another of Stuart's favorites. Lee had commanded the 1st Virginia cavalry early in the war and had participated in most of Stuart's campaigns since. Both men survived the fighting at Gettysburg, and after Stuart was mortally wounded at the Battle of Yellow Tavern almost a year later, Hampton and Fitz Lee shared command of the Confederate cavalry.

Despite his manifest talents, Jeb Stuart (left) was not at his best during the Gettysburg campaign. Aware of his errors in judgment during the advance into Pennsylvania and hurt by Robert E. Lee's less-than-enthusiastic welcome when he finally arrived at Gettysburg, he no doubt hoped to erase the memory of those errors by achieving a grand success against the Federal rear on July 3. Though afterward he claimed that his only objective was to guard the left flank of the army, almost certainly his real purpose was to strike at the enemy rear in conjunction with the infantry charge against its front. Shown here is Stuart's cavalry pistol (above), his gauntlets (below left), and his famous plumed hat (below right).

who commanded the two brigades that made up the 2nd division of Federal cavalry. Because Stuart's plan relied heavily on catching his Federal counterparts by surprise, his chances of success were significantly reduced almost from the beginning.

Three miles east of Gettysburg, Stuart turned his column off to the right onto a farm road that led to a tree-covered piece of high ground called Cress Ridge, named for a local farmer. From its summit, Stuart surveyed the terrain in front of him. The ground fell away gradually down to the Hanover Road—one of the ten roads that ran into the town square at Gettysburg like the spokes of a wheel. He could see Federal cavalry pickets on the road, and a little further south, where Hanover Road intersected Low Dutch Road, he saw a larger mass of Yankee cavalry—Gregg's force, though Stuart did not yet know it. Perhaps in an effort to find out what other enemy forces were in the vicinity, Stuart ordered his horse artillery to unlimber a single gun atop the ridge and fire off a number of random shots in various directions. It is possible that this ploy was designed to attract Federal attention and encourage the Union cavalry to ride out toward Cress Ridge in an effort to capture the gun. Stuart could then sweep down off the ridge with his three brigades and ambush the Federals.

That single piece of artillery, however, provoked no reaction from the Yankees along Hanover Road, and at one o'clock, when the thunderous crash of the Confederate artillery bombardment against Meade's center reached his ears, Stuart tried another gambit. He instructed his three veteran brigades to remain concealed in the trees atop the ridge and sent most of Jenkins's men forward—on foot—to

David McMurtrie Gregg was the man on the spot when he saw Stuart's troopers moving toward him from Cress Ridge. Under orders to send half his force elsewhere, he assumed the responsibility to countermand those orders and keep his force at full strength. Soon afterward, the Confederate cavalry charged his position, and he ordered a countercharge.

occupy a fence line at the foot of the ridge that bordered the property of a local farmer named Rummel.

Gregg saw this force moving down off the ridge and decided to respond. He sent elements of three regiments, armed with carbines, forward on foot to contest possession of the Rummel Farm. Stuart fed in more troops from his other units, the horse artillery of both sides joined in, and the skirmishing around the Rummel Farm welled up into a brisk little fight. At that moment, just as things were getting serious, Gregg was confronted with a crisis in command. One of the two brigades he had with him at the crossroads was George Armstrong Custer's Michigan brigade of Judson Kilpatrick's division, on loan to him for temporary service. At just this moment, Gregg received an order from Pleasonton to send Custer's brigade south to rejoin Kilpatrick. Custer was only 23 years old at Gettysburg—another member of the West Point Class of 1861—and he had been elevated from captain to brigadier general only days before. As he received his new orders, Custer remarked that he was sorry to leave, for it looked like Gregg had a fight on his hands. Gregg agreed and asked Custer if he was willing to postpone obeying his orders long enough to deal with this imminent threat. "If you give me the order," Custer replied, "I will be only too happy to stay." Gregg then took it upon himself to instruct Custer to ignore the orders from Pleasonton and remain. It was a courageous, and possibly decisive, move.

While this conversation was taking place, the skirmish at the Rummel Farm had turned into a full-fledged battle. Jenkins's men soon fired off all their ammunition and had to fall back, which left the rest of the Confederate skirmishers to face long odds. Having lost the element of surprise when Hampton's and Lee's brigades came

"A CRASH, LIKE THE FALLING OF TIMBER"

Captain William E. Miller of the Pennsylvania 3rd cavalry was a participant in the cavalry action east of Gettysburg on the afternoon of July 3. His firsthand account, written for *Century* magazine in the 1880s, is one of the most vivid eyewitness descriptions of this engagement. Here he describes Stuart's charge off Cress Ridge and the countercharge by Custer's Wolverines:

About half a mile distant . . . there appeared moving toward us a large mass of cavalry, which proved to be the remaining portions of Hampton's and Fitzhugh Lee's brigades. They were formed in close column of squadrons and directed their course toward the Spangler House. A grander spectacle than their advance has rarely been beheld. They marched with well-aligned fronts and steady reins. Their polished saber-blades dazzled in the sun. All eyes turned upon them. . . . Shell and shrapnel met the advancing Confederates and tore through their ranks. Closing the gaps as though nothing had happened, on they came. As *they drew nearer, canister was substituted by our artillerymen for shell, and horse after horse staggered and fell. Still they came on. Our mounted skirmishers rallied and fell into line; the dismounted men fell back, and a few of them reached their horses. The 1st Michigan, drawn up in close column of squadrons near Pennington's battery, was ordered by Gregg to charge. Custer, who was near, placed himself at its head, and off they dashed. As the two columns approached each other the pace of each increased, when suddenly a crash, like the falling of timber, betokened the crisis. So sudden and violent was the collision that many of the horses were turned end over end and crushed their riders beneath them. The clashing of sabers, the firing of pistols, the demands for surrender and cries of the combatants now filled the air.*

SOURCE: William E. Miller, "The Cavalry Battle Near Gettysburg," *Battles and Leaders of the Civil War* (New York: The Century Company, 1884–88) vol. 3, p. 404.

The Cavalry Charge at Gettysburg by H. C. Bispham

forward out of the tree line prematurely, Stuart decided to commit his mounted force at once to succor the dismounted troopers at the Rummel Farm. At about three o'clock, just as the Confederate infantry was emerging from the tree line along Seminary Ridge for the assault on Hancock's corps, Stuart committed two of his brigades. Most of Hampton's and Fitz Lee's regiments charged down off the top of Cress Ridge toward the Rummel Farm. But the troopers did not stop there; they galloped forward into the open fields between Cress Ridge and Hanover Road as if determined to punch through the Federal cavalry holding the road. With evident pride, Stuart reported that "the impetuosity of those gallant fellows, after two weeks

George Armstrong Custer had been a notoriously bad student at West Point. He was nearly expelled a number of times for excessive demerits and graduated last in the class in June 1861. Despite that, his courage and dash brought him to the attention of his superiors, and two years later (and only two days before the Battle of Gettysburg), he was promoted in one step from captain to brigadier general at age 23. Ordered by Gregg to countercharge the Confederate cavalry, he called out to the men of the 1st Michigan, "Come on, you Wolverines!" and led the charge personally.

of hard marching and hard fighting on short rations, was not only extraordinary, but irresistible. The enemy's masses vanished before them like grain before the scythe, and . . . elicited the admiration of every beholder."

Among the admiring beholders was an officer in the 3rd Pennsylvania who admitted that "a grander spectacle than their advance has rarely been beheld." But the Federals were not so impressed that they were willing to give up the field. The Union horse artillery fired away at the oncoming horde with a will—first with shell, then with canister. Despite that, the rebel horsemen came on undaunted almost as if they were unconsciously duplicating the drama that was even then being played out on the far side of Cemetery Ridge three miles to the west. Unwilling merely to stand and receive that charge, Gregg ordered the 1st Michigan to countercharge. Custer placed himself at the head of the regiment, drew his sword, called out, "Come on, you Wolverines!" and led the charge personally. Most of Custer's brigade, unwilling to be left out, charged as well. Thus it was that the cavalry forces of both armies, with more than a thousand men on each side, galloped toward each other at full speed. Neither side slackened its speed, neither side shied away, and they collided "with a crash, like the falling of timber."

The contest then became a frantic melee with horses wheeling and falling, sabers slashing into flesh and bone, pistols discharging at close range, and men shouting for surrender or quarter. It was all but impossible to exercise effective command over such a scene. Gregg sent couriers dashing off to bring more forces into the fight, but often those couriers could not find the units to which they were sent, and junior officers had to make independent decisions. Watching the melee, Captain William Miller of the 3rd Pennsylvania turned to his lieutenant and told him, "I have been ordered to hold this position, but if you will back me up in case I am court-martialed for disobedience, I will order a charge." The lieutenant assured the captain of his support, and Miller drew his saber and led his command into the left flank of the rebel column. On the other flank, elements of the 1st New Jersey likewise charged into the roiling mass of men and horses. Like their infantry colleagues struggling to capture the Angle at almost the same time, the rebel cavalry found itself assailed from three sides.

The fighting was fierce and hand to hand. After the battle, a local farmer found the bodies of two men, one from Virginia and one from Pennsylvania, each grasping a bloody saber in his right hand, each holding onto the other with his left, their fingers clenched so tightly in a death grip that the two bodies could hardly be separated. Watching the fight from the top of Cress Ridge, Stuart could see his charge had lost its momentum, and he ordered a recall. He claimed later that "the enemy were

driven from the field," but in fact the Confederate horsemen were fortunate to extricate themselves from the fight and make their way safely back to their starting positions on Cress Ridge.

Stuart put the best face on it that he could. He claimed a victory, noting that Union losses in the fight (254) were greater than Confederate losses (181). He admitted that his cavalry charge fell short of complete success, which he attributed to the exhaustion of the horses, which were "jaded by long marching." Nevertheless, he insisted that the charge had swept the enemy from the field before him and allowed him to remain in position all afternoon. On Cress Ridge, he declared, he "held such a position as not only to render Ewell's left entirely secure. . . but [which] commanded a view of the routes leading to the enemy's rear. Had the enemy's main body [of infantry] been dislodged, as was confidently hoped and expected, I was in precisely the right position to discover it and improve the opportunity." But, of course, the enemy's main body of infantry was not dislodged, and after dark Stuart withdrew his four brigades and led them back to Seminary Ridge to report to Lee.

While Stuart's cavalry assailed the Federal rear, elements of the Federal cavalry were trying to do the same to the Confederates. This initiative was the brainchild of Alfred Pleasonton, the mustachioed Federal cavalry commander whose performance in the campaign so far had been less than exemplary. That morning he ordered Judson Kilpatrick, the impetuous 27-year-old commander of his 3rd division and yet another member of the West Point class of 1861, to cooperate with the brigade of U.S. regulars

This engraving based on Waud's 1863 sketch depicts the charge of the 1st Virginia cavalry and the countercharge of the 1st Michigan. A Federal participant recalled that "a more determined and vigorous charge than that made by the 1st Virginia it was never my fortune to witness."

The men of the 3rd Pennsylvania cavalry, part of Colonel John McIntosh's brigade of Gregg's division, pose here for a formal portrait with their sabers drawn. Along with the 1st New Jersey, it was the 3rd Pennsylvania that Gregg sent forward to contest possession of the Rummel Farm with Stuart's skirmishers. Each side fed supports to the skirmish until it became a full-fledged battle. The men of the 3rd Pennsylvania finally had to fall back when they ran out of ammunition.

under Wesley Merritt in an attack on the Confederate right south of the Round Tops. It was for this mission that Pleasonton had recalled Custer's brigade from Gregg that afternoon, an order Gregg had seen fit to postpone. But even without Custer, Kilpatrick intended to go ahead.

Like Custer, Kilpatrick had been recently promoted to general, but he had already earned a reputation for ferocity that was not entirely complimentary. Behind his back, his own troopers called him Kill-Cavalry, not in testimony to his prowess in battle but for his recklessness. He had already demonstrated this character trait during the campaign in the several skirmishes along the Blue Ridge (see chapter 2). Now,

with or without Custer, Kilpatrick was ready to hurl his division at the rebel right. He set off with his other brigade, that of Elon J. Farnsworth, to rendezvous with Merritt's brigade of regulars.

Farnsworth was not a West Pointer. At the outset of war he had enlisted in a regiment raised by his uncle in Illinois, was elected a lieutenant, then got a spot on Pleasonton's staff as a captain. Only days before the battle at Gettysburg, he was elevated from captain to brigadier general at age 26 and given command of a brigade; at Gettysburg, Pleasonton had to lend him an officer's blouse with brigadier's straps on the shoulders so that he could appear in proper uniform. Farnsworth had led his brigade

THE CLASS OF 1861

In the nineteenth century, the single-most important factor in determining whether an officer achieved high rank in the U.S. Army was not courage, intelligence, leadership, or even friends in high places. It was timing. Graduates in the West Point class of 1820, however brilliant, could not be sure of obtaining a commission upon graduation because the demand for active-duty officers was so small in the 1820s and 1830s. On the other hand, graduates in the West Point class of 1861 not only received commissions, most were elevated almost at once to stratospheric heights of responsibility that would have been unimaginable only months before, because the demand for professionally trained officers was so great.

In fact, there were two West Point classes of 1861. In the 1850s, when Robert E. Lee had been superintendent, he had sought to strengthen (and lengthen) the curriculum by changing the program at West Point from four years to five. Even without the press of civil war, that experiment was ending in 1861, and as a result, two classes graduated that spring: one in the first week of May, composed of forty-five men who had enrolled in the summer of 1856 and who completed the five-year program, and another six weeks later in June, composed of thirty-four men who had enrolled in 1857 and completed the four-year program. Dozens of others, mostly Southerners, resigned in April, just before graduation, in the wake of Fort Sumter and Lincoln's call for volunteers.

The seventy-nine men who graduated from West Point that spring soon found themselves endowed with responsibilities far beyond their years. Many commanded regiments, several commanded brigades, and more than a few commanded divisions—two of them at Gettysburg. Adelbert Ames (who graduated fifth in the May class) commanded Barlow's division after

Barlow fell wounded and was captured on the first day, and it was Ames, holding a major general's billet, who defended Cemetery Hill against Jubal Early's assault on the evening of July 2. In that same class, Judson Kilpatrick (who graduated seventeenth) also held a divisional command at Gettysburg, leading one of the three Union cavalry divisions.

Two members of the class lost their lives in the fighting for Little Round Top on the second day. The popular and promising Patrick "Paddy" O'Rorke, who had graduated first in the June class, was killed while leading the 140th New York regiment in a dramatic counterattack that very likely saved the position for the Union army. Not long afterward, Charles E. Hazlett (fifteenth in the May class), who had helped drag his four-gun battery to the crest of that hill, was tending to the mortally wounded Stephen Weed when he was shot in the head.

Two more were killed in the Union defense of Cemetery Ridge on the third day. George Woodruff (sixteenth in the June class) fell mortally wounded while commanding a battery of Hazlett's artillery battalion, and Alonzo Cushing (twelfth in that same class), whose battery was at the literal apex of Pickett's Charge, died even as he fired a final round from the last of his working guns.

Three miles to the east on that same day—indeed at almost the same moment—Thomas Rosser, who resigned from West Point only two weeks before he would have graduated in the May class, led the 5th Virginia cavalry as it charged down Cress Ridge to collide head-on with the 1st Michigan, led by his classmate George Custer, who graduated thirty-fourth (and last) in the June class.

The average age of these men, several of whom lost their lives, and all of whom made life-and-death decisions on the field of battle, was 25.

Adelbert Ames

Alonzo Cushing

George Woodruff

Patrick "Paddy" O'Rorke

Charles E. Hazlett

George Custer

Judson Kilpatrick

Thomas Rosser

Judson Kilpatrick was almost as unpopular with his own soldiers as he was with the enemy. A fierce fighter, he was quick to action but also occasionally impetuous and even rash. One of Meade's staff officers described him as "a frothy braggart without brains." His own men dubbed him Kill-Cavalry for his tendency to throw them into a fight without (in their opinion) sufficient concern for their chances of success or even survival. Nowhere was that tendency more evident than at Gettysburg, where Kilpatrick ordered Elon Farnsworth to make a foolish and unnecessary charge against the Confederate right wing.

during the search for Stuart in the days leading up to Gettysburg, and it was his force Stuart had skirmished with at Hanover on July 1. Now Farnsworth's small command, composed of three regiments from New York, Pennsylvania, and Vermont, plus ten companies of the 1st West Virginia, headed around the Union left flank at about the same time that Stuart was heading around the Union right. Kilpatrick and Farnsworth met up with Merritt's men south of the Round Tops at about one o'clock, just as the Confederate artillery bombardment began.

Alerted by skirmishers of this threat to his flank, Evander Law, commanding Hood's division, ordered Tige Anderson's Georgia brigade to change front; that is, to turn around and face southward blocking Emmitsburg Road. Law placed two more regiments in a long skirmish line in front of the stony hill and Devil's Den, where so much blood had been spilled the day before.

Kilpatrick and Merritt decided to dismount their men and attack this line on foot, essentially using their commands as mounted infantry rather than cavalry. Merritt's brigade advanced up the Emmitsburg Road, while Kilpatrick sent Farnsworth's brigade to assail the rough terrain to the east. Since the cavalrymen carried breech-loading carbines rather than muzzle-loading rifles, they could fire faster than their infantry foes, but the Confederate muzzle-loading Enfields had a greater range, and the dismounted troopers found it hard going against the Georgians. Farnsworth's men found the going particularly tough, advancing as they were through the thick forest of Bushman's Woods on the shoulder of Big Round Top. Before very long, their advance bogged down.

Then sometime after four o'clock, Kilpatrick learned that the Confederate infantry assault on Cemetery Ridge had failed. A courier dashed past him yelling, "We turned the charge! Nine acres of prisoners!" Eager—even desperate—to be in on the kill, Kilpatrick ordered Farnsworth to lead the 1st Vermont and the 1st West Virginia in a mounted charge straight through the rebel defenses. Farnsworth objected, pointing out that the terrain was unsuitable for cavalry and that the defenders had good position and probably numbers as well. Kilpatrick brushed these objections aside. "The whole [rebel] army is in full retreat," he insisted. "Our cavalry there is gobbling them up by the thousands." When Farnsworth still balked, Kilpatrick asked him, "Do you refuse to obey my orders? If you are afraid to lead this charge, I will lead it." Having made it a point of honor, there was nothing Farnsworth could do now but reply tersely, "I will obey your order."

The West Virginians struck first, but their charge was first blunted and then turned back by the 1st Texas regiment firing from behind a stone wall. To their right, Farnsworth personally led the Vermonters. With saber drawn, he put the spurs to his horse and charged with about three hundred Vermonters hard on his heels. They hit a line of Alabama skirmishers, burst through, and found themselves behind the enemy

lines. Farnsworth turned right toward Big Round Top and emerged directly behind the Confederate forces on Law's main line. With so little strength, however, there was little he could do but continue past them, northward now, toward Devil's Den.

Alerted that enemy cavalry was in their rear, the Confederate soldiers along the main line swung around, took aim, and shot them down. "Cavalry boys, cavalry!" shouted a lieutenant of the 4th Alabama, "This is no fight, only a frolic, give it to them!" Men and mounts went down, but Farnsworth galloped onward. He had broken through, but he was now in a box. Strong infantry forces were to his left, right, and rear. Farnsworth ordered his troopers to break into two groups and try to fight their way back. One group headed south and after taking heavy casualties, broke through the 1st Texas to relative safety. Farnsworth led the other group back the way they had come. On the shoulder of Big Round Top, he found the way blocked by the 15th Alabama, the same regiment that had failed to drive the 20th Maine from Little Round Top the day before. The Alabama soldiers took careful aim and emptied a dozen saddles. Farnsworth went down with multiple wounds. As he lay on the ground, he drew his pistol. A half dozen Alabama soldiers approached him with leveled muskets to demand his surrender. He declined and raised his pistol. Afterward, some Confederates claimed Farnsworth killed himself. Even if he did not in fact put the pistol to his head, his refusal to surrender was, in effect, a decision to die.

The attack achieved nothing. A Confederate soldier later described the Federal cavalry as galloping "around and round . . . until most of them were either killed or captured." Sixty-seven of the three hundred who made the charge never returned, Farnsworth among them. Kilpatrick was unrepentant. In his official report, he said only that "In these various attacks . . . the enemy was known to have sustained great loss." He even made the absurd claim that his actions that afternoon had compelled the Confederates to withhold forces from Pickett's Charge, thus claiming partial credit for the repulse of the grand assault.

Farnsworth's charge against the Confederate infantry near Devil's Den (above) was magnificent but contributed nothing to the outcome of the battle. Farnsworth knew the charge was ill-advised but felt that honor would not allow him to refuse. That conviction cost him his life.

Overleaf: The drawing by William Waud shows surgeons working by the light of lanterns hung from trees in the aftermath of battle. Those wounded who could, made their painful way back to their own lines; others had to be helped or dragged to safety by their friends. With so many men badly wounded, many had to simply bear the pain. One Confederate officer later recalled watching a friend whose leg had been mangled by an artillery shell leaning stoically against a tree awaiting help. "I have watched this officer pretty closely," he wrote, "and although I have seen much pain and agony in his expression, I haven't heard a single word of complaint. . . . Only once I heard him ask some negro camp attendant in a tone of piteous expostulation to make a little fire near him, for the night was cold. . . . [But] no fires were made. . . ."

In this nineteenth-century drawing by A. C. Redwood, a
wagon of Confederate wounded prepares to leave on the
long journey to friendly Virginia as comrades bid one
another farewell, uncertain if they will ever meet again.

Despite the failure of the Union cavalry thrust against the Confederate left, July 3 was a disaster for Southern arms. Pickett had reported to Lee that he had no division left. If that was not literally true, it was true enough. Of his three brigadiers, Garnett was dead, Armistead was mortally wounded and a prisoner, and Kemper was not expected to live through the night. Indeed, of the entire complement of officers in the division above the rank of major, only one, besides Pickett himself, survived unscathed. Among the rank and file, losses were less catastrophic, but they were bad enough. Moreover, the division was scattered. Though Pickett ordered cooks and teamsters into arms in order to beef up the ranks, fewer than a thousand men could be mustered the next morning out of the 5,400 in his division who had made the charge.

Lee fully expected Meade to follow up his advantage, and he put his army in position to defend against a counterattack. It was an unnecessary precaution. Though Hancock suggested a counterstrike, Meade was completing only his sixth day in command of the army, and he was not inclined to press his luck. He rode up and down the length of his line that evening, assessing his losses and the condition of the army, and he resolved to wait one more day to see what Lee had in mind.

On the southern side of the field, it now was evident to everyone, Lee included, that retreat was the only viable option left. The army had barely enough artillery ammunition for one day's fighting. Food was scarce as well; an army living off the land must move to survive, and the Army of Northern Virginia had been pinned at Gettysburg for three days. Finally, there were the wounded. Those with a chance of surviving had to be evacuated; others, too badly injured to move, would have to be left behind; still others had fallen too near enemy lines to be retrieved and would have to depend on the mercy of the Yankees. Altogether, some 6,800 would be left behind. That was hard.

When Lee returned to his headquarters tent that night, he was so physically and emotionally exhausted that he could barely dismount. He sent for Brigadier General John Imboden to ask him to take command of the army's wagon train of wounded, and Imboden was shocked to see Lee so worn down. Then, even as they talked, Imboden recalled, Lee straightened himself, as if by an act of will, and staring into the unseen middle distance, he declared, "I never saw troops behave more magnificently than Pickett's division of Virginians did today . . . If they had been supported . . . we would have held the position. . . ." But the transformation was temporary. As if he were watching the failure of that magnificent attack all over again, he exclaimed in a voice that rose gradually to an agonized wail, "Too bad! *Too bad!* OH, TOO BAD!"

CHAPTER FOURTEEN

The Endgame
Retreat and Pursuit
(July 4 – July 14, 1863)

On July 4 the sun rose on a scene that was an image of war itself. Looking out over the battlefield that morning, a captain in the 20th Maine tried to describe it in a letter to his wife, "Heaven save you from the distress of such scenes," he wrote, "blackened and mangled corpses—dead horses—guns and equipment broken and strewn—trees cut and mangled—fences demolished—the grounds trodden, muddy and messy—and an almost unbearable stench—confusion all about—burying dead—hauling away wounded, etc., etc. Oh, what scenes."

Cautiously, the townspeople ventured out of their homes. Though Lee's army remained defiantly on Seminary Ridge, the Confederates had abandoned the town during the night. Liberated from unfriendly occupation, residents sought out missing pets, a stray horse or cow, even an absent family member who had waited out the battle in the home of a neighbor. They did not go far, however, without a bottle of pennyroyal or peppermint oil to hold to their noses to combat the overpowering stench of rotting flesh. One Gettysburg family was surprised to encounter the black woman who did their washing. Three days before, when Confederate soldiers had first occupied the town, they had rounded up the few dozen black residents who remained and marched them through town under guard en route to Virginia and slavery. But this woman had managed to slip away from her guards and hide in the belfry of the Lutheran Church, where she stayed for three days, crouching there without food or water until the shooting stopped and the Confederates gave up the town. Then she climbed down exclaiming, "Thank God, I's alive yet."

Many others, of course, were not. Union soldiers kept busy throughout the morning digging shallow trenches to get the thousands of dead bodies underground. Later, most of those bodies would be exhumed and reburied more conventionally in coffins, but for now the threat of disease made haste more important than convention. For the wounded, the doctors set up surgical stations in barns and tent hospitals—even in the open air—and often used doors suspended between chairs as operating tables. Piles of amputated arms and legs began to grow as the thousands of wounded stoically waited their turn. Altogether some 20,000 men were treated in these ad hoc hospitals. At one, of the 3,260 who were treated (2,308 Federals and 952 Confederates), 437 died (245 Union and 192 Confederate)—a loss rate of 13.6 percent.

Opposite: Few places on earth are as depressing as a battlefield the day after a fight, as illustrated in this photograph taken on July 5, 1863. U.S. Army ordnance wagons are being used to "clean up" the battlefield—gathering discarded arms and ammunition, separating the wounded from the dead, and dead Federals from dead Confederates. The shallow grave in the foreground contains four Confederate bodies. The presence of individual headboards suggests that these graves near the Rose's Farm were dug by Southern soldiers on the evening of July 2. Most soldiers—on both sides—were buried anonymously in shallow trenches. A soldier assigned to burial duty after the battle wrote home that "the ground here is very hard, full of rocks and stones, the digging is very laborious work, the dead are many, the time is short, so they got but very shallow graves."

A dead horse lies next to a ruined caisson (right), and others litter the landscape near the Trostle barn (below). "Heaven save you from the distress of such scenes," a Federal officer in the 20th Maine wrote to his wife the day after Pickett's Charge. Indeed, images of death and destruction were omnipresent during the ensuing week. In addition to the more than six thousand soldiers who were killed at Gettysburg, more than three thousand horses died, and the smell of their rotting flesh in midsummer permeated the air. After the Army of the Potomac left Gettysburg in pursuit of Lee's army, militia units moved in and assumed the burden of cleaning up. The tents pitched just below Cemetery Hill (opposite bottom) belonged to a militia unit that arrived in Gettysburg on July 7. In addition to caring for the human dead and wounded (opposite top) their duties included the burial of thousands of horses.

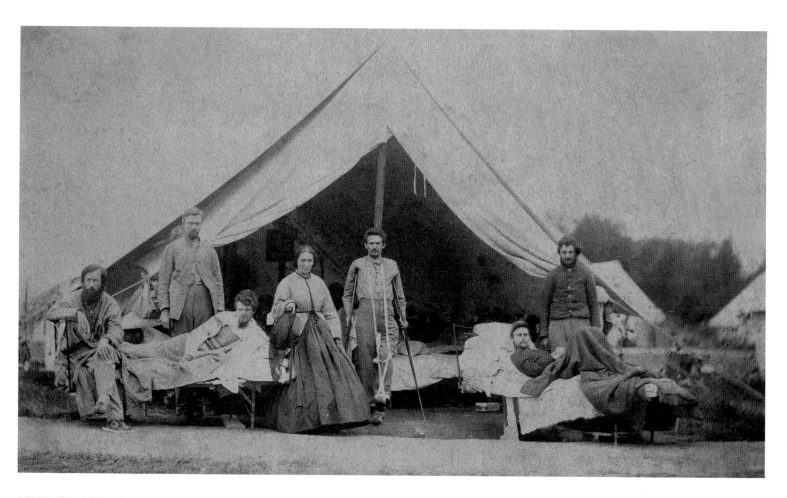

This surgeon's kit above was typical of the kind used by field surgeons at Gettysburg. It contains a bone saw (which looks very much like a modern hacksaw), knives for amputating limbs, and probes to search for bullets.

In the drawing below, a long line of Confederate prisoners who have survived the assault on Cemetery Ridge are escorted away from the battlefield on the afternoon of July 3. Nearly eight hundred Southern soldiers were captured from the three divisions that participated in the attack.

In the afternoon, it began to rain—gently at first, then harder. Almost as if the heavens were determined to wash the blood from the land, the rain fell heavily, washing the faces of the living and the dead, and running off roofs and tentflys to be absorbed by the soil, itself scarred by shot and shell and littered with the accoutrements of war. For the wounded, the rain was a mixed blessing. It tempered the oppressive heat, but because there was not enough room indoors to shelter them all, many awaited the surgeon's probe or saw in the open air and simply had to abide the rain.

Before that melancholy dawn, Lee already knew he had to retreat. He had faced up to that fact the night before. Before he had gone to bed—finally—sometime after 1 A.M., he had recalled the troops from both flanks to shorten his line and given instructions for the wagon trains to be ready to start the next day, especially those carrying the army's wounded. In the morning, Lee sought to unburden himself of several thousand Federal prisoners, most of them taken on the first day of the battle. He had already granted parole to several hundred of them, and now he sent a flag of truce across the field to propose a prisoner exchange. Meade held several thousand prisoners, too, most of them taken on the third day of the battle, but he had already started them eastward toward Federal prison camps, and in any case he was not eager to enhance Lee's strength by returning several thousand soldiers to his ranks or increase

his mobility by unburdening him of the responsibility of caring for several thousand Federals. So Meade declined the offer.

Throughout the morning, Lee worried that Meade might attack or that he might send his cavalry to seize the passes through the mountains that now constituted Lee's only line of escape. But Meade's army remained immobile, and in the afternoon, as the rain fell, a Confederate wagon train seventeen miles long, filled to overflowing with the wounded and dying, began its lugubrious journey westward up the Chambersburg Pike escorted by two brigades of cavalry and several batteries of artillery, though many of those guns had little or no ammunition. Later that same afternoon, toward twilight, another wagon train, this one bearing supplies as well as more wounded, headed southwest toward Fairfield. Once the wagons were well away, after full dark, Lee started the infantry: Hill's corps in the lead, then Longstreet's, and finally Ewell's. They marched southwest toward the passes through South Mountain. Once through the mountains, they would turn south, down the fertile Cumberland Valley to the Potomac River and the relative safety of friendly Virginia. To screen his movement, Lee ordered Stuart, with two brigades, to occupy Emmitsburg Road, thus

This famous Mathew Brady photograph shows three Confederate prisoners on Seminary Ridge still in possession of their kits and bedrolls. Since most Confederate prisoners were immediately marched off to prison camps, these men may have been stragglers captured during the pursuit. By the time the armies reached the Potomac River, nearly 12,000 Confederates had been taken prisoner. Combined with Lee's battlefield casualties, these further losses reduced the Southern army by a full third.

Edwin Forbes portrays the Federal army plodding southward through the rain in pursuit of Lee. The weather that plagued Lee's retreating columns slowed the pursuers as well.

staying between the retreating infantry and the Federal army. After the infantry made good on its escape, Stuart, too, would turn west to cross the mountains and find the road south.

The rain slowed the march. Lee had hoped to be well on his way before the Federals discovered that he was gone. But sending three corps along a single road at night in a driving rain was a prescription for delay. Ewell's corps, the last in line, did not leave Seminary Ridge until the next afternoon (July 5). Meade did not try to stop them.

Meade's disadvantage on July 4 was that, unlike Lee, he did not know that the battle was over. After the bloodletting of Pickett's Charge, a Confederate retreat certainly seemed called for, but Lee had a well-deserved reputation for doing the unexpected, as Hooker had learned at Chancellorsville. Meade's uncertainly was evident in the report he sent to Halleck that morning, in which he stated that although Lee was apparently on the move, it was not yet clear whether it was "a retreat or a maneuver for other purposes." Uncertain of Lee's plans or intentions, Meade kept his army in its famous "fishhook" defensive line until he was sure that his enemy was retiring.

Meade later received confirmation that Lee was evacuating his position late that afternoon. By then the rain was falling in sheets, and Meade decided to wait until

BATTLEFIELD WOUNDS AND CIVIL WAR MEDICINE

One of the enduring images for visitors to any Civil War battlefield was the horror of the field hospital. At Gettysburg, some 20,000 young men, many of them maimed in ghastly ways, awaited the attention of the handful of surgeons who attempted to save their lives and alleviate their pain. Perhaps the most vivid image was the pile of discarded appendages—arms and legs—tossed aside by the surgeons after amputation. That and the large number of amputees who survived the war (and the many who did not) led some to conclude that Civil War surgeons were butchers whose answer to most medical problems was amputation. Such a conclusion is unfair.

The real culprit was the minié ball. In order for the hollow base of the bullet to expand and engage the rifling of the musket, it had to be made of soft lead, so soft that it was not unheard of for soldiers to use them as pencils to write letters home. And because they were made of soft lead, they had much the same effect as a modern dum-dum bullet: they flattened and expanded upon impact. A minié ball might make a hole the size of dime going in and one the size of a fist going out. Worse, when a minié ball struck bone, the bone did not break; it shattered. Surgeons amputated so many limbs in the Civil War in large part because the bones of arms and legs had been so ruined by minié balls that even the best surgeon had no hope of saving them.

Lead minié balls could also poison the system if not removed. Lacking the benefit of X rays, surgeons had to find them by probing for them—inserting instruments, or even their fingers, into the bullet hole and groping around until they found it. Like amputation, such a procedure was horribly painful, and though the extent to which surgeons operated without painkillers has been somewhat exaggerated, it was not unknown, especially on the Confederate side.

The treatment of the wounded also suffered from the fact that doctors on both sides were ignorant of how diseases were transmitted. (In France, Louis Pasteur was even then conducting the experiments that would lead to acceptance of the germ theory.) Though disease was by far the largest cause of death in the Civil War, most doctors could do little about it for they believed that illness came from unhealthy humors in the air, and they did not fully understand the critical importance of hygiene or the role of microbes. In operating on the wounded, it was common for them to use the same knife or saw on hundreds of patients in succession, the only concession to hygiene being an effort to wipe off the blade between operations.

On the Union side, some of the worst such conditions were ameliorated by the work of the U.S. Sanitary Commission, founded in the first summer of the war, whose volunteer workers were known as Sanitarians. In addition to raising money for the care of the wounded, they also encouraged officers to pay more attention to cleanliness and diet in camp, and they supervised a number of rehabilitation centers where wounded soldiers could recover.

A battlefield wound was not necessarily a ticket home. Lightly wounded Confederates were expected to return to the ranks. So desperate was the South for manpower that within a year of the Battle of Gettysburg, Confederate commanders largely stopped listing the ambulatory wounded among their casualties in battle reports; if they could walk and carry a gun, they were still carried on the rolls as "effectives," able to do their duty. Similarly, the Union army created an Invalid Corps for their walking wounded, and these veterans were mainly used as garrison troops in fortifications.

Still, for all its shortcomings, the practice of Civil War medicine generated tremendous interest in the treatment of both wounds and disease, and in the postwar years that interest would trigger a number of important medical advances.

An amputation procedure at a Union field hospital

morning before initiating his pursuit. Only his cavalry was busy that night. Kilpatrick found elements of the rebel wagon train at Monterey Pass just beyond Fairfield. He attacked up a narrow defile that limited the fighting to a handful on each side and made a breakthrough difficult. Amid the confusion of a summer thunderstorm in the pitch-black darkness, Kilpatrick resorted to his customary tactic: he ordered a charge. It broke through the Confederate rear guard and led to the seizure of 150 wagons and some 1,500 prisoners. Characteristically, Kilpatrick inflated his accomplishments, reporting that he had captured Lee's entire wagon train.

That same night back on Cemetery Ridge, Meade met with his corps commanders to satisfy himself about the readiness of their commands for the morning march. Rather than simply launching the army in a pell-mell pursuit of Lee's retiring column, Meade outlined a three-part design. The cavalry would continue to harry the Confederate wagon train; Sedgwick's relatively fresh VI Corps would undertake a direct pursuit of the enemy along Fairfield Road to conduct what amounted to a reconnaissance in force; and the rest of the army would march not west, but south, on the eastern side of South Mountain, paralleling Lee's route in the Cumberland Valley, before turning west across the mountains to the Potomac River crossings, where it would cut Lee off from his line of escape. It was not an unreasonable plan; it avoided having to confront the rebel rear guard in the passes of South Mountain, where the defenders would have all the advantages. The problem was that Lee had both a head start and a shorter route, though Meade hoped to make up for that by ordering forced marches.

Sedgwick's corps started out after the retreating Confederates on July 5 only a few hours behind Ewell's rear guard, and he caught up with it just beyond Fairfield where the road snaked up the side of South Mountain. Most of the rebel army had already

Another Edwin Forbes drawing shows the Federal army in pursuit. Here a team of horses hauls a 3-inch Ordnance rifle along the muddy roads.

Overleaf: Sedgwick's corps leaves the battlefield and heads southward the afternoon of July 5, as seen in an 1863 colored lithograph entitled *Leaving the Field* by an unknown artist. Though the fighting at Gettysburg ended on July 3, the rain—and Meade's uncertainty about Lee's intentions—kept both armies in camp for another day. Not until July 5 did Federal forces begin their pursuit of Lee's retreating column.

out.

"IT WAS A SAD SIGHT"

The human carnage that followed the battle made a profound impression on soldiers and civilians alike. The veterans in the ranks were used to such sights, of course, but the more than 40,000 dead and wounded at Gettysburg taxed even their equanimity. One Confederate soldier who kept a diary later recounted his impressions of his first night as a wounded prisoner of war in the hands of the Yankees:

The whole ground for miles around is covered with the wounded, the dying and the dead. Confederate and Yankee are often promiscuously thrown together, although the officials separate us as much as is convenient. . . . This is a horrid night, cold and wet and rainy. Groans and shrieks and maniacal ravings; bitter sobs, and heavy sighs, piteous cries; horrid oaths; despair; the death rattle; darkness; death. . . . All night long I lie awake shivering with cold save when my wearied eyes droop for a moment, again to be opened by a convulsive start as the wheels of the ambulance all but run over my feet. And the infuriated drivers curse and whip their refractory horses. . . . All night long these ambulances move among us, still bringing more and more from the field of blood.

There is one poor youth near by whose agonies are frightful, especially at night. Both his thigh bones have been broken by a ball, and really his anguish is enough to move a heart of stone. The worst is that he lingers in this terrible agony for three days, and it was a real satisfaction to learn that the unfortunate boy had died.

For the local civilians, such scenes were almost unfathomable. The immediate problem was sanitation. With thousands of corpses lying about in midsummer, the smell became overpowering, and the threat to public heath obvious. Men labored around the clock to get the bodies underground; surgeons worked just as frantically probing wounds for bullets or amputating shattered limbs. The Gettysburg civilians found such scenes almost overwhelming. The following is an excerpt from Albertus McCreary's memoirs of his boyhood days in Gettysburg.

In going over the field that first day after the fight [July 4], the many strange and terrible sights made a strong and lasting impression on my mind. In one place there were as many as forty dead horses—where a battery had been

Edwin Forbes's drawing of caissons and dead horses

General hospital at Camp Letterman, located just outside Gettysburg

placed; the bodies were much swollen, the feet standing up in the air. Broken wagons and guns, belts, cartridge-boxes and canteens, blankets, and all sorts of soldier equipment were lying around everywhere. The fences were all down; only a few posts, here and there, were left, like sentinels on guard.

Dead soldiers were everywhere. . . . The stench from the battle-field after the fight was so bad that every one went about with a bottle of pennyroyal or peppermint oil. The burial of the dead commenced at once, and many were buried along the line where they fought and fell, and, in many cases, so near the surface that their clothing came through the earth.

We made a long tramp that first day and did not reach home until late in the afternoon. There we found plenty to take up our time and attention. The surgeons were at work in the hospital that adjoined our back yard. I spent hours on the fence watching them operating on the wounded. On a table out of doors operations of all kinds were performed. I must say I got pretty well hardened to such sights.

One day shortly after the battle, as we were walking over the field, we came to a squad of soldiers who had opened a trench where some of the dead had been hastily buried. They were taking up the bodies and placing them in coffins to be buried in the National Cemetery. The sight became so horrible that we could not endure it and quickly left the spot. . . .

It was a sad sight to see relatives visiting the fields in search of some dear one. Sometimes they would find him in one of the many hospitals, but more often among the dead. One young lady came to our house in search of a brother who had been wounded. She came on the late train and stayed at the house until morning. When morning came she went with my brother to find him, but he had died during the night.

SOURCE: (1) John Dooley, *Confederate Soldier: His War Journal*, edited by Joseph T. Durkin (Washington: Georgetown University Press, 1943), pp. 111–12, 114; (2) Albertus McCreary, "Gettysburg: A Boy's Experience of the Battle," *McClure's Magazine* (July 1909), 33: pp. 251–52.

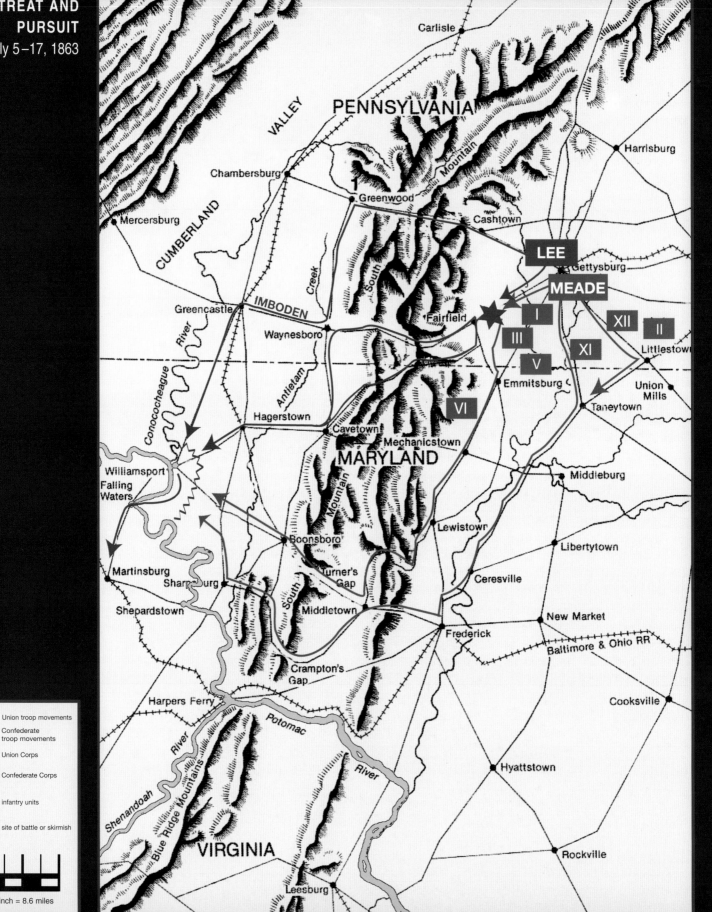

RETREAT AND PURSUIT
July 5–17, 1863

Carlisle

PENNSYLVANIA

Harrisburg

Chambersburg

Greenwood

Cashtown

Mercersburg

CUMBERLAND

LEE Gettysburg

MEADE

Greencastle IMBODEN River

Waynesboro

Fairfield

I

XII

II

III

XI

Littlestown

V

Conococheague River

Creek

South

Mountain

Antietam

VI

Emmitsburg

Union Mills

Taneytown

Hagerstown

Cavetown

Mechanicstown

MARYLAND

Middleburg

Williamsport
Falling
Waters

Lewistown

Libertytown

Martinsburg

Boonsboro

Ceresville

New Market

Sharpsburg

South Mountain

Turner's Gap

Middletown

Frederick

Baltimore & Ohio RR

Shepardstown

Cooksville

Crampton's Gap

Hyattstown

Harpers Ferry

Potomac River

River

Shenandoah River

Blue Ridge Mountains

VIRGINIA

Rockville

Leesburg

Union troop movements

Confederate troop movements

I Union Corps

EWELL II Confederate Corps

infantry units

★ site of battle or skirmish

1 inch = 8.6 miles

filed through the mountains, but the pass was being held by John B. Gordon's brigade. Gordon was apparently uncowed by the appearance of a Federal corps on his front and showed no willingness to give way. Sedgwick did not like the circumstances despite his numerical superiority, for the terrain dramatically favored the defenders. Meade, on the other hand, was inclined to force the issue and directed Sedgwick to press ahead, promising him support from two more corps. Sedgwick declined. Gouvernor Warren, who was accompanying him, supported his decision to abandon the direct pursuit and march the VI Corps back to Emmitsburg. Gordon watched him go, then slipped over the mountain to join the rest of Lee's army in the Cumberland Valley.

⚔ ⚔

All this time, the Confederate wagon trains were moving south under the command of Brigadier General John D. Imboden. In an ordeal that lasted all night and all the next day, the wagons rumbled through the mountains, the agonized cries of the wounded rising above the ceaseless drumming of rain on canvas as the wagons bumped and jostled along the rutted roads. The column struck the main north-south road at Greencastle by daylight, but there they found that the local citizens, who had seemed so benign when the army had marched northward along this same route only a week before, were much less so now that the invaders were crippled and in retreat. Bands of civilians armed with axes attacked the wagons, smashing the spokes of the wheels and even tipping some of them over in the streets. Imboden's cavalry drove them off, but only a few miles further on, Federal cavalry appeared. The Yankee horsemen struck at the column in small groups, picking their targets and taking several hundred prisoners and some sixty more wagons. Nevertheless, late on the afternoon of July 5—at about the time that Gordon was fending off Sedgwick's tentative probings in the mountain passes behind Fairfield—the head of the Confederate wagon train reached the Potomac River at Williamsport.

They had reached the river, but they could not cross. The heavy rains had raised the level of the water by several feet, and the shallow fords where the Confederate infantry had splashed across the river going north were now too deep for either men or wagons to cross. Worse, the only pontoon bridge, which Lee had left in place as the army moved north, had been destroyed by Federal raiders. Imboden found himself with his back to a river, burdened by several thousand wounded, and able to field only two small cavalry brigades, two infantry regiments, and some artillery with limited ammunition. If the Federals arrived before Lee's infantry, he would not be able to put up much of a fight. "Our situation," he wrote later, "was frightful."

The next day, Yankee cavalry arrived. It was John Buford, whose troopers had initiated the fight on McPherson's Ridge five days and several lifetimes ago, with a total of about 4,000 men. Imboden ordered his 2,100 troopers to dig in alongside his two regiments of infantry, deployed his artillery, and put up as bold a front as he could. He even organized the teamsters into companies, armed them with whatever was available, and appointed some of the ambulatory wounded to command them. Buford dismounted his troopers and attacked on foot. Imboden used his artillery to good effect until his guns began to run low on ammunition. As it happened, however, Lee had ordered that artillery ammunition be sent up from Winchester to meet the army. That supply train was waiting across the river, and Imboden was able to ferry enough ammunition across in small lighters to keep his guns in service. It probably saved his command. The arrival of Fitzhugh Lee's brigade at nightfall ended the immediate cri-

Opposite: Lee began his retreat from Gettysburg late on July 4, sending the wounded and much of his artillery with Brigadier General Imboden due west toward Cashtown and Greenwood. The rest of his army decamped the next day, passing through South Mountain and heading south toward the river crossings. Meade followed on parallel roads, but he hesitated to attack his cornered foe at Williamsport, and on July 15, Lee escaped back into Virginia.

Overleaf: Lee's army cross the bridge over the Chesapeake and Ohio Canal, then ford the Potomac River into friendly Virginia in this Edwin Forbes painting. A few of the army's wagons can be seen being swept away by the high water, but Lee's determination, and the timidity of Meade's subordinates, allowed most of the Army of Northern Virginia to cross the river unmolested. Lincoln was hugely disappointed. Convinced that Lee could have been destroyed, he said that "our army held the war in the hollow of their hand and they would not close it."

sis and ensured that the rebel cavalry could hold the river crossings, at least for now.

Meanwhile, the head of Lee's long column of infantry was approaching Hagerstown, only five miles away. Lee and Longstreet rode together in the van and had plenty of opportunity to discuss the recent battle. Lee accepted full responsibility for the outcome of the fight, ensuring Longstreet that "it was all my fault," and making it clear that he held Longstreet guiltless. For his part, Old Pete did not belabor the subject—that would come later. For now, his duty was to support his commander and help the army make it safely back to friendly soil.

At Hagerstown Lee learned that the pontoon bridge over the Potomac had been

destroyed and that the river was too high for the army to ford. With the rain still falling, it was unlikely that the river would drop anytime soon. The Confederate engineers would have to build another bridge. Meanwhile, the army would have to hold the bridgehead. The engineers laid out a defensive line that stretched in an arc from Downsville, three miles south of Williamsport, to the Conocoheague River, which drained into the Cumberland Valley and flowed into the Potomac just north of the town. It was a strong position, and as the troops arrived, they made it stronger, digging with entrenching tools, bayonets, canteens—anything at hand. By July 9, Lee had some 56,000 men with him at Williamsport, and despite the rain and the circumstances, their morale had largely recovered from the effects of the battle at Gettysburg—a testament to the resilience of human nature. The sight of Virginia just across the river was also a boost. If the Yankees wanted to try them again, let them come.

The Yankees were coming as fast as they could. Meade's pursuit got under way in earnest on the morning of July 7. He sent his seven corps southward on parallel roads to expedite their progress, and despite the rain, they performed some heroic feats of marching. The men of Howard's XI Corps, almost as if they were trying to compensate for their poor showing on the battlefield, covered more than thirty miles that day, most of it in a driving rainstorm, collapsing into their bivouacs after seventeen hours on the march. The next day, the Army of the Potomac climbed up through the passes in South Mountain at Turner's Gap and Crampton's Gap, which the army had used in its approach to Antietam the previous fall. By July 9, the Federals were near enough to Williamsport to begin to feel the enemy. The river was still swollen; Lee's army was still in place on the north bank. An opportunity beckoned to finish off the rebel army and end the war.

Or so it seemed in Washington. There General Halleck and other distant observers, including the president, eagerly read the dispatches from the front, and in their col-

This Edwin Forbes sketch depicts a probing attack by two companies of the 6th Michigan cavalry against Lee's defensive enclave on the north bank of the Potomac River, near Falling Waters. The partially dismantled barn might have been a victim of war damage, or it could have been cannibalized by Lee's engineers who tore down several structures in order to build a pontoon bridge over the river.

A "Charge of the 6th Michigan cavalry over the rebel earthworks nr. Falling Wat[ers]"

lective imaginations they perceived a golden opportunity. They ordered reinforcements from a variety of sources to converge on Williamsport, and they peppered Meade with telegrams that, however they were phrased, all carried the same message: Don't let Lee get away! Most of the Federal reinforcements they sent were useless, consisting of militia or new recruits without experience, supplies, or reliable leadership. Meade would just as soon not have had the responsibility of looking out for them. Moreover, he was fully aware of both the opportunity and the dangers presented by the strategic circumstances, and he began to resent the hectoring tone of the telegrams.

For most of three days, Meade cautiously maneuvered his army, numbering perhaps 80,000 men, to within striking distance of Lee's defensive lines. By July 12 the two armies were once again facing each other on parallel lines within long artillery range. The Federals had a numerical advantage, but the Confederates were well placed and entrenched, and Meade, as well as his soldiers, remembered all too well the consequences of charging well-positioned veterans across open ground. That night, Meade called a meeting of his corps commanders—the third since he had assumed command only two weeks earlier. He outlined a plan to send a strong reconnaissance in force against Lee's line the next morning that could turn into a general assault if any weakness were discovered. Meade's new chief of staff, A. A. Humphreys, who had replaced the wounded Dan Butterfield, expressed immediate support for the idea. But of the unit commanders, only Wadsworth and Howard thought it was worth trying; all the others opposed it as too risky. A more confident army commander, or one with more than two weeks' tenure in the job, might have been willing to override the advice of his juniors and order the assault anyway, but Meade did not. Unlike Lee, who had overridden Longstreet's objections to an offensive at Gettysburg, Meade calculated that an assault carried out by officers who had no faith in the outcome was a bad bet. He bowed to the majority and postponed the attack until he could make a personal reconnaissance.

The next day, Meade and Humphreys rode out to do exactly that. They saw that

the Confederate defenses were certainly imposing—well constructed and designed to give the defenders interlocking fields of fire—but Meade determined that the chance to achieve something decisive justified the risks, and he directed Humphreys to write out orders for a forward movement at seven the next morning, July 14.

🜨   🜨

While Meade's army slowly worked its way to within striking distance of the rebel army, Lee used the respite to improve his defensive lines, evacuate his wounded and his prisoners, and hasten the completion of a new bridge. The Confederate wounded and the Federal prisoners were evacuated across the river in small lighters and flatboats, then those same boats ferried artillery ammunition back to the northern bank. Each day, morning to night, boats plied back and forth across the river carrying men in one direction and shot and shell in the other. Meanwhile, his engineers labored on the new bridge. They salvaged some of the pontoons from the old bridge, built new ones from wood that they scavenged by tearing down old warehouses, and linked these together to make a serviceable floating bridge at Falling Waters, a few miles downstream from Williamsport. The bridge was completed on the thirteenth, and that night Lee choreographed a carefully planned evacuation. Now that the moment had come, Longstreet wondered if the army shouldn't stay. After all, here was a chance to fight a defensive battle from prepared positions. With the artillery resupplied and a secure bridge to the southern bank, why not stay and let the Yankees hurl themselves to destruction against strong defensive lines as they had at Fredericksburg? But once again Lee overruled him, and the evacuation began as soon as it was dark enough to disguise his movement.

Some of the infantry, particularly Ewell's corps, was able to use the ford, the river having dropped several feet. The shorter men had some trouble with the deep water and took some good-natured ribbing from their comrades as they struggled against the current, but all successfully made the crossing. The rest of the army, along with the wagons and the guns, used the new bridge, the wagons rumbling precariously across the planks in single file. A handful of wagons and a few guns, mired in the thick mud, had to be abandoned, but on the whole it was a successful decampment.

At 7 A.M. on July 14, the hour Meade had appointed for the forward movement, the Federal skirmishers noted an absence of activity in the Confederate lines. Union patrols went forward to find them empty, and Meade at once ordered a general pursuit. Led by Buford's cavalry, the Federals charged through the abandoned defenses into the Confederate bridgehead. There they encountered evidence of a hasty evacuation. Only Heth's division was still present on the northern bank of the river to serve as a rear guard. It was nearly overrun. Johnston Pettigrew, who had survived the carnage of Pickett's Charge, received a mortal wound in the ensuing fight, and some seven hundred other Confederates were killed, wounded or captured. But cavalry alone could not break an infantry division, and the rest of Pettigrew's command, bearing their mortally wounded commander, conducted a fighting retreat to the far bank. By midday, the Army of Northern Virginia stood once again on Virginia soil.

Opposite: David Gilmour Blythe's painting illustrates the crossing of the I Corps that, ironically, used the same ford in its pursuit of Lee's army after the Battle of Antietam the previous fall. The Federal army crossed the canal and the Potomac in pursuit of Lee's escaping army on July 18.

EPILOGUE

The Last Full Measure

O n the very day that Lee hurled the flower of his army against Hancock's line on Cemetery Ridge, a thousand miles to the west, Confederate General John C. Pemberton sent a message through the siege lines to ask Grant if they might meet for the purpose of discussing the surrender of Vicksburg. After enduring a forty-seven-day siege characterized by dwindling food supplies and nearly constant bombardment, Pemberton hoped that Grant would be in a generous mood on the anniversary of American independence. But "Unconditional Surrender" Grant lived up to his nickname, and in the end Pemberton had to surrender both the city and the Army of Mississippi, nominally numbering some 30,000 men. The fall of Vicksburg was decisive. It sundered the Confederacy not quite in half and regained the Mississippi River for the Union. As Lincoln expressed it, "The father of waters once more flows unvexed to the sea." Combined with the defeat at Gettysburg, these twin blows staggered the Confederacy and, in retrospect at least, marked a turning point from which the South would never quite recover.

Lee offered to resign. A month after recrossing the Potomac, he wrote Jefferson Davis a thoughtful letter that was clearly more than a pro forma apology for his lack of success in the recent campaign. Disappointments, he wrote to the Confederate president, are inevitable in war. But the failure of the recent campaign had triggered an erosion of public confidence that might easily spread to the army and thereby weaken its future effectiveness. The cause was too important to risk it merely for the sake of one individual's feelings. "I therefore, in all sincerity, request your Exc[ellenc]y to take measures to supply my place." His sense of anguish was evident when he added, "I cannot even accomplish what I myself desire. How can I fulfill the expectations of others?" Davis would not hear of it. He knew full well that there was no better general in the Confederacy to lead the army in Virginia, especially when the road ahead was dim with uncertainty.

By late summer, Lee's army was back behind the line of the Rappahannock and Rapidan Rivers. New officers replaced those who had fallen in battle, new recruits—conscripts primarily—filled out the ranks of the regiments, and, by November, the Army of Northern Virginia was again a confident and dangerous instrument of war, ready for the next assault across the "dare mark."

Opposite: A stone sentry stands a silent vigil over the graves of thousands of veterans who are buried on Cemetery Hill. More than 50,000 men were casualties in this three-day battle, and those who survived knew that their lives had been changed forever. In November, Lincoln came to this hilltop to dedicate the cemetery but even more to articulate the meaning of those veterans' sacrifices.

More than four months after the battle, President Lincoln visited
Gettysburg to participate in the dedication of "a final resting
place" for Union soldiers on the aptly named Cemetery Hill. This
photo shows the procession moving southward along Baltimore
Street just above the turnoff onto Emmitsburg Road.

The photo below shows a crowd at the Gettysburg dedication ceremony. After a two-hour drum-and-trumpet narration of the Battle of Gettysburg by Edward Everett, the president got up to speak. He stood hatless at the front of the stand (inset, left) and spoke from a text he held in his hand. The impact of his profound and eloquent speech was felt even at the time and was soon widely printed in newspapers, eventually becoming recognized as the purest and most eloquent statement on the Union cause.

B-4975

Two veterans, enemies during the Civil War, discuss their great adventures at a Gettysburg reunion held in 1913—the fiftieth anniversary of the battle. The event brought together 57,000 veterans of the war. In time, the events that took place at Gettysburg during three July days in 1863 took on a mythic quality. Americans preferred to remember the courage and valor that was shared by the men on both sides rather than the differences that divided them.

Meade, too, offered to resign. His offer was prompted by a telegram from Halleck that stating that "the escape of Lee's army without another battle has created great dissatisfaction in the mind of the President." In part, Lincoln's dissatisfaction was a measure of how desperately he had hoped for an end to the bloodshed. The destruction of Lee's army would have shortened the war, maybe ended it altogether, and thereby saved tens of thousands of lives that would now have to be expended in finishing the job. In part, too, the president's distress was the result of his experience with Meade's several predecessors, especially George McClellan, who had failed on several occasions to seize opportunities that lay before them. In particular, McClellan had declined to commit his reserves at the Battle of Antietam when doing so might have won a decisive victory. It seemed to Lincoln that Meade had done much the same thing at Williamsport.

Meade responded by asking "to be immediately relieved from the command of the army." He would have been far more distressed had he read the letter Lincoln wrote that same afternoon but did not send. It was a therapeutic act by the president to write out his true feelings, then fold up the letter and put it in his pocket. "I do not believe you appreciate the magnitude of the misfortune involved in Lee's escape," Lincoln wrote. "He was within your easy grasp, and to have closed upon him would, in connection with our other late successes, have ended the war. As it is, the war will be prolonged indefinitely. . . . Your golden opportunity is gone, and I am distressed immeasurably because of it."

Instead of sending the letter, the president authorized Halleck to send a soothing telegram to Meade assuring him that no censure was intended and that no grounds existed for him to offer his resignation. His honor satisfied, Meade retracted his resignation. He followed Lee into Virginia and made several efforts to move between him and Richmond, but by the fall he found himself back on the north bank of the Rappahannock occupying the ground the army had held when the campaign began in late May. When the Army of the Potomac next crossed the dare mark the following spring, Meade would still be its commander, but traveling with him and guiding the army's movements would be a new general in chief named Ulysses S. Grant.

That same November Lincoln was invited to travel to Gettysburg to be present at the dedication of the National Cemetery, where so many of the dead had been reinterred on the hill they had defended. It was an opportunity for the president to honor and acknowledge the sacrifice of the soldiers and a chance, too, to redefine the purpose and meaning of the conflict. A few days after the battle, when a crowd of citizens serenaded him outside the White House, Lincoln had responded with a short extemporaneous talk in which he asked rhetorically, "How long ago was it?—eighty odd years—since . . . a nation by its representatives, assembled and declared as a self-evident

At the fiftieth anniversary, survivors reenacted Pickett's Charge, though their numbers had been substantially reduced since the battle.

Executive Mansion,

Washington, , 186 .

Four score and seven years ago our fathers brought
forth, upon this continent, a new nation, conceived
in liberty, and dedicated to the proposition that
"all men are created equal"

Now we are engaged in a great civil war, testing
whether that nation, or any nation so conceived,
and so dedicated, can long endure. We are met
on a great battle field of that war. We have
come to dedicate a portion of it, as a final resting place for those who died here, that the nation
might live. This we may, in all propriety do. But, in a
larger sense, we can not dedicate — we can not
consecrate — we can not hallow, this ground —
The brave men, living and dead, who struggled
here, have hallowed it, far above our poor power
to add or detract. The world will little note, nor long
remember what we say here; while it can never
forget what they did here.

It is rather for us, the living, we here be dedicated to the great task remaining before us —
that, from these honored dead we take increased devotion to that cause for which
they here, gave the last full measure of devotion — that we here highly resolve these
dead shall not have died in vain; that
the nation, shall have a new birth of freedom, and that government of the people by
the people for the people, shall not perish from the earth.

This is the earliest known draft of Lincoln's
Gettysburg Address. Known as the Nicolay copy
because it was owned for years by one of
Lincoln's two private secretaries, John G. Nicolay,
it may be the one Lincoln read from at the
cemetery on November 19, 1863. The address
printed on page 293 is the the commonly
accepted, modern version of the speech, although
these may not be the exact words Lincoln said
that day.

Four score and seven years ago our fathers brought forth, upon this continent, a new nation, conceived in Liberty, and dedicated to the proposition that all men are created equal.

Now we are engaged in a great civil war, testing whether that nation, or any nation, so conceived, and so dedicated, can long endure. We are met here on a great battle-field of that war. We have come to dedicate a portion of it as a final resting place for those who here gave their lives that that nation might live. It is altogether fitting and proper that we should do this.

But in a larger sense we can not dedicate—we can not consecrate—we can not hallow this ground. The brave men, living and dead, who struggled here, have consecrated it far above our poor power to add or detract. The world will little note, nor long remember, what we say here, but can never forget what they did here. It is for us, the living, rather to be dedicated here to the unfinished work which they have, thus far, so nobly carried on. It is rather for us to be here dedicated to the great task remaining before us—that from these honored dead we take increased devotion to that cause for which they here gave the last full measure of devotion—that we here highly resolve that these dead shall not have died in vain; that this nation shall have a new birth of freedom; and that this government of the people, by the people, for the people, shall not perish from the earth.

This painting by an unknown artist captures the heady sense of relief in the
Northern states when the Civil War finally ended. When news of the Union
victory at Gettysburg and of the fall of Vicksburg hit, it spread like wildfire across
the North, and some who heard the news expected (or at least hoped) that it

would be followed by news of an end to the war itself. Unfortunately, the conflict had two more years to run—years during which the loss of life exceeded the losses up to and including Gettysburg. Only in the spring of 1865 would America's bloodiest war finally come to an end.

This nineteenth-century illustration depicts Lincoln giving his address at Gettysburg. Though Ward Lamon, who introduced Lincoln that day, later claimed that Lincoln was disappointed by his speech, Lamon's testimony is suspect. Except for opposition newspapers, most contemporaries recognized its poetic brilliance at once. The *Providence Journal* declared that no speech could be "more beautiful, more touching, more inspiring than those thrilling words."

truth that 'all men are created equal.'" He noted that "this is a glorious theme, and the occasion for a speech, but I am not prepared to make one worthy of the occasion."

To ensure that he was prepared for a speech on that theme at Gettysburg, Lincoln wrote out his ideas on White House stationery. "Eighty odd years" became "four score and seven," and from that opening, he crafted a short speech (only 272 words) that was not so much about the battle (though he did pay moving tribute to "those who here gave their lives that this nation might live") as it was about the *meaning* of the war. What was at issue in this conflict, Lincoln would assert, was the very idea of self-government. The war was a test of those principles articulated by the Founding Fathers: that a free people could make their own government and defend it not only against external invasion but against internal dissent and rebellion. A failure now would suggest to the world that those principles were little more than foolish vanities, that the notion of self-government had proved unable to survive the test of time and changing circumstances. Those who gave their lives at Gettysburg offered the nation—and, more importantly, the principles on which it was founded—a chance to survive. Now it was up to the living to see the task through to the end, to ensure the triumph of the concept of self-government.

Lincoln traveled by train, arriving in Gettysburg at five in the afternoon on November 18. He spoke a few words to the crowd that met him, then went to his hotel to write out a fair copy of the speech. The next morning he rode to the cemetery on horseback as part of a lengthy procession and joined the crowd there in listening to the music of several military bands. Then he settled in to attend to the address by the featured speaker of the day, Edward Everett of Massachusetts. Everett spoke for two hours. He offered a dramatic narrative account of the fighting that had taken place at Gettysburg more than five months before, describing the ebb and flow of battle and successfully engaging his large audience. At its conclusion, Lincoln congratulated him and expressed his gratitude. Then Ward Lamon introduced the president.

The audience was just settling down after Everett's lengthy discourse. It was a brisk fall day, and the wind fluttered the paper that Lincoln held in his hand as he read his prepared remarks in his high, reedy voice:

Four score and seven years ago our fathers brought forth, on this continent, a new nation, conceived in Liberty, and dedicated to the proposition that all men are created equal.

Now we are engaged in a great civil war, testing whether that nation, or any nation so conceived and so dedicated, can long endure. We are met on a great battlefield of that war. We have come to dedicate a portion of that field, as a final resting place for those who here gave their lives, that this nation might live. It is altogether fitting and proper that we should do this.

But in a larger sense, we cannot dedicate—we cannot consecrate—we cannot hallow this ground. The brave men, living and dead, who struggled here, have consecrated it far above our poor power to add or subtract. The world will little note, nor long remember what we say here, but it can never forget what they did here. It is for us the living, rather, to be dedicated here to the unfinished work which they who fought here have thus far so nobly advanced. It is rather for us the living to be here dedicated to the great task remaining before us—that from these honored dead we take increased devotion to that cause for which they here gave the last full measure of devotion—that we here highly resolve that these dead shall not have died in vain—that this nation, under God, shall have a new birth of freedom—and that government of the people, by the people, for the people, shall not perish from the earth.

ARMY OF THE POTOMAC • Order of Battle

Major General George Gordon Meade

Maj. Gen. Daniel Butterfield, Chief of Staff
Brig. Gen. G. K. Warren, Chief of Engineers
Brig. Gen. Henry Hunt, Chief of Artillery

I CORPS	**II CORPS**	**III CORPS**	**V CORPS**
Maj. Gen. John F. Reynolds	Maj. Gen. Winfield S.	Maj. Gen. Daniel Sickles	Maj. Gen. George Sykes
Maj. Gen. Abner Doubleday*	Hancock	Maj. Gen. David Birney*	
Maj. Gen. John Newton*	Maj. Gen. John Gibbon*		1ST DIVISION
		1ST DIVISION	Brig. Gen. James Barnes
1ST DIVISION	1ST DIVISION	Maj. Gen. David Birney	
Brig. Gen. James S. Wadsworth	Brig. Gen. John C. Caldwell	Brig. Gen. J. H. Hobart Ward*	2ND DIVISION
			Brig. Gen. Romeyn Ayres
2ND DIVISION	2ND DIVISION	2ND DIVISION	
Brig. Gen. John C. Robinson	Brig. Gen. John Gibbon	Brig. Gen. Andrew A.	3RD DIVISION
	Brig. Gen. William Harrow*	Humphreys	Brig. Gen. Samuel Crawford
3RD DIVISION			
Brig. Gen. Thomas A. Rowley	3RD DIVISION		
Maj. Gen. Abner Doubleday*	Brig. Gen. Alexander Hays		

*Officers who succeeded command of units during the battle are indicated by an asterisk.

VI CORPS
Maj. Gen. John Sedgwick

1ST DIVISION
Brig. Gen. Horatio Wright

2ND DIVISION
Brig. Gen. Albion Howe

3RD DIVISION
Maj. Gen. John Newton
Brig. Gen. Frank Wheaton*

XI CORPS
Maj. Gen. Oliver Otis Howard
Maj. Gen. Carl Schurz*

1ST DIVISION
Brig. Gen. Francis Barlow
Brig. Gen. Adelbert Ames*

2ND DIVISION
Brig. Gen. Adolph von
Steinwehr

3RD DIVISION
Maj. Gen. Carl Schurz
Brig. Gen. A. Schimmelfennig*

XII CORPS
Maj. Gen. Henry W. Slocum
Brig. Gen. Alpheus
Williams*

1ST DIVISION
Brig. Gen. Alpheus Williams
Brig. Gen. Thomas Ruger*

2ND DIVISION
Brig. Gen. John W. Geary

CAVALRY CORPS
Maj. Gen. Alfred Pleasonton

1ST DIVISION
Brig. Gen. John Buford

2ND DIVISION
Brig. Gen. David McM. Gregg

3RD DIVISION
Brig. Gen. Judson Kilpatrick

Total Union Army Strength at Gettysburg: 88,000

Total Union Casualties (killed, wounded, missing, captured): 23,000

A 10-pound Parrott rifle of Battery D 5th U.S. Artillery on Little Round Top

ARMY OF NORTHERN VIRGINIA • Order of Battle

General Robert E. Lee

Col. R. H. Chilton, Chief of Staff
Brig. Gen. W. N. Pendleton, Chief of Artillery
Col. A. L. Long, Military Secretary
Lt. Col. Walter Taylor, Aide-de-Camp
Capt. S. R. Johnston, Staff Engineer

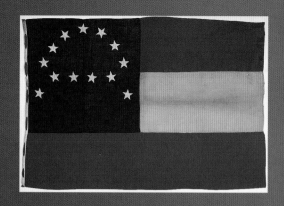

I CORPS Lt. Gen. James Longstreet	II CORPS Lt. Gen. Richard S. Ewell	III CORPS Lt. Gen. Ambrose Powell Hill	CAVALRY GRAND DIVISION Lt. Gen. James E. B. Stuart
1ST DIVISION Maj. Gen. Lafayette McLaws	1ST DIVISION Maj. Gen. Jubal A. Early	1ST DIVISION Maj. Gen. R. H. Anderson	BRIGADE COMMANDERS
2ND DIVISION Maj. Gen. George Pickett	2ND DIVISION Maj. Gen. Edward Johnson	2ND DIVISION Maj. Gen. Henry Heth Brig. Gen. James J. Pettigrew*	Brig. Gen. Wade Hampton Col. R. S. Baker* Brig. Gen. Fitz Lee
3RD DIVISION Maj. Gen. John Bell Hood Brig. Gen. Evander Law*	3RD DIVISION Maj. Gen. Robert Rodes	3RD DIVISION Maj. Gen. William D. Pender Brig. Gen. James H. Lane* Maj. Gen. Isaac Trimble*	Brig. Gen. Beverly Robertson Brig. Gen. Albert G. Jenkins Col. M. J. Ferguson* Brig. Gen. William E. Jones Col. J. R. Chambliss

*Officers who succeeded command
of units during the battle are
indicated by an asterisk.

Total Confederate Army Strength at Gettysburg: 73,000

Total Confederate Casualties (killed, wounded, missing, captured): 28,000

Bronze statue of Major General
Gouvernor Warren on Little Round Top

A PORTFOLIO
OF
GETTYSBURG
BATTLEFIELD
MONUMENTS

9th Pennsylania Reserves Monument
on Big Round Top

Pennsylvania Memorial

Two 10-pound Parrott rifles of Battery D
5th U.S. Artillery on Little Round Top

The Battle of Gettysburg has been the object of detailed and critical study for more than a hundred years. The foregoing synthesis is therefore necessarily dependent on the scholarly work of many others. Just in Chapter One, for example, Dan Sutherland will recognize my use of his term—"the dare mark"—to describe the line of the Rapidan-Rappahannock Rivers, and Archer Jones (along with the late Tom Connelly) first coined the phrase "the western concentration bloc" to describe that group of Davis's critics who urged greater Confederate efforts in the western theater. It would be impossible for me to list here every student of the battle whose work contributed to this narrative, but fairness requires me to name at least some of the most important. Edwin B. Coddington's *The Gettysburg Campaign: A Study in Command* (New York, 1968) remains the most thorough and reliable one-volume narrative of the events of July 1–3. A useful collection of thoughtful essays on some of the more controversial aspects of the battle is Gary Gallagher, ed., *Three Days at Gettysburg: Essays on Confederate and Union Leadership* (Kent, Ohio, 1999). For comprehensiveness and detail, there is no better source than the three volumes (so far) by Harry W. Pfanz, former chief historian at Gettysburg National Military Park: *Gettysburg: The First Day* (Chapel Hill, 2001), *Gettysburg: The Second Day* (Chapel Hill, 1987), and *Gettysburg: Culp's Hill and Cemetery Hill* (Chapel Hill, 1993).

Biographies are a particularly compelling way to approach any battle, for in the end, all battles are the result of a myriad number of personal decisions made by individuals at almost every level. In this category, the place to start is with Douglas Southall Freeman, whose worshipful biography *R. E. Lee* (New York, 1935) is still a good read despite the author's unwillingness to write anything critical about Marse Robert. (A more balanced view is offered by Emory Thomas in *Robert E. Lee, A Biography* [New York, 1995], but Thomas emphasizes the man rather than the soldier and passes over Gettysburg rather quickly.) Another indispensable work is Freeman's *Lee's Lieutenants* (New York, 1944), volume III of which is titled *Gettysburg to Appomattox*. For Meade, the best work remains Freeman Cleaves, *Meade of Gettysburg* (Norman, Okla., 1960).

There has been a great deal of recent biographical scholarship of Lee's corps commanders. The best of these are James I. Robertson's biography *A. P. Hill: The Story of a Confederate Warrior* (New York, 1987), Jeffry Wert's *General James Longstreet: The Confederacy's Most Controversial Soldier* (New York, 1993), and Donald C. Pfanz's *Richard S. Ewell: A Soldier's Life* (Chapel Hill, 1998). Curiously, with the exception of Joshua Lawrence Chamberlain and George Armstrong Custer, there has been less attention paid to leaders on the Union side. Edward J. Nichols's book on Reynolds (*Toward Gettysburg: A Biography of General John F. Reynolds* [University Park, Pa., 1958]) is still the best book on the I Corps commander, Glenn Tucker's *Hancock the Superb* (Indianapolis, 1960) has not been surpassed, and W. A. Swanburg's appropriately named *Sickles the Incredible* (New York, 1956) remains the best work on that controversial officer.

One book that has had an extraordinary impact on popular perceptions of what happened at Gettysburg is Michael Shaara's novel *The Killer Angels,* which won the Pulitzer Prize for fiction in 1979 and which was not only widely read, but was subsequently made into a popular film as well. It is a great read and not to be missed, though readers must remember that it is a novel and not history. Shaara's sympathy for Longstreet's professional dilemma, his presumption that Lee's physical ailments affected his decision making during the battle, and his admiration of Chamberlain's personal heroism are the key interpretive elements of this work. In composing it, Shaara relied heavily on the personal memoirs of both Longstreet and Chamberlain, and like all memoirs, both of those works are subject to all the pitfalls of memory. Chamberlain subsequently embellished his own role in the famous counterattack of the 20th Maine of Little Round Top (see sidebar, pp. 150–51), and as for Longstreet, one critic opined in 1904 that "If Longstreet . . . says so, it is most likely not true."

The most famous event at the Battle of Gettysburg is Pickett's Charge, which many scholars suggest should properly be called "Longstreet's Charge" or even the less euphonious "Pickett-Pettigrew-Trimble Charge." (The monument to the 26th North Carolina on Cemetery Ridge refers to the assault as the "Pettigrew-Pickett Charge.") A detailed narrative of that assault is George R. Stewart's *Pickett's Charge: A Microhistory of the Final Attack at Gettysburg, July 3, 1863* (Boston, 1959; Dayton, Ohio, 1983). Those interested in how this near mythic event has permeated the American, and particularly the Southern, consciousness, should read Carol Reardon's thoughtful *Pickett's Charge in History and Memory* (Chapel Hill, 1997).

For those willing to make the effort, the one indispensable source for every historian of the Civil War is the extensive collection of Official Records accumulated in the 1880s by the Department of War and published as *The War of the Rebellion: A Compilation of the Official Records of the Union and Confederate Armies*. Volume 27, which is actually three volumes (parts 1, 2, and 3), includes the reports (from both sides) concerning the Battle of Gettysburg in just over 3,000 pages. It is important to remember, however, that many of the after-action reports contained in these volumes were written several months (and in a few cases even years) after the battle. Nevertheless, when used with caution, these documents can be deemed primary sources.

Caution must also be used in reading the firsthand memoirs of many of the participants published in such nineteenth-century periodicals as *Confederate Veteran, The Southern Historical Society Papers,* and *Century* magazine. (Most of the pertinent articles in the last of these were subsequently republished in a four-volume collection called *Battles and Leaders of the Civil War* [New York, 1884–88].) Though these are indisputably firsthand accounts, they need to be read in conjunction with other accounts in order to filter out the self-serving or time-damaged memories. Excerpts from several firsthand accounts are included in the sidebars of this volume, notably those of Edward Porter Alexander (published as *Fighting for the Confederacy*, edited by Gary Gallagher [Chapel Hill, 1989]), Rufus R. Dawes (published as *A Full Blown Yankee of the Iron Brigade*, edited by Alan T. Nolan [Lincoln, Nebr., 1962, 1999]), and Frank Haskell and William C. Oates (published together as *Gettysburg*, edited by Glenn LaFantasie [New York, 1992]).

For those who envision battles most effectively by examining maps of the battlefield, two books are of special interest: my own short booklet titled *Gettysburg: A Battlefield Atlas* (Baltimore, 1992) and the much more detailed and colorful volume by John D. Imhof on the second day's fighting, *Gettysburg, Day Two: A Study in Maps* (Baltimore, 1999).

Finally, some of the best recent scholarship on the Battle of Gettysburg is in the specialized articles of such modern publications as *Civil War Times Illustrated, North & South,* and especially *The Gettysburg Magazine*, which are devoted exclusively to various aspects of the Civil War's most important, and most exhaustively studied, military engagement.

ACKNOWLEDGMENTS

I must acknowledge a number of personal debts: My friend Howard Bahr, who is the best living novelist on the Civil War era, first urged me to tackle this project. D. Scott Hartwig, the chief historian at Gettysburg National Military Park, whose knowledge of the battlefield is unsurpassed, read the entire manuscript and offered many important corrections and suggestions, for which I am grateful. Likewise I am grateful to Park Historian John Heiser, who was very helpful in identifying battlefield landmarks. Several tours of the battlefield with veteran tour guide Gary Kross sharpened my understanding of the battle. My editor at Byron Preiss Visual Publications, Dwight Zimmerman, who kept me focused on the project, as editors will do; Valerie Cope, who gathered the hundreds of images that adorn the text and put up with my demanding requests for just the right images to illustrate the battle; Gilda Hannah, who designed this beautiful book; Kathy Huck, who signed me on to the project and played an important role during production; Barbara Strauch, Richard Snow, and Frederick Allen at American Heritage, an institution whose products have maintained the highest of standards of scholarship and readability for nearly a half century; Cathy Hemming, Tim Duggan, Roni Axelrod, and Cindy Achar at HarperCollins; and Ann Abel and Jan Miles, who copyedited and proofread this work.

Most importantly, I once again offer thanks to my wife, Marylou, who has walked the battlefield with me countless times, who listened patiently as I read aloud to her each chapter of the manuscript—in several iterations—and who has disproved the adage that an author and a critic cannot live together happily.

—Craig L. Symonds

ILLUSTRATION CREDITS

ABBREVIATIONS
CS: Craig Symonds
GNMP: Gettysburg National Military Park, NPS, Gettysburg, Penn.
LC: Library of Congress, Washington, D.C.
MASS-MOLLUS/USAMHI: Massachusetts Commandery of the Military Order of the Loyal Legion of the United States and the U.S. Army Military History Institute, Carlisle, Penn.
NA: National Archives, Washington, D.C.
USAMHI: U.S. Army Military History Institute, Carlisle Barracks, Penn.
WPC: Frank & Marie-Therese Wood Print Collection, Alexandria, Va.

FRONT MATTER
1 Top: Barlow's Knoll, July 1, 1863, photo by James Pierce, NA #NWDNS-200-M-276(2); bottom: Pickett's Charge, WPC. **2–3** James Walker, *First Day at Gettysburg*, ca. 1865, West Point Museum Collection, United States Military Academy, photo by Anthony Mairo.

PROLOGUE
6 WPC. **8** Top: Courtesy David Humiston Kelley; bottom: Courtesy Mark H. Dunkelman. **9** Both: Courtesy of the N.C. Division of Archives and History. **10** Adams County Historical Society, Gettysburg, Pennsylvania. **11** Top: Don Troiani; bottom: Adams County Historical Society, Gettysburg, Pennsylvania.

CHAPTER ONE
12 The Museum of the Confederacy, Richmond, Virginia, copied by Katherine Wetzel. **14** NA #NWDNS-111-B-326. **15** © Medford Historical Society Collection/CORBIS. **16** LC-USZC4-1760. **18** Chicago Historical Society, neg. #ICHi–09975. **19** WPC. **20** NA. **21** LC-B8172-1562. **22** LC-USZ62-39901. **24** LC-USZC4-2058. **25** MASS-MOLLUS/USAMHI. **26** From left to right: Virginia Historical Society, Richmond, Virginia; Valentine Museum/Richmond History Center; The Museum of the Confederacy, Richmond, Virginia. **27** Top left: NA #NWDNS-111-B-4717; top right: NA #NWDNS-111-B-2774; center left: NA #NWDNS-111-B-4165; center right: NA #NWDNS-111-B-2372; bottom, from left to right: LC-B8172-1702; NA #NWDNS-111-B-3685; NA #NWDNS-111-B-3542.

CHAPTER TWO
28 Virginia Historical Society, Richmond, Virginia. **30** NA #NWDNS-165-SB-73. **31** Valentine Museum/Richmond History Center. **32** LC-BH-831-1329. **33** WPC. **34** LC-B8172-2009. **35** NWDNS-111-B-4481. **36** LC-USZ62-7902. **37** NA #NWDNS-165-SB-32. **38** LC. **39** © David Muench/CORBIS. **41** LC-USZC2-3761. **43** pfMS Am 1585 by permission of the Houghton Library, Harvard University. **44** WPC. **45** LC-B8171-7649. **46** The Abraham Lincoln Foundation of the Union League of Philadelphia. **47** David J. Eicher/Well-Traveled Images.

CHAPTER THREE
48 WPC. **50** From *The Soldier in Our Civil War,* published by Stanley-Bradley Pub. Co., New York, 1894. **51** Public domain. **52** USAMHI. **53** The Maryland Historical Society, Baltimore, Maryland. **54** Top: from *The Soldier in Our Civil War,* published by Stanley-Bradley Pub. Co., New York, 1894; bottom: LC-USZ62-33816. **55** Top: LC-USZ62-110269; bottom: Adams County Historical Society, Gettysburg, Pennsylvania. **56** LC. **57** LC-BH821-5900. **58–59** The York County Heritage Trust, PA. **60** LC-B813-6785. **61** Top: General Research Division, The New York Public Library, Astor, Lenox and Tilden Foundations; bottom: LC-B8171-2393. **62–63** GNMP. **64** USAMHI. **67** Guns courtesy of Don Troiani; bottom: CS.

CHAPTER FOUR
68 Alan T. Nolan Collection. **70** Top: NA #NWDNS-111-B-17; bottom: from the Pettigrew Family Papers #592, Southern Historical Collection, Wilson Library, University of North Carolina at Chapel Hill. **71** LC. **72** WPC. **73** General Research Division, The New York Public Library, Astor, Lenox and Tilden Foundations. **74** Wisconsin Veterans Museum, Madison, Wisc. **75** LC-USZC4-1041. **76–77** Courtesy, Museum of Fine Arts, Boston. Reproduced with permission. © 2000 Museum of Fine Arts, Boston. All Rights Reserved. **78** WPC. **79** Left: WPC; right: CS. **80** Top: Chicago Historical Society, neg. #ICHi–07906; bottom: CS. **82** LC-B8172-3719. **83** NA #NWDNS-111-B-3516. **84–85** State Museum of Penn., Pennsylvania Historical and Museum Commission. **86** Top: USAMHI; bottom: Wisconsin Veterans Museum, Madison, Wisc.; Collection of Old Capitol Museum, Mississippi Department of Archives and History. **87** NA #NWDNS-111-B-5173.

CHAPTER FIVE
88 Valentine Museum/Richmond History Center. **90** LC-USZ62-89454. **91** Top: LC-D4-37052 L and LC-D4-37052 R; bottom: NA #NWDNS-111-B-1786. **92** The Historic New Orleans Collection, accession no. 1977.137.2.7. **93** Left: NWDNS-111-B-21; right: NWDNS-111-B-3949. **94** Left: USAMHI; right: WPC. **95** USAMHI. **96** NWDNS-111-B-5060. **97** Public domain. **100** CS. **101** USAMHI. **102** NA #NWDNS-111-B-21. **103** GNMP **104–105** West Point Museum Collection, United States Military Academy, photo by Anthony Mairo. **107** Don Troiani.

CHAPTER SIX
108 CS. **110** GNMP. **111** USAMHI. **112** LC-B8171-7330. **113** NA #NWDNS-111-B-1884. **114** NA #NWDNS-111-B-4683. **115** NA #NWDNS-111-B-1333. **116** LC-USZ62-102514. **117** Top: LC-USZ62-102514; bottom: Adams County Historical Society, Gettysburg, Pennsylvania. **118** GNMP. **119** The Museum of the Confederacy, Richmond, Virginia, photography by Katherine Wetzel.

CHAPTER SEVEN
120 Archive Photos/Kean Collection. **122** Left: WPC; right: LC-USZ62-54709. **123** NA #NWDNS-111-B-4553. **124** CS. **125** NA #NWDNS-111-B-5819. **128** NA #NWDNS-111-B-4332. **129** Top: LC-B8184-B-29; bottom: NA #NWDNS-111-B-2456. **130** Adams County Historical Society, Gettysburg, Pennsylvania. **131** Virginia Historical Society, Richmond, Virginia. **132** LC-B8184-10387. **132–133** R. Scott Dann.

CHAPTER EIGHT
134 © CORBIS. **136** Brian C. Pohanka. **137** © David Muench/CORBIS. **138** USAMHI. **139** LC-USZC4-1825. **140** WPC. **142** USAMHI. **143** Courtesy of the National Infantry Museum, Fort Benning, Ga. **144** USAMHI. **145** General Research Division, The New York Public Library, Astor, Lenox and Tilden Foundations. **146** Virginia Historical Society, Richmond, Virginia. **146–147** LC-USZC4-976. **147** USAMHI. **148** NA #NWDNS-165-SB-44. **150** Top: courtesy of The Pejepscot Historical Society, Brunswick, Maine; bottom: Don Troiani. **151** Maine State Archives. **152** Maine State Museum, Augusta, Maine; Maine State Archives. **153** State Museum of Penn., Pennsylvania Historical and Museum Commission.

CHAPTER NINE
154 CS. **156** USAMHI. **157** Virginia Historical Society, Richmond, Virginia. **158** MASS-MOLLUS/USAMHI. **159** Top: Don Troiani; bottom: University of Notre Dame Archives, Notre Dame, Indiana. **160–161** The Snite Museum of Art, University of Notre Dame, Notre Dame, Indiana. **162** LC-USZ62-

18156. **164** LC. **165** Top: USAMHI; bottom: NA #NWDNS-165-SB-36. **166** Top: USAMHI; bottom: LC-B813-1423. **167** CS. **168–169** Rufus Zogbaum, Minnesota Historical Society. **170** Virginia Historical Society, Richmond, Virginia. **171** National Museum of Health & Medicine, Armed Forces Institute of Pathology, #379085.

CHAPTER TEN
172 © David Muench/CORBIS. **174–175** © CORBIS. **176** LC-B8172-2033. **177** LC. **178–179** LC-USZC4-1859. **180–181** USAMHI. **182** NA. **183** Anne S. K. Brown Military Collection, Brown University Library. **184–185** State Museum of Penn., Pennsylvania Historical and Museum Commission. **186** Top: LC-B8171-0254; bottom: LC. **187** Top: LC-USZ62-7030; bottom: LC-USZ62-18175. **188** General Research Division, The New York Public Library, Astor, Lenox and Tilden Foundations. **189** GNMP. **192** WPC. **193** David J. Eicher/Well-Traveled Images.

CHAPTER ELEVEN
194 The Seventh Regiment Fund, Inc. **196** MASS-MOLLUS/USAMHI. **197** Top: CS; bottom: NA #NWDNS-111-B-5108. **198** General Research Division, The New York Public Library, Astor, Lenox and Tilden Foundations. **199** Virginia Historical Society, Richmond, Virginia. **200** Both: USAMHI. **201** Craig Haffner, courtesy William A. Frassanito's *Early Photography at Gettysburg*. **202** LC-B8172-2179. **203** NA #NWDNS-111-B-1564. **204** The Maryland Historical Society, Baltimore, Maryland. **206–207** State Museum of Penn., Pennsylvania Historical and Museum Commission. **208** Top: LC-USZ62-117573; bottom: General Research Division, The New York Public Library, Astor, Lenox and Tilden Foundations. **209–210** CS. **211** Top: R. Scott Dann; bottom: Virginia Historical Society, Richmond, Virginia.

CHAPTER TWELVE
212 WPC. **215** Top: Virginia Historical Society, Richmond, Virginia; bottom: USAMHI. **216** LC-B8171-0259. **217** USAMHI. **218** USAMHI. **219** WPC. **220** LC. **221** Left: David J. Eicher/Well-Traveled Images; right: NA #NWDNS-111-B-2522. **222** NA# NWDNS-111-B-3338. **223** GNMP. **224–225** LC-USZC4-978. **228–231** GNMP. **232–233** New Hampshire Historical Society. **234** Both: The Museum of the Confederacy, Richmond, Virginia, photography by Katherine Wetzel. **235** USAMHI. **236–237** WPC. **238** Both: CS. **239–241** WPC.

CHAPTER THIRTEEN
242 Wadsworth Atheneum Museum of Art, Hartford. The Ella Gallup Sumner and Mary Catlin Sumner Collection Fund. **244** Left: Valentine Museum/Richmond History Center; right: The Museum of the Confederacy, Richmond, Virginia. **245** Top left: NA #NWDNS-64-M-9; top right and bottom left and right: The Museum of the Confederacy, Richmond, Virginia. **246** LC-B8172-1756. **247** Soldiers and Sailors Memorial Hall and Military Museum, Pittsburgh, Pennsylvania. **248** NA #NWDNS-111-B-192. **249** WPC. **250–251** LC-B8171-7389. **252** Both: United States Military Academy Archives, West Point. **253** All: United States Military Academy Archives, West Point (except bottom right: Museum of the Confederacy, Richmond, Virginia). **254** LC-B8171-0340. **255** WPC. **256–257** LC-USZC4-3609. **258** WPC.

CHAPTER FOURTEEN
260 LC-B811-233. **262** Top: © CORBIS; bottom: USAMHI. **263** Top: courtesy of the Atlanta History Center; bottom: AP/Wide World Photos. **264** Top: Don Troiani; bottom: LC-USZC4-2622. **265** USAMHI. **266–267** LC-USZC4-1003. **268** NA #NWDNS-79-T-2265. **269** LC-USZC4-2916. **270–271** Anne S. K. Brown Military Collection, Brown University Library. **272** LC-USZ62-18156. **273** Manuscripts and Archives, The New York Public Library, Astor, Lenox and Tilden Foundations. **276–277** LC-USZC4-979. **278** LC-USZ62-15990. **279** LC-USZ62-9222. **280** National Baseball Hall of Fame and Museum, Inc./Cooperstown, N.Y.

EPILOGUE
282 © Farrell Grehan/CORBIS. **284** NA #NWDNS-111-B-357. **285** Both: NA #NWDNS-111-B-4975. **286** Brown Brothers. **287** Pennsylvania State Archives, RG-25 Records of Special Commissions. **288** LC-LSMS-30189-76. **289** LC-LSMS-30189-77. **290–291** United States Military Academy. **292** WPC/Bob Marcus.

BACK MATTER
294 From left to right: NA #NWDNS-111-B-4717; NA #NWDNS-111-B-4165; LC-B8172-1702; NA #NWDNS-111-B-4683. **295** Top: Harpers Ferry Center/NPS; bottom, from left to right: NA #NWDNS-111-B-2774; NA #NWDNS-111-B-2372; NA #NWDNS-111-B-3542; NA #NWDNS-111-B-4481. **296** Photography by D&D Griggs, Topsham, Maine. **297** Top: The Museum of the Confederacy, Richmond, Virginia; bottom, from left to right: NA #NWDNS-111-B-1333; Valentine Museum/Richmond History Center; The Museum of the Confederacy, Richmond, Virginia; NA #NWDNS-64-M-9. **298–307** Photography by D&D Griggs, Topsham, Maine.

INDEX

Page numbers in *italics* indicate an illustration of the subject mentioned.

Absolution Under Fire (Wood), *160–161*
Adams, Charles Francis, Jr., on Alfred Pleasonton, 35
African-Americans
    in aftermath of Gettysburg, 261
    in Army of the Potomac, 25
    Confederate enslavement of Northern, 53–57
Alabama, 74, 90–91, 126, 132, 144, 145, 149–152, 167, 170–171, 238, 255
Alamogordo, New Mexico, 214
Aldie, 43
    battle at, 35, 39–40
Alexander, Colonel Edward Porter, 126, 131, 211, *211*, 214, 215, *215*, 219–220, 222, 226–232
Alleman, Mrs. Tillie Pierce, 56
Almshouse, 116, *117*, 118–119
Ames, Brigadier General Adelbert, 93, 152, *174–175*, 176, 188, 252, *252*, 295
Ammunition, 218, 219. *See also* Balls; Bullets
Amputation, 268, *268*, 272, 273. *See also* Surgeons
Anderson, George T. "Tige," 153, 156, 158, 159, 166, 254
Anderson, Major General Richard H., 119, 155, 167, 198, 297
Antietam Creek, battle of, 8, 24, 27, 33, 90, 91, 135, 152, 155, 162, 193, 218, 222, 278, 281, 286
Archer, James J., 71, 75
Archer's Brigade, 71, 74–75
Arkansas, 142
Armistead, Brigadier General Lewis, *212–213*, *232–233*, 238
    death of, 239, 241, 259
Armistead Monument, *238*
Arms technology, revolution in, 66–67
Army of Mississippi, 21
    surrender of, 283
Army of Northern Virginia, 16, 23, 26, 50, 55, 87, 213, 220
    in aftermath of Gettysburg, 259
    escape of, 281
    morale of, 25
    organization of, 297
    reconstitution of, 283
    retreat of, 260–281, *275–277*
Army of the Potomac, 12–16, *15*, 23, 44, 47, *60*, 65, 115, 128, 135, 150, 155, *186–187*, *194–195*, 262, 287
    field strength of, 25
    at Frederick, 45–47
    organization of, 294–295
    pursuit of Robert E. Lee by, 278–281, *280–281*
Army of Virginia, 13
Arnold's battery, 222

Artillery, 214–219, *216*, *223*, *224–225*, 226–232. *See also* Ammunition; Cannonballs; Gun crews; Muskets; Napoleon gun; Parrott gun
    shortcomings of, 214–217
    sound of, 214, 217
Ashby's Gap, 38, *41*
    battle at, 39–40
At Gettysburg: or What a Girl Saw and Heard of the Battle (Alleman), 56
Atlanta, 132
Atomic bomb, first, 214
Attack at Seminary Ridge, Gettysburg, 75–77
Avery, Colonel Isaac E., 9, 9–10, 92, *174–175*, 182–191
    death of, 188
Ayres, Brigadier General Romeyn, 294

Baker, Colonel R. S., 297
Balls, for shoulder arms, 66, 67. *See also* Bullets; Cannonballs; Minié balls; Musket balls
Baltimore, 11, 49, *53*, 57
    Gettysburg and, 45
Baltimore Pike, *10*, 56, *97*, 106, 173, 191, 192, 202, 217
Baltimore Street, 95, *284*
Barksdale, Brigadier General William, 162, *162–163*, 166, 166–167, 171, 198
    death of, 166, 170
Barlow, Brigadier General Francis C., 92, 93, *93*, *102*, 175, 252, 295
Barlow's Knoll, 92, *92*, 93, 102
Barnes, Brigadier General James, 138, 156, 158, 294
"Battle and Campaign of Gettysburg, The" (Trimble), 101
Battle of Gettysburg, The (Haskell), *217*
Battle of Seven Pines, 82
Battle of South Mountain, 74
Battles and Leaders of the Civil War, 247
Baxter's Fire Zouaves, *209*
Bayonets, 66, 150, 151, 152, 170, 222–223
Bellew, F. H., 54
Benjamin, General Judah P., *19*
Benner's Hill, 176, 182
Benning, Brigadier General Henry, *140*, 142, *143*
Berdan, Colonel Hiram, 125, *125*, 126
Beverly Ford, 33
Biesecker's Woods, *132–133*, 137, 139, 145, 157
Bigelow, Captain John, *162*
Big Round Top, *132–133*, 145, 149, 173, 254, 255
Birney, Major General David, *102*, 125, 133, 135, 158, 159, 196, 294
Bispham, H. C., 247
"Black Hat boys," 74–75
Black Horse Tavern, *130*, 131
"Bleeding" Kansas, 176, 177
Bloody Angle, The, *212–213*

Bloody Lane, 90, 91
Blue Ridge Mountains, *38*, *39*, 40, *42–43*
Blythe, David Gilmour, 280–281
Bolivar Heights, *45*, *47*
Boone, Daniel, 66
Boston, 229
Bostwick, B. O., 45
Brady, Mathew, 14, 20, 21, *62–63*, 70, *138*, 180–181, 200, 265
Bragg, General Braxton, 8, 19
Brandy Station, battle at, 30–36, *33*, *36*
Breastworks, 177, *177*, *178–179*, *180–181*, 182, 189, 192–193, 210
Breech-loading carbines, 71
Breech-loading muskets, 66–67
Briarfield, 18
Brickyard Road, 188
Brigades, organization of, 26
Bristoe Station, 43
Broadsheets, *159*
Brockenbrough, J. M., 226
Brooke, John Rutter, 159, 162–166, 167
Brooklyn, 78
Brooks, Adjutant Edward P., 86
Browne, William Garl, 70
Brown's battery, 222
Bryan Farm, 222
Buford, Brigadier General John, *32*, 33, 60–61, *62–63*, 64–65, 66, 69, 71–72, 80, 87, 98, 111, 112, 275, 281, 295
    Alfred Pleasonton and, 35
    at Brandy Station, *33*, 33–34
    at McPherson's Ridge, 69–72, *73*, 87
    rifles used by troops under, 67
Bugle calls, 10–11
Bulger, Lt. Colonel Michael, 145
Bullets, for shoulder arms, 66–67, *67*. *See also* Balls
Bull Run Creek (Manassas), 30
    first battle of, 8, 26, 27, 31, 89, 90, 156, 157
    second battle of, 13, 90, 111, 126, 222
Bull Run Mountains, 40
    battle at, 39–40
Burnside, Ambrose, 13, 23
Burnside carbine, *73*
Bushman Farm, *132–133*
Bushman's Woods, 254
Butler, Benjamin, 122
Butterfield, Major General Daniel, *113*, 128, *129*, 196–197, *197*, 279, 294

Caldwell, Brigadier General John C., *158*, 158–166, *162–163*, 167, 170, 222, 294
California, 177
Campaigns of the Army of the Potomac (Swinton), 115
Camp Letterman, 273
Candy and Kane, 202–203

Cannonballs, damage from, *171*
Carbines, 67, 254. *See also* Burnside carbine; Sharps carbine; Spencer carbine
Carlisle, 61, 90, 98–99, 199
    Confederate capture of, 57
    Gettysburg and, 45
Carlisle Barracks, 57
Carlisle Road, 10–11, *10–11*, 64, *91*
Carroll, John, 222, 223, 226
Carroll, Samuel, *174–175*, *183–185*, 191
Cartes de visite, 200
Cashtown, 65, 69, 90, 275
    Confederate occupation of, 57
Cashtown Turnpike, 86
Cavalry, 29, *242–243*, 242–259, *247*, *249*, *250–251*
    casualties among, *272*
    Confederate, 56
    muskets for, 66–67
    in Robert E. Lee's strategy, 243–244
"Cavalry Battle Near Gettysburg, The" (Miller), 247
Cavalry Charge, A (Forbes), *36*
Cemetery Hill, 9–10, 82–87, 96, *96,* 98, 100, 101, *103,* 107, 109, 110, *110,* 111, 112, 119, 121, 123, 125, 133, 137, 152, 171, *172–173,* *174–175, 183–185, 186–187, 188, 190–191,* 198, 209, 214, *216,* 221, 222, 223, 226, 244, 252, *262–263, 282–283*
    battle at, 102–106, 172–193
    George G. Meade at, 113–114
Cemetery Ridge, 102, 113–114, 121, *124,* 125, 137, 159, 167, 168–169, 170, 171, 173, 195, 196, 198, 208, 209, *209, 211,* 214, 215, *216,* 217, 221, *223, 224–225,* 234, 235, *236–237,* 238, *239, 240–241,* 243, 244, 248, 252, 254, 264, 269, 283
Chamberlain, Colonel Joshua Lawrence, 142, 145–152, *150,* 171
Chamberlain, Thomas, 150
Chambersburg, 11, 40, 60, 119
    burning of, 52
    Confederate occupation of, 50–51, *52*
    Robert E. Lee's entry into, 57–60
Chambersburg Pike, 8, 71, 86, 137, 265
Chambersburg Road, 64, 70, *70,* 72, 73–74, *78,* 78–79, 109
Chambliss, Colonel John R., 43, 244, 297
Champion's Hill, battle of, 21
Chancellorsville, 73, 82, 90, 94, 119, 121, 133, 156, 157, 182, 244, 266
    battle at, 12–16, *16,* 22–23, 24, 27, 35, *94*
Chase, Salmon P., 22, 23
Chesapeake and Ohio Canal, *275–277*
Chester Gap, 37
Chickamauga, 126
Chilton, Colonel R. H., 297
Civil War
    end of, *290–291*

meaning of, 292
medical care during, 268
photography during, 200–201
progress of, 8
spying during, 29
Civil War Recollections of General Ellis Spear, The (Spear), 151
Clarke, Major John, 116
Codori House, 171, *220,* 235, 241
Colvill, Colonel William, *168–169,* 170–171
Communications, battlefield, 121
Confederacy
    formation of, 8
    "high tide" of, 171, 213–214, 238, 239
    Robert E. Lee's resignation offer and, 283
Confederate Army, *118, 220, 258*
    abandonment of Gettysburg by, 261
    invasion of Pennsylvania by, 48–65
    organization of, 26
    prisoners from, *264,* 264–265, *265*
    seizure of Gettysburg by, 88–107
    surgeons with, *255–257*
    wounded soldiers in, *6–7*
Confederate Army Corps, *10–11*
    Cavalry Grand Division, *44,* 243–249, 254–259, 297
    I Corps, 22, 26, 38, 109, 115, 126–133, *127,* 203, 211, 214, 265–266, 297
    II Corps, 10, 22, 26, 30, 38–39, 40, 49, 51, 57, 87, 89–91, 98, *98–99,* 100–102, *103–105,* 111, 119, 203, 265–266, 297
    III Corps, 22, 26, 30, 38, 49, 60, 64, 69–71, 98, 119, 265–266, 297
Confederate money, 49–50
    used by occupying Confederate troops, 50–52, *51*
Confederate Soldier, His War Journal (Dooley), 273
Conocoheague River, 277
Conscription, by Confederacy, 16–18
Cooke, General Philip St. George, 31
Cooksville, 43
Corby, Father William, *160–161*
Corlies, Samuel Fisher, 201
Cornfield, the, 155
Corps, organization of, 26, 294–295, 297
Coster's brigade, 191
Couch, Darius N., 23–24
    Winfield Scott Hancock and, 27
Cowan, Captain Andrew, 222
Crampton's Gap, 278
Crawford, Brigadier General Samuel, 294
Cress Ridge, 246–249, 252
    casualties at, 249
Cromwell, Major James, death of, 142
Cross, Colonel Edward, 159–162
    death of, 162
Culpeper, 29–31, 37, 38, *44, 112*
Culp's Hill, *70, 91, 97, 100,* 100–102, *103–105,*

111, 114, 123–124, 167, *177, 178–179, 180–181, 189, 190–191, 192,* 195, 197, 198, 199, *200,* 202–203, *204,* 205, 208, 209, 210, 211, 244
    battle at, 106–107, 172–193
    photography of, 200
Cumberland Valley, 265, 275, 277
Curtin, Andrew, 50
Cushing, Lt. Alonzo H., 222, 238, 239, *252*
    death of, 235, 252
Custer, Brigadier General George Armstrong, 246, 247, 248, *248,* 250, 251, 252, *253, 279*
Cutler, Lysander, 73–74, 75–78, 86
Cyclorama canvas, *223, 228–229, 230–231*

Daniel, Junius, 205
"Dare mark," 283
    crossing of, 13–16
Davis, Jefferson, 18, *18,* 19, *19,* 214
    in preparations for Gettysburg, 21, 22
    Robert E. Lee's resignation and, 283
Davis, Joseph R., 71, 75–78, 79, 226
Davis, Theodore, 284
Dawes, Colonel Rufus R., 78, 79–82, 86, 189, 191–192
Death of General Reynolds, The (Rothermel), *84–85*
Democrats, 20
de Thulstrup, Thure, 236–237
de Trobriand, Colonel Philip Regis Denis de Kerendern, 135, 136, 155–156, *156,* 158
Devil's Den, 125, *132–133, 139, 140,* 152, 155, 156, 166, 171, 254, 255, *255*
    assault on, 132–144, *140–141*
    photography of, 200
Devin, Thomas, *64,* 64–65
Diamond, the, 10
Disease, 268
Divisions, organization of, 26
Dooley, John, 273
Doubleday, Major General Abner, 75, 78, *83,* 87, 90, 107, 196n, 196, 294
Douglas, Henry Kyd, 98
Downsville, 277
Duffie, Alfred N.
    at Brandy Station, 33–35
    at Middleburg, 40
Durkin, Joseph T., 273

Early, Major General Jubal A. "Old Jube," 51–53, 64, 92, 97, 98, 100, *111,* 114, 173, 175, 176, 182, 187, 188–191, 209, 239, 252, 297
    Gettysburg strategy of, 111–112
    occupation of York by, 57, *58–59*
Early Photography at Gettysburg (Frassanito), 201
East Cemetery Hill, 97, *183–185*
Eastern Theater, *16–17*
Edward's Ferry, 44
Emmitsburg, 11, 65, 71, 125, 275

Emmitsburg Road, *10*, 65, 74, 116, 118, 119, 121, 124, 125, 128, 131, 132, 133, 135, 136, 140, *154–155*, 157, 159, 166, *166*, 167, 170, 171, 233–234, 235, 238, 254, 265–266, *284*
Enfield muskets, 244, 254
Enfield rifle, *67*
Ensworth, Philinda, 8–9
Espionage, 29, 59–60
Everett, Edward, 285, 292–293
Evergreen Cemetery, *96*, 173, *174–175*
Ewell, Lizinka Brown, 90
Ewell, Lt. General Richard Stoddert "Dick," 10–11, 22, *26*, 37, 38–39, 40–41, 50, 53, 60, 87, *88–89*, 98–99, 101, 109, 110, 114, 116, 118–119, 126, 133, 173–176, 177, 191, 199, 202–203, 204, 205–208, 209, 215, 244, 249, 265, 266, 281, 297
   advance on Gettysburg by, 30
   conduct at Gettysburg of, 96–98, 99–102
   crossing of Mason-Dixon Line by, 49
   at Culp's Hill, 106–107
   encampment at Gettysburg of, 45–47, 90
   Gettysburg strategy of, 111
   military career of, 89–90
   occupation of Chambersburg by, 51–52, 57

Fairfax, 43
Fairfield, 265, 269, 275
Fairfield Road, 269
Falling Waters, *278*, *279*, 281
Farnsworth, Brigadier General Elon J., 251–255, *255*
   death of, 255
Faulkner, William, 213
Ferguson, Colonel M. J., 297
Field hospitals, 268, 272–273, *273*
Fieldworks, 177–178
Fight for the Standard, The, *242–243*
Fighting for the Confederacy: The Personal Recollections of General Edward Porter Alexander (Gallagher, ed.), 215
Flags, 152, *159*, *208*, 234, *234*
Fleetwood Hill, 34, 35
Florida, 167, 170
Forbes, Edwin, 24, 36, 38, 110, 132–133, 146–147, 174–175, 177, 178–179, 198, 208, 224–225, 266–267, 269, 272, 275–277, 278, 279
Fort Sumter, 8, 9, 31, 156, 214, 222, 252
Frank Leslie's Illustrated Newspaper, *54*
Frassanito, William A., 201
Frederick, 44, 59–60
   Army of the Potomac at, 45–47
Fredericks, C. D., 121
Fredericksburg, 24, 26, 30, 37, 131, 152, 156, 281
Freeman, Douglas Southall, 90, 97
Front Royal, 37
Fry's brigade, 238
Fugitive Slave Law, 53–57

Gallagher, Gary, 215
Gamble, Colonel William, 71, 80
Gardner, Alexander, *95*, 139, 164–165
Garnett, Richard, 220, 239
   death of, 259
Gauntlets, Jeb Stuart's, *245*
Geary, Brigadier General John W., 106, 114, 123, 125, *176*, 177–178, 179, 192, 202, *205–207*, 295
George Weikert House, *124*, 170
Georgia, 91, 92, 93–94, 130, 131, 132, 142, 156, 158, 159, 162, 164, 166, 167, 170, 171, 254
German immigrants, Carl Schurz and, 87
Gettysburg, *70*, *80*, *91*, *116–117*, *201*, *228–231*
   aftermath of, 259, *260–261*, 260–281, 282–293
   aftermath of battle at, 8–10
   battle of McPherson's Ridge at, 68–87
   battles leading up to, 13–16
   casualties at, 193, *260–261*, 261, *262–263*, 272, *272–273*, *273*, 295, 297
   cavalry at, 242–259
   civilians at battle of, 95
   Civil War and, 8
   Confederate retreat from, 7, 260–281
   Confederate seizure of, 88–107, *98–99*, 111–112
   Daniel Sickles at, 121–126
   dedication ceremony at, *284*, *285*
   James Longstreet at, 108–119, *126–127*, 126–133
   layout of, 10–11
   photography at, 200–201
   Pickett's charge at, 212–241
   plans for Union evacuation of, 114
   preparations for battle of, 16–23, 28–47
   regiments at, 26, 45–47
   Richard S. Ewell ordered to, 90
   timing of battle of, 107
"Gettysburg: A Boy's Experience of the Battle" (McCreary), 272–273
Gettysburg: A Journey in Time (Frassanito), 201
Gettysburg (LaFantasie, ed.), 217
Gettysburg (motion picture), 115
Gettysburg address, 285, 287–293, *288–289*, *292*
   text of, 293
Gettysburg & Hanover Railroad, *80*
Gettysburg reunion, *286*
Gibbon, Brigadier General John, *102*, 171, 196, 217, 222, 235, 241, 294
Gifford, Sanford Robinson, 194–195
Goldsborough, Major William H., 204
Gone with the Wind (Mitchell), 115
Gordon, Brigadier General John B., 57, *91*, 92, 93, *93*, 97, 98, 187, 188–191, 275
Gordon, General J. B., 93
Graham, Charles K., 135
   death of, 166
Grand Assault. *See* Pickett's Charge

Granite Schoolhouse Road, 192
Grant, General Ulysses S. "Unconditional Surrender," 8, 18, 19, 20, 21, 287
   capture of Vicksburg by, 283, *284*
Greencastle, 275
Greene, George S., 178, *178–179*, 179, 182, 189, 191, 192–193, 205, 208
Greenwood, 275
Gregg, Brigadier General David McMurtrie, 61, 244–246, *246*, 247, 248, 250, 295
   at Brandy Station, 33–35
Groveton, 74
   battle of, 22
   Richard S. Ewell wounded at, 90
Gun crews, *198*
Guns. *See* Artillery; Napoleon gun; Muskets; Pistol; Rifles

Hagerstown, 11, 276–277
Hagerstown Road, 61, *130*, 131
Hall, Captain James A., 74, 78, *78*
Hall, Captain James S., 137–138
Hall, Norman, 241
Halleck, Major General Henry Wager, 30, 47, 197, 267, 278–279, 286, 287
   Joseph Hooker's resignation and, 44
Hampton, Brigadier General Wade, 43, 244, *244*, 246–247, 297
Hancock, Major General Winfield Scott, 24, *27*, *102*, 103–106, 107, 109, 112, 114, 124, 126, 129, 137, 158–159, 168–169, 170, 171, *172–173*, 191, 196, 218, 219, *221*, 222, *230–231*, 233, *236–237*, 239, *239*, 241, 243, 247, 283, 294
   in aftermath of Gettysburg, 259
Hanover, 11, 61, 65, 254
   battle at, 60
Hanover Road, 246, 247
Hardee-model hat, *68–69*, 74, *74*
Hardie, Colonel James A., 44–45
Harpers Ferry, 44, *45*, 47, 222
Harper's Weekly, 186–187
Harrisburg, 10, *54*, 57, 58, 60, 65, 90, 211
Harrisburg Road, 92, *92*
Harrison, James, 59
Harrow, Brigadier General William, 294
Harvest of Death (Gardner), *165*
Haskell, Lt. Frank A., 217, *217*
Hat, Jeb Stuart's, 245
Hays, Brigadier General Alexander, 211, *222*, 222–223, 226, 234, 238, 241, 294
Hays, Harry, 92, *174–175*, 182–191, *183*, *186–187*. *See also* Louisiana Tigers
Hazard, Captain John G., 218
Hazlett, Lieutenant Charles E., 144, *146–147*, *253*
   death of, 135, 147, 252
"Head logs," 178
Herbst's Woods, 74

Herr's Ridge, 64, 71, 74, 79, 82, 91, 92–93, 131

Heth, Major General Henry "Harry," 71, 80, 82, 87, 98–99, 203, 211, 220, 281, 297
    at Herr's Ridge, 91
    at McPherson's Ridge, 69–71, *103–105*

"High tide" of Confederacy, 171, 213–214, 238, 239

Hill, Lt. General Ambrose Powell, 22, *26*, 30, 37, 40, 49, 60, 64, 69–71, 89, 98, 101, 111, 203, 209–211, 265, 297
    encampment at Gettysburg of, 45
    at Herr's Ridge, 91

Hill's Corps, 26, 111, 119

"Historicus," 128–129

Hoffbauer, Charles, 28–29

Hoke, Robert, 9–10, 92, 182

Hood, Major General John Bell, 29, 118, 119, 126, 131–133, *132*, 136, 155, 198, 203, 297
    military career of, 131–132

Hood's division, *132–133*

Hooker, General Joseph "Fighting Joe," *14*, 21, 23–24, 25, 29, *36*, 41, 43, 59, 113, 196, 197
    advance on Gettysburg by, 37–40
    Alfred Pleasonton and, 35
    at Chancellorsville, 13–16, *16–17*, 266
    Daniel Sickles and, 27, 122–123
    encampment at Gettysburg of, 45–47
    Lincoln's advice to, 30
    resignation of, 44

Hospitals, 268, 272–273, *273*

Houck's Ridge, 136, *140*, 142, 149

"Housewife" kit, *119*

Howard, Major General Oliver Otis, 14–15, 23, 24, *27*, 74, *82*, 82–87, 96, 103–106, 107, 112, 139–140, 173, 176, 191, 278, 279, 295

Howard, Private David R., 210

Howe, Brigadier General Albion, 295

Humiston, Amos, *8*, 8–9, 10

Humphreys, Brigadier General Andrew A., 125, 144, *166*, 167, 170, 279, 281, 294

Hunt, Brigadier General Henry Jackson, 125, 129, 218, *218*, 226, 294

Hygiene, 268

Imboden, Brigadier General John D., 7, 8, 259, 274–276

Indiana, 74, 136

Infantry
    Confederate, 56, *56*
    flags of, *86*
    in Robert E. Lee's strategy, 243–244
    tactics of, 66–67

Insanity plea, by Daniel Sickles, 122

Intelligence gathering, 29

Intruder in the Dust (Faulkner), 213

Invalid Corps, 268

Irish Brigade, *159*, 159–162, *160–161*, 166

Iron Brigade, *68–69*, 74–75, 78, 94, 107, 177, 192, 195

Iron Works, burning of, 57

Iverson, Brigadier General Alfred, 91

Jackson, General Thomas J. "Stonewall," *16–17*, 23, 27, 34, 97, 98, 106, 111, 119, 121, 133, 205
    at Chancellorsville, 12–16
    death of, 16, 21–22
    at Rappahannock River, 12
    Richard S. Ewell and, 26, 89–90

Jenkins, Brigadier General Albert Gallatin, *48–49*, *55*, 244, 246, 297
    occupation of Chambersburg by, 50–51

J. L. Schick's Dry Goods Store, *55*

Johnson, Major General Edward "Allegheny," 98, 100, 107, 176, 177, *178–179*, 179, 182, 202, 203, 205–208, 297

Johnston, Captain Samuel R., 116–118, 121, 124, 130, 131, 297

Johnston, General Joseph E., 13, 19

John Weikert House, 114

Jones, Brigadier General William E. "Grumble," 43, 297

Joseph Weikert House, 159

Julio, E. B. D., 12–13

Kane, Thomas L., 205. *See also* Candy and Kane

Kansas, 176, 177, 192

Keeler, Private Charles P., *68–69*

Kelly, Patrick, 159–162

Kelly, Thomas, 19

Kelly's Ford, 33

Kemper, James, 220, 239, 259

Kentucky, 8

Kershaw, Brigadier General Joseph Brevard, *153*, 156–158, *157*, 162, 166, 167

Key, Francis Scott, 122

Key, Philip Barton, 122, *122*

"Kill-cavalry," 250, 254

Killer Angels, The (Shaara), 115, 151

Kilpatrick, Brigadier General Judson, 39–40, 60, 61, 65, 246, 249–251, 252, *253*, 254, *254*, 255–259, 269, 279, 295

Knight, Daniel Ridgway, 46

Knox, David, 30

Kryzanowski, Colonel Wladimir, 191

LaFantasie, Glenn, 217

Lafayette, Marquis de, 156

Lafayette Guards, 156

Lafayette Square, 122

Lamon, Ward, 292, 293

Lane, Brigadier General James H., 297

Lane's brigade, 238

Last Meeting of Lee and Jackson, The (Julio), *12–13*

Latimer, Major Joseph W., *182*
    death of, 182

Law, Brigadier General Evander, 126–130, 132, 133, 140–142, 144, 145, 149, 155, 254, 255, 297

Law, George, 48–49, 50

Lee, Brigadier General Fitzhugh, 43, 244, *244*, 246–247, 275–276, 297

Lee, General Robert Edward, 7, 8, 19, 36–37, 43, 47, 51, 52–53, 61, 70, 89, 90, 100, 112, 113, 114, 121, 125, 126–130, 131, 132–133, 137, 167, 173, 174, 175, 176, 195, 202, *203*, 214, 220, 222, 241, *241*, 243, 244, 245, 249, 261, 262
    Abraham Lincoln on escape of, 286–287
    advance on Gettysburg by, 29–30, 37–40
    in aftermath of Gettysburg, 259
    at Brandy Station, 30–32
    as Chancellorsville, 12–16
    encampment at Gettysburg of, 45
    at Fredericksburg, 13
    in Gettysburg preparations, 21–23
    Gettysburg strategy of, 109–111, 198–199, 203–204, 208–211, 215, 226–232
    at Herr's Ridge, 91, 92–93
    invasion of Maryland by, 49
    invasion of Pennsylvania by, 49–50, *50*, 54, 55, 57–60
    James Longstreet and, 115, 116–119, 126, 130
    Jeb Stuart and, 31
    on Jeb Stuart's Maryland campaign, 40–41
    northward advance of, *42–43*
    offer of resignation by, 283
    order to Richard S. Ewell from, 97–98, 101
    post-Gettysburg strategy of, 264–266, 267–275
    pursuit of, *266–267*, 269–275, *274–275*, *280–281*, 287
    retreat of, *6–7*, 275–277, *275–278*, *278*
    at West Point, 252

Lee's Lieutenants (Freeman), 90

Leister House, 195–196, *196*, 197, 216, 217

Lilly, Sergeant William C., *208*

Lincoln, Abraham, *20*, 22, 27, 43, 47, 87, 128, 201, 275, 279, 283, 284, *292*
    Civil War volunteers and, 9
    formation of the Confederacy and, 8
    on George Meade's resignation offer, 286–287
    Gettysburg address by, 285, 287–293
    Joseph Hooker's resignation and, 44
    in preparations for Gettysburg, 23–24, 30, 37

Little Round Top, *116–117*, 116–118, 124, 128, 130, 131, *132–133*, *134,* 135–137, *137*, *138*, 139, 142, 143, *146–147*, *153*, 155, 156, 159, 167, 171, 196, 209, 226, 252, 255
    assault on, *140–141*, 144–153
    photography of, 200

Littleton, 61

Local times, during Battle of Gettysburg, 107

Long, Colonel Armistead L., 116, *116*, 297

Longstreet, Lt. General James "Old Pete," 21, 22, *26*, 37, 40–41, 59, 91, *108–109*, *115*, 125, 128, 135, 137, 145, 155, *162–163*, 166, 167, 173, 174–175, 176, 178, 189, 191, 192, 198, 199,

202–203, 208, 209–211, 214, *219*, 219–220, *232–233*, 241, 265, 276, 279, 281, 297
advance on Gettysburg by, 29–30
conduct at Gettysburg of, 108–119, *126–127*, 126–133
encampment at Gettysburg of, 45
Gettysburg strategy of, 203–204
Looting, by occupying Confederate troops, 50–52
"Lost Cause" revisionism, 98
James Longstreet in, 115
Pickett's Charge and, 213–214
Louisiana, 179, 180
Louisiana Tigers, 182–188, *183*, *184–185*, *186–187*, *188*
Low Dutch Road, 246
Lowell, Charles Russell, on Alfred Pleasonton, 35
Lunettes, *110*
Lutheran Church, 261
Lutheran Seminary, *60–61*, 71, 78, 137, 214

Mackenzie, Lt. Ranald, 138
Maine, 74, 106, 125, 136, 142, 145, 149–152, 156, 158, 171, 183, 255, 261, 262
Maine State Museum, 152
Mallory, Stephen R., *19*
Manassas. *See* Bull Run Creek (Manassas)
Manassas Gap Railroad, 38
Marshall, J. K., 238
Marsh Creek, 71, 126, 130, 145
Marsh Creek Bridge, *130*
Marye's Heights, 26, 131
Maryland, 90, 101, 182, 191, 204, 205, 210, 211
in Civil War, 8, 10–11, 49
Jeb Stuart's campaign through, 40–43, *44*
Maryland Heights, *47*
"Masked battery," 218
Mason-Dixon Line, 10, 52
crossing of, 49
Massachusetts, 192, 208
Mayo, Colonel Robert, 226
McAllister's Mill, 182
McCausland, General John, 52
McClellan, George Brinton, 29, 30, 31, 33, 286
McCreary, Albertus, *95*, 272–273
McGilvery, Colonel Freeman, 218, 226, 232
McIntosh, Colonel John, *250–251*
McLaws, Major General Lafayette, 29, 40, 118, 119, 125, 126, 130–132, *131*, 155, 156, *162–163*, 166, 198, 203, 297
McMillan House, *224–225*
McPherson, Edward, farm of, *62–63*
McPherson's Farm, *72*, 74n, 74, *83–85*, 94
McPherson's Ridge, 64, *73*, *80–81*, 91, 94, 103, *103–105*, 189, 243, 275
battle at, 68–87
McPherson's Woods, *72*, 74n, 74–75, *83–85*
Meade, Captain George, Jr., 124

Meade, Major General George Gordon "Old Snapping Turtle," 23, 24, *27*, *46*, 59, 61, 64, 65, 83, 103–106, 109, 110, *112*, 116, 119, 121, 124, *129*, 135, 137, 156, 158, 166, 167, 177n, 178–179, 191, 192, 195–197, *196*, 196n, 198, 199, 203, 216, 217, 218, 239, *240–241*, 244, 246, 254, 259, 264–265, 266, 267–269, 275, 294
in aftermath of Gettysburg, 259
Daniel Sickles and, 122–123, 125–126, 128–129
offer of resignation by, 286–287
pursuit of Robert E. Lee by, 278–281
strategy at Gettysburg of, 112–116
as Union Army commander, 44–45, 47
Medicine, 268. *See also* Surgeons
Melcher, Lt. Holman S., 150, 151
Memminger, Christopher G., *19*
Mending the Flag (Forbes), *208*
Meredith, Solomon "Long Sol," 74
Merritt, Wesley, 250, 251, 254
Mexican War, 135, 136, 177, 222, 239
Michigan, 74, 144, 158, 246, 247, 248, *249*, 252
Microbes, 268
Middleburg, battle of, 35, 40
Miller, Captain William E., 247, 248
Miller, Louis, 58–59
Milroy, Major General Robert H., 38–39
Minié, Claude-Etienne, 66
Minié balls, 66, *67*, 93, 98, 143, 147, 158, 159, 180, 205, 239, 264
destructive nature of, 268
Minnesota, 167, 168–169, *170–171*
Mississippi, 78, 79, 96, 131, 166, 167, 170, 171, 198, 226
in Civil War, 8
infantry flag of, *86*
infantrymen from, *56*
regimental flag of, *234*
Mississippi River, 18, 283
Missouri, in Civil War, 8
Mitchell, William, 241
Mobile telegraphic stations, *30*
Monterey Pass, 269
Monuments, *210*, *238*, *298*
Morrill, Captain Walter G., 145, 152
Morris, Lt. Colonel William, 238
Mosby, John Singleton, 41
Mudge, Lt. Charles R., 208
Mummasburg, 10
Mummasburg Road, 87, 90
Musket balls, 66, *67*
Muskets, 66–67, 189, *224–225*, 234
Enfield, 244, 254

Napoleon Bonaparte, 25
Napoleon gun, *198*
National Cemetery, dedication of, 9
New Jersey, 144, 234, 248, 250

Newton, Major General John, 83, 196, 196n, 294, 295
New York, 75, 78, 136, 137, 142, 144, 156, 159, 170, 171, 180, 182, 191, 192–193, 195, 205, 234, 239, 254
Daniel Sickles in, 122
New York City, Mathew Brady in, 200
New York Light Artillery, 136
Nicholl's brigade, 180
Nicolay, J. G., 288
Nicolay copy of Gettysburg address, *288*
Night Bivouac of the Seventh Regiment New York at Arlington Heights, Virginia (Gifford), *194–195*
North Anna River, 13
North Carolina, 78, 79, 91, 94, 182, 188, 191, 205, 238
in Civil War, 9–10
regimental flag of, *234*
North Carolina Monument, *238*
Northern Central Railroad, 57

Oak Hill, *91*
Oak Knoll, 98, 101, 191
Oates, Colonel William B., *145*, 145–149
Official Records of the Union and Confederate Armies in the War of the Rebellion, 129, 143
Ogden, H. A., 220, *240–241*
Ohio, 223, 226
"Old Army," 71, 75
"Old Bald Head," 89, 90, 111. *See also* Ewell, Lt. General Richard Stoddert "Dick"
"Old Jack," 89, 98. *See also* Jackson, General Thomas J. "Stonewall"
"Old War Horse," 115, 203. *See also* Longstreet, Lt. General James "Old Pete"
O'Neal, Colonel Edward A., 90–91
Orange & Alexandria Railroad, 30, 38
Orange Turnpike, 121
Ordnance rifle, *269*
O'Rorke, Colonel Patrick H. "Paddy," *144*, 145, 171, 176, 252, 253
death of, 144, 145, 252
O'Sullivan, Timothy, 37, 112, 148, 186
Overland Campaign, 93

Pardee, Lt. Colonel Airo, 205
Pardee's Field, *204*, 205, *205–207*, 210
Parrott gun, 143
Pasteur, Louis, 268
Peace Democrats, 20
Peach Orchard, 116, 125, 131, 135, *154–155*, *162*, 198, 211, *211*, 214
battle in, 154–171, *162–163*
Pegram, Major William "Willie," 91
Pemberton, General John C., 8, 19, 21
surrender of, 283, *284*
Pender, Major General William D. (Dorsey), 49, 91, 93, 94, 203, 211, 297

Pendleton, Brigadier General William Nelson "Old Mother," 214, *215*, 218, 232, 297
Pendleton, Colonel Alexander "Sandy," 98
Peninsular Campaign, 29, 31, 32
Pennsylvania, 90, 103, 136, 142, 156, 159, 166–167, 176, 189, 199, 205, 209, 213, 222, 230, 233, 235, 239–241, 244, 248, *250–251*, 254
  in Civil War, 10–11
  Confederate invasion of, 48–65
Pennsylvania College, *91*
Pennyroyal, 261, 273
Peppermint oil, 261, 273
Perry's brigade, 170, 226, 241
Peters, John J., 19
Petersburg, Virginia, *30*
Pettigrew, Brigadier General James Johnston, *70*, 94, 98–99, 211, 220, 222, 226, 233, 234–235, 238, 239, 243, 297
  death of, 281
  at McPherson's Ridge, 69
Philadelphia, 49
Philippoteaux, Paul, 223, 228–231
Photography, 200–201
Pickett, Major General George, 119, 126, 167, 198–199, *199*, 203, 211, *219*, 243, 259, 297
  conduct at Gettysburg of, 212–241
Pickett's Charge, 212–241, *226–227*, *235*, *236–237*, 252, 262, 266, 281
  fiftieth anniversary of, 287
  high-water mark of, 238
  Judson Kilpatrick and, 259
Piedmont, *39*
Pierce, Franklin, 18
Pinkerton, Alan, 29
Pipe's Creek, 65, 112, 123
Pipe's Creek Circular, 65
Pistol, Jeb Stuart's, *245*
Pitzer School, 131, 140
Pitzer's Woods, 125, 126
Pleasonton, Major General Alfred, 21, 29, 30–31, 32, 33, *35*, 39, 61, 65, 246, 249–250, 254, 295
  at Upperville, 40
Plum Run, 136, 137, *138*, 142–144, 152, 156, 159
Pope, Major General John, 13
Potomac River, *45*, 47, 265, 275, *275–277*, 277, *278*, *280–281*, 283
  Jeb Stuart's crossing of, 43
  Jenkins's brigade's crossing of, *48–49*
  Robert E. Lee's crossing of, 49, *50*
Potter, Clarkson, 93
Powers Hill, 202, 217
Prison camps, 264–265
Prisoners
  Confederate, *264*, *265*, 272–273
  proposed exchange of, 264–265
Private property, Confederate treatment of, 50–52, 56, 57–60
Pye, Major Edward, 78

Radicals, 22, 23
Rapidan River, 13–16, 18, 283
Rappahannock River, 13–16, 18, 29–30, 33, 35, 38, 283, 287
  battle at, 8
  bridges across, 37, *37*
Read, Charles W., 60
Reagan, John H., 19, *19*
Redwood, Allen Carter, 6–7, 33, 72, 94, 118, 204, 258
Reed, Charles, 162, 220
Regiments, organization of, 26
Regular Union troops, *25*
Reminiscences of the Civil War (Gordon), 93
Repulse of General Johnson's Division by General Geary's White Star Division (Rothermel), *205–207*
Repulse of Longstreet's Assault at the Battle of Gettysburg (Walker), *232–233*
Repulse of the Louisiana Tigers (Rothermel), *183–185*
Reynolds, Major General John F., 10, 24, *27*, 64, 65, 71, 73, 80, 111, 112, 195, 294
  death of, 74, *75*, *79*, 82, 83, *83–85*, 103
  at McPherson's Ridge, 71–72
Reynolds Tree, *79*
Rice, Colonel James, 144
Richmond, 18–21, 82, 243, 287
  Jeb Stuart at, 32–33
  Joseph Hooker's plan for, 37
Ricketts, Captain R. Bruce, 187, 188
Ride Around McClellan, 31
Rifles, 66–67, *67*, 254
Rifling, 66
Rigby, James A., 204
Rittenhouse's battery, 226
Robertson, Brigadier General Beverly H., *34*, 41–43, 297
  at Brandy Station, 34
Robertson, Jerome, 139–140
Robinson, Brigadier General John C., 294
Rock Creek, 173, 182
Rock Creek Bridge, 192
Rockville Pike, 43
Rodes, Major General Robert Emmett, *90*, 90–91, 92, 97, 98, 100, 176, 187, 202, 297
  military career of, 191
Rosecrans, General William S., 8
Rose's Farm, 261
Rose's Run, 166
Rose's Woods, 136, 140, 142, 156, 157, 158, 162, 164, 166, 167
Rosser, Thomas, 252, *253*
Rothermel, Peter Frederick, 83–85, 153, 183–185, 187, 205–207
Round Tops, *103–105*, 121, 125, 128, *130*, 132, *132–133*, 133, 136, 139, 140, 142, 149, 151, 171, 173, *220*, 226, *232–233*, 250, 254. *See*

also Big Round Top; Little Round Top
  George G. Meade at, 113–114
Rowley, Brigadier General Thomas A., 294
Rowser's Ford, 43, 47
Ruger, Brigadier General Thomas, 177, 177*n*, 179, 182, 192, 202–203, 295
Rummel Farm, 246–247, 250
Runaway Limber, The (Shelton), *103*
Russell, Andrew J., 15

San Francisco, 176, 177, 192
Sanitarians, 268
Sanitary Commission, 268
Sanitation, 272–273
Sawyer, Colonel Franklin, 223, 226
Saylor's Creek, 157
"Scallywag," James Longstreet as, 115
Schick, J. L., 55
Schimmelfennig, Brigadier General Alexander, *94*, 295
Schurz, Major General Carl, 87, *87*, 90, 295
Scouts, 29, 59–60, 202, 203
Seasons of the Confederacy—Autumn (Hoffbauer), *28–29*
Sedgwick, Major General John, *27*, 114–116, *269–271*, 269–275, 295
Sellers, W. H., 143
Seminary Ridge, *60–61*, *70*, 83, 94, 98, 102–103, *108–109*, 109, 111, 115, 116–118, 119, 126, 132–133, 137, *154–155*, 171, 198, *199*, 203, 208, 211, 218, 220, 235, 239, 241, 247, 249, 261, *265*, 266
  battle at, 75–77
Semmes, Paul, *153*
  death of, 164, 166
Semmes's Brigade, *164–165*, 166
Service with the Sixth Wisconsin Volunteers (Dawes), 86, 189
Seven Days' Battles, 24, 26
Seven Pines, battle of, 82
Shaara, Michael, 115, 151
Sharpsburg, battle at, 8
Sharps carbine, 67, 71, *73*, 125
Sharpshooter regiments, 125
Sharpshooters, 125, 126, 136, 139, 145, 147, 152, *153*
Sharpshooters at Roundtop (Rothermel), *153*
Shelton, W. H., 103
Shenandoah River, 37, *45*
Shenandoah Valley campaign, 89
Sheppard, William L., 189
Sherfy peach orchard. *See* Peach Orchard
Sheridan, Philip, 27
Sherman, General William Tecumseh, 82, 115, 132
Shoulder arms, *67*
  manufacturing accurate, 66–67
Sickles, Major General Daniel E., 13, 24, *27*, 102, 112, 114, 116, *120–121*, *123*, *128*, 133, 135,

136–137, 155, 156, 159, 166, 170, 189, 196–197, 221, 294
  conduct at Gettysburg of, 121–126
  injury of, 171
  killing of Philip Barton Key by, *122*
  military career of, 122–123
  postwar assessment of, 128–129
  right tibia and fibula of, *171*
  scandals involving, 122
  temporary insanity plea by, 122
Sickles, Theresa, 122, *122*
Slaughter Pen, *137, 148*
Slavery, 57
  in aftermath of Gettysburg, 261
  Salmon P. Chase on, 22, 23
Slaves, Confederate seizure of, 53–57, 261
Slocum, Major General Henry W. "Slow Come," 27, 101, 106, 112, 114, 167, 177, 177*n*, 178–179, 196, 202, 295
Smith, Captain James, 129, 136
Smith, Major General William "Extra Billy," 57, *57*
Smith, Orland, 106
Smith's battery, 129, 144
Snicker's Gap, 39
Snyder's Wagon Hotel, *10*
South Carolina, 131, 156–158, 164
South Mountain, 137, 269, 275, 278
  battle of, 74
Spain, 87
Spangler House, 247
Spangler's Meadow, *208*
Spangler's Spring, 192, *192, 193*
Spanish-American War, 162
Spear, Major Ellis, 149, 151
Spencer carbine, *67*
Sperryville, 37
Springfield rifle, *67*
Spying. *See* Espionage
Stannard, Brigadier General George J., *235*, 235–239
Stanton, Edwin, 122
Steinwehr, Brigadier General Adolph von, 106, 295
Stephens, Alexander H., *19*
Steuart, Brigadier General George Hume "Maryland," 182, 191, *204, 205–207*, 205–208, 210
Stevens, Captain Greenleaf T., *186–187*, 187
Stevens, Thaddeus, 52
Stone, Colonel Roy, 94
Stoneman, General George, *21*, 23, 29
Stonewall Brigade, 239
Stony hill, 166, 171, 254
Stuart, Flora Cooke, 31, 34
Stuart, Lt. General James Ewell Brown "Jeb," 22–23, *28*, 29, *31, 41, 43, 44*, 61, 65, 89, 110, 199, 243, 244, *245*, 246–248, 248–249, 250, 254, 266, 297

at Aldie, 40
Alfred Pleasonton and, 35
in battle at Hanover, 60
on Beverly Robertson, 34
at Brandy Station, 30–36
death of, 244
encampment at Gettysburg of, 47
Maryland campaign of, 40–43, 44, *44*, 47
at Upperville, 40
Sugar Loaf Hill, 128. *See also* Round Tops
Surgeons, *255–257*, 261, 264, 272, 273
  kits for, *264*
Susquehanna River, *54*, 57, 65
Sweitzer, Jacob, 156, 158
Swinton, William, 115
Sykes, Major General George, 27, 114, *114*, 129, 138, 156, 159, 294

Tammany Hall, 24, 122
Taneytown, 11, 65, 112
Taneytown Road, 114, 116, 167, 170, *216*
Tate, Major Sam, 9–10, 188
Taylor, Major Walter, 98, 109, 208–209, 297
Telegraph station, *30*
Tennessee, 8, 74, 132, 238
Terrell, Captain Leigh, 149
Texas, 132, 139–140, 142, 144
"Through Blood and Fire at Gettysburg" (Lawrence), 150–151
Tilton, William, 156, 158
Time, during Battle of Gettysburg, 107
Tippin, Colonel Andrew, 166–167
Toombs, Robert A., *19*
Traveller, 203
Trimble, Major General Isaac, 90, 100–102, *101*, 107, 211, *224–225*, 234–235, 238, 243, 297
Trostle barn, *262*
Trostle Farm, 164, *165*
Trostle's Woods, 158, 159
Turner's Gap, 278
"20th Maine at Little Round Top, The" (Melcher), 151
Tyson, Charles John, 97, 200–201
Tyson brothers, 273

Union Army, 279. *See also* Army of the Potomac
  organization of, 26, 27
  prisoners from, 264–265
Union Army Corps
  Cavalry Corps, 40, 41, 246–259, 295
  I Corps, 10, 24, 27, 40, 64, 80, 83, *83–85*, 87, 94, 96, 102–103, 114, 173, 193, 196, 196*n*, 294
  II Corps, 23, 27, *102*, 114, 124, 158–166, 170, 191, 196, 218, 221, 222, 294
  III Corps, 13, 27, 65, 74, *102*, 114, 116, 121–126, 128–129, 133, 135–136, 294
  V Corps, 24, 27, 61, 65, 114, 116, 138, 156,

294
  VI Corps, 27, 114–116, 269, 275, 295
  XI Corps, 14, 27, 65, 74, 82, 87, 94, *94*, 95, 96–97, 98, 102–106, 114, 173, 176, 188, 193, 244–246, 278, 295
  XII Corps, 27, 101, 106, 116, 123, 167, 177*n*, 177–179, 193, 196, 202, 295
Unknown soldiers, 8
Upperville, 138
  battle of, 35, *38*, 40, *41*
Urban warfare, 94–96

Valley Campaign, 37
Vast Procession of Misery, A (Redwood), *6–7*
Venable, Colonel Charles, 116, 119, 175
Vermont, 235–239, 254–255
Vicksburg, 290
  battle at, 8, 18, 19, 21
  surrender of, 283, 284
Videttes, 43
Vincent, Colonel Strong, 40, 137, 138–139, *142*, 144–145
  death of, 142, 144, 145
Vincent's Spur, 144, 149
Virginia, 18–21, *39*, 93, 126, 192, 195, 198–199, 211, 226, 238, 244, 248, *249*, 252, 258, 259, 261, 265, 275, *275–277*, 287
  in Civil War, 8
Vizetelly, Frank, 43, 44
Voices of the Civil War: Gettysburg, 210
Volunteering, 9
von Amsberg's brigade, 191

Wadsworth, Brigadier General James S., 73, 78, 87, 107, 176–177, 279, 294
Wainwright, Colonel Charles, 188
Walker, Brigadier General James A., 103–105, 205
Walker, Colonel Elijah, 136
Walker, James, 232–233
Walker, Leroy Pope, *19*
Ward, Brigadier General J. H. Hobart, 129, 135, *136*, 140, *140*, 142–144, 156, 294
  military career of, 135–136
Warren, Brigadier General G. K., 294
Warren, Major General Gouvernor, 136–138, *137*, 145, 196, 275
Washington, DC, 38, 41, 43, 110, 222, 278–279
  Mathew Brady in, 200
Waud, Alfred, 41, 75, 92, 140, 186–187, 239, 249
Waud, William, 255–257
Webb, Brigadier General Alexander, *221*, 222, *230–231*, 233, 235, 239–241
Weed, Stephen H., *146–147*, 152, *153*
  death of, 135, 147
Weikert House, 192
Western concentration bloc, 18
West Point, graduates of, *252–253*

West Virginia, 254–255

Wheat, C. R., 183

Wheat Field, 125, 135, 136, *138*, *160–161*
    battle in, 154–171, *162–163*

Wheatfield Road, 145, 158, 167

Wheaton, Brigadier General Frank, 295

White, Colonel E.V., 56

Wiedrich, Captain Michael, 188

Wilcox, 126, 170–171, 226, 241

Wilderness, the, 13, 29

Wilkeson, Lt. Bayard, *92*

Willard, George, 170

Williams, Brigadier General Alpheus S. "Old Pap,"
    177, 177*n*, 196, *202*, 202–203, 204, 295

Williamsport, 275, *275*, 277, 278, 279, 281, 286

Willoughby Run, 75, 131

Winchester, 275
    Richard S. Ewell at, 90
    second battle of, 38–39

Wisconsin, 74, 78, 79–82, 86, 96, 189, 192
    infantry colors of, *86*

Wofford's brigade, *153*, 167

Wolverines, 247, 248

Wood, Paul, 160–161

Woodruff, George, *253*
    death of, 252

Wright, Brigadier General Ambrose R., *170*, 171,
    195, 198, 209

Wright, Brigadier General Horatio, 295

Wright, Sergeant Philander, 74

Wrightsville, 57
    battle at, 54

Yellow Tavern, battle of, 244

York, 11
    Confederate occupation of, 51–52, 53, 57,
    58–59
    Gettysburg and, 45

York Road, 98, 244

Ziegler's Grove, 222–223, *232–233*, 234

Zogbaum, Rufus Fairchild, 168–169

Zook, Samuel Kosciuzko, 159–162
    death of, 162

Zouaves, *153*, *209*